NEW YORK CENTRAL SYSTEM
4214
NEW YORK
3819
NEW YORK CENTRAL

New York Central System Diesel Locomotives

by
William D. Edson
with
H.L. Vail Jr. and C.M. Smith

1995
TLC Publishing, Inc.
Route 4, Box 154
Lynchburg, Virginia 24503-9711

Front Cover Illustration: In this scene New York Central E8 No. 4082 leads one of the line's crack passenger trains past Alco FA No. 1031 stopped with its freight, symbolizing the twin pillars of NYC's traffic and the variety of its motive power. The original painting by noted railroad artist Andrew Harmantas was specially commissioned for this book .

Library of Congress Catalog Number 95-61244
ISBN 1-883089-16-6

Layout and Design by
Kenneth L. Miller, Miller Design & Photography, Salem, Virginia

Printed by
Walsworth Publishing Co.
Marceline, Missouri 64658

Contents

Louis A. Marre

The diversity of the New York Central's fleet is represented here in this Louis A. Marre photo at Elkhart, Indiana. The three major builders from left are an EMD F7, No. 1733, Class DFA-2g; Alco PA-2, P&LE No. 4214; Class DPA-4c, and a Baldwin RF-16, Sharknose No. 3819, Class DFA-8a.

EMD E-7 No. 4000, Class DPA-1a is ready to pull out of La Salle Street station in Chicago with train 26 *The Twentieth Century Limited* on sunny September 8, 1945.

NYC Photo, NYCSHS Collect

Introduction

The first edition of *Diesel Locomotives of the New York Central System* was published in 1978 by the New York Central System Historical Society, Inc. of Cleveland Ohio. Actually it was printed in serial form starting in May, 1975 as a continuing article in the *Central Headlight*, the quarterly publication of the Society. Originally, the work was intended to be simply a roster book, with a diagram and builders photo for each major class. When published as a book several technical discussions were added, as well as a selection of service photos of various diesels in action.

Much of the material in the first edition has been retained in this one. The principal change is in the roster data, which is presented in more detail by individual unit rather than by group. Also new is material made available only recently, along with photos from many additional sources including the New York Central's collection now in the possession of the NYCSHS. Special thanks go to Dr. Louis A. Marre who furnished numerous important photographs.

The New York Central's numbering system for its diesels requires explanation. The general locomotive renumbering scheme of 1936 provided the 500, 600, and 700 blocks for early diesels. Additional switchers soon overflowed into the 800 and 900 series, forcing the renumbering of light steam engines into higher numbers. Still more switchers opened up the 8500 series and higher.

Numbers assigned to the first road diesels were puzzling. The FT units were numbered 1600-1603, right in the middle of many H-5 steam Mikados. A little later, Alco B units were numbered 2300's surrounded by H-10 Mikados. As new units arrived, renumberings were precipitated repeatedly.

As the roster shows, almost every NYC diesel was renumbered at least once, sometimes four or five times. The largest renumbering occurred in 1966, in anticipation of the Penn Central merger. The purpose was to group together similar locomotives from both the NYC and the Pennsylvania, still leaving room for future additions. The actual merger took place almost two years after the renumbering was completed.

Presentation of roster material in this edition stops with February, 1968, the effective date of the PC merger. Now almost 27 years later, there are still some former NYC units in service on Conrail. The final chapter cannot be written until these units are retired. Perhaps there will be a third edition to record the details.

William D. Edson
Chief Mechanical Engineer
New York Central System
1965-1968

Charles M. Smith
Mechanical Engineer-Locomotive
New York Central System
1963-1968

H. Lansing Vail Jr.
Trustee,
NYCS Historical Society
1968-1995

The Diversity of New York Central's Diesel Fleet

Just before the New York Central completed dieselization in the mid 1950s, the railroad seemed to have "one of everything". As soon as any of the locomotive builders came out with a new model, the Central apparently couldn't resist the temptation to add to its collection. By 1954, there were no less than seventy separate and distinct designs of diesel locomotives operating on NYC rails. They were supplied by Alco , Baldwin, EMD, Fairbanks Morse, GE and Lima, with horsepower ranging from 330 (for the DES-1) to 2400 (for the DPA-6). The locomotive roster which follows will give the details of this fascinating fleet. The reasons for this variety were many - some compelling, some subtle, and some baffling. To those of us who watched it happen, there didn't appear to be any rhyme nor reason to the way this power was accumulated. Actually, there was a period when the motive power department was not in complete control of the situation.

In the earliest days of dieselization, just before World War II, only two designs of locomotives were being purchased, the Alco high hood 600 (NYC class DEs-7) and EMD's version of the same thing, their SW1 (Class DEs-5 and 6). At that stage, of course, the railroad was interested in the diesel for switching service only. Steam reigned supreme out on the road; the J-3s were still new and a new class of Mohawks,the L-3, was on the drawing board. The American Locomotive Company enjoyed a good reputation with the New York Central, after building most of its steam power for years. More important, Alco had teamed up with General Electric to supply a good fleet of electrics for New York and Detroit, as well as the experimental diesels of 1928 and the remarkable DEs-3 "three-power" units of 1930.

So it was natural that the Central looked to Alco for its first straight diesel-electrics late in 1938, assigning them to Buffalo and Boston.

The Electro-Motive Corporation (later EMD) had gained a foothold on the NYC System in 1936 when it delivered a group of seven 600 HP Model SC switchers (class DEs-4) to the affiliated Chicago River & Indiana. These units,with Winton 201A engines, were never duplicated on the NYC proper, but their performance was so good it was not difficult for General Motors salesmen to convince 230 Park Avenue they should try an improved version with the new 567 engine. After that, the EMDs sold themselves, and the Central soon had equipment trust agreements for a very respectable fleet of both Alco and EMD 600s. Many of those early EMD units incidentally worked at Buffalo Central Terminal and were painted gray.

Then, in 1940, it was Alco's turn to change horses, introducing at the New York World's Fair the new S-1 model with 539 engine, rated at 660 HP. The New York Central bought this unit, No. 590, which became the first of its class, DEs-8. (The DEs-9 was identical except for ballasting to increase weight on drivers). Here was an example of what happened over and over again on every major road - the builders themselves introduced changes improving reliability and performance, but often at a cost of losing interchangeability and standardization of parts.

Another factor contributing to variety was the special situation which could be handled only by a particular design. Such was the case with the 70-ton class DEs-1, specially built by GE in 1940 to operate on very light track with sharp curvature, such as at Auburn, NY where the 506 replaced the NYC's only steam Shay engines. This class DEs-1, by the way, is not to be confused with the first class DEs-1 design of 1927, never actually built, although road number 1520 was assigned.

Still another model appeared on NYC rails in April, 1941, the Baldwin VO switcher. This one is not so easy to explain, for the Central had never been a good Baldwin customer. At any rate, something or someone persuaded the management to try a single unit, which was numbered 501, class DEs-10a. Shortly thereafter, the War Production Board made its famous ruling that restricted diesel switcher production to Alco and Baldwin only, and all through the war the Central did everything it could to obtain more DEs-8 and DEs-10 600 HP units, along with 1000 HP units from the same builders. The first higher power DEs-11 Alco units were assigned to Albany passenger station, where they took over all the switching at this critical bottleneck, including pusher duty on West Albany hill. The Baldwin 1,000 HP units, class DES-12, were assigned to Syracuse and the Michigan Central.

Meanwhile, at the direction of the War Production Board Electro-Motive was concentrating on road power only. Just before the war, EMD had developed the FT freight unit, and had gone into mass production. Literally hundreds of these units were soon demonstrating remarkable performances on the Santa Fe, Great Northern, Southern, as well as some eastern roads uncomfortably close to the NYC, such as the B&O and Boston & Maine. Finally, in June 1944, a pair of four-unit FTs appeared on the Central almost secretly and without fanfare. They were thoroughly tested in regular main line freight service on both Line East and Line West, soon piling up mileage records with almost perfect availability. Yet it took over two years for NYC management to believe in the evidence, and by the time it was ready to place an order in quantity, the FT was no longer in production. So the railroad accepted two new F2 units which were immediately available, and then awaited delivery of 28 more units which arrived in 1947 as F3 units, still another design!

Electro-Motive also continued to build passenger power for other lines all during the war and in March 1945 succeeded in delivering four E7 units to the Central, which were promptly assigned to the Century - a crushing blow to steam power. These first class DPA-la units were followed a few months later by four more A units and four B units, enough to hint at what was to come.

Alco's answer to the F3 and E7 appeared long after the war ended. When they finally went into production, the NYC was only too willing to buy as many as they could afford, despite the fact they were new models with lots of bugs. Why? Partly because of traffic considerations. Alco and General Electric were, after all, on-line at Schenectady, and they generated a very significant amount of freight revenue for the railroad. Naturally, the purchasing and motive power departments were frequently encouraged to consider their options very carefully.

Once the policy was formulated to embark upon full dieselization as rapidly as possible, the situation became chaotic. Every day of delay replacing steam power meant considerable loss of savings. Some builders offered earlier deliveries, and suddenly this factor became almost overriding, despite the inferiority of some models compared with others. New diesels weren't supposed to require maintenance; those problems were minor, anyway, and far in the future.

Soon management learned how to play a subtle game which involved purchasing a few "off-brand" models now and then to demonstrate to the major builders that the railroad meant to maintain independence and would entertain any reasonable pricing arrangement. This practice had much to do with the decision to acquire many of the Baldwin, Fairbanks-Morse, and finally the Lima-Hamilton units.

There was an element of true wisdom in all this, of course, for the result was to encourage the development of new designs which just might turn out to be real improvements. The diesel locomotive, after all, was still in relative infancy. True competition is supposed to foster progress.

Eventually it became obvious that not all the competing builders could survive, and the purchasing policies of the New York Central and other roads were just prolonging the agony. But for the NYC Mechanical Department of 1952, it was too late; the damage had already been done. The Transportation Department had insisted on assigning new power wherever it was needed most, regardless of make or model, and many maintenance terminals ended up with locomotives of every builder. The repair problems were almost overwhelming, as evidenced in the variety of spare parts, tools, catalogs, manuals, and know-how required to keep everything moving. Almost as serious was the confusion of engine crews faced with the differing controls and performance characteristics of so many types of diesels.

Only one category of diesel never appeared on the pre-merger New York Central: the six-motor unit. The Water Level Route was not supposed to need high-tractive force machines. The truth was, of course, they could have been useful on the Boston and Albany and Ohio Central, at least.

Finally a plan evolved which alleviated the maintenance problems somewhat. Pools were set up to concentrate like units together at home terminals. For example, all the EMD E7s and E8s would cycle into Harmon on a regular basis, at least once every four days. All the EMD freight power would operate on the Line West, with maintenance at Collinwood. The GP7 and GP9 fleet would cover the Ohio Central, Michigan Central and Big Four, through freight and regional passenger runs included. All EMD switchers were supposed to move west of Buffalo.

Alco power of all kinds was to stay on the Line East, or at least east of Cleveland. With heavy maintenance based at De Witt, access to the Alco parts supply was supposed to be easier. The troublesome Alco PAs continued to be pooled with the EMD passenger units out of Harmon, although for a short time Collinwood got stuck with the 4208-4211 for the New England States service.

The early Baldwin freight units failed miserably in service out of Collinwood, and finally went east to work the hump at Selkirk yard. The later shark-nose Baldwins worked out of De Witt, mercifully confined to the Line East. The 1500 HP combination units and road switchers were eventually re-engined with EMD horses, but only the road switchers survived very long, these in the Chicago "cowhide" service. The Baldwin switchers clustered around De Witt, Selkirk, and North Bergen, while the smaller road switchers handled the West Shore and Harlem Division commuter service.

The adventures of NYC's Fairbanks-Morse power would fill several chapters, but except for the passenger units they stayed east of Buffalo. Both the Erie-built and the big C-Line freight units seemed to knock about the B&A and Line East, for the most part, although some units got EMD engines and moved west. The 1600 HP C-Line units operated on the Pennsylvania Division, maintained at Arvis along with most of the road switchers and the early 2000 HP "transfer units" as the NYC called their DFT-1 class. Most of the 9100 series FM switchers stayed on the B&A or the Buffalo yards. As for those passenger units, the original Erie-builts were pooled with the EMD and Alco units out of Harmon, but they were always in trouble and it was decided to move them west, first to Collinwood then to Englewood. The 2400 HP C-Liners joined them at Englewood sharing regional passenger run work with the boiler-equipped GP9s.

The Lima road switchers which predictably proved too small for B & A through passenger service proved satisfactory in commuter service, both on the B & A and West Shore. Eventually they moved west to the Big Four to finish out their days in company with the 1000 HP switchers. Except for two units, that is, which got EMD engines and ran Chicago "cowhide" assignments.

In later years, of course, these general allocations changed somewhat, but once the general idea was established, togetherness did become a way of life for the New York Central's fascinating fleet.

The remainder of this chapter deals with the 1957-1967 period which saw the acquisition of 366 second-generation units. These same years also witnessed the disappearance of most of the odd and minority classes which made the early New York Central diesel roster so interesting. Gone in those years were the DES-3 diesel-storage battery-electrics, the Winton engined EMD switchers, the EMD FTs and F-2s, Alco high-hood switchers, PA and PBs all Baldwin and Fairbanks road power, and all Lima's except the two EMD re-engined 1200 HP road switchers. Truly a period of change.

After the elimination of steam in 1957 with the delivery of 47 GP9s from EMD and 9 RS-11s from Alco, plus the acquisition of 17 second-hand EMD NW2s from the New York, Ontario and Western, a period of four years elapsed without the acquisition of additional motive power. While there was some demand for additional road freight units, this was met by the regearing and reassignment of RS-3 and GP7 units which were made available as a result of the continuing program of local passenger train discontinuance during this period.

The first sign of a break came in 1960 when negotiations were held with Alco for the lease of 6 additional RS-11 units to be numbered 8009-8014. While these

Lamar M. Kelley photographed this three-power DES-3 switcher in Chicago in May, 1937 following renumbering from MC 7533.

Collection of Louis A Marre

units were completed and delivered to Selkirk the lease was never consummated, the units never saw service on the Central, and in 1961, Alco shipped them off to the Delaware & Hudson as their 5000-5005.

This was only a momentary diversion however. The early 1960s saw a large increase in the number of high - speed freight trains being operated, particularly Flexi-Van trains, and to maintain schedule, it was necessary to assign as many as seven of the 1500-1600 horsepower road switch units to each train. Simultaneously, the locomotive builders were developing second-generation high-horsepower units, and the earlier first generation units were showing signs of advancing age.

Consequently, in 1962 EMD delivered 15 GP20s and Alco delivered 15 RS-32s, for which a like number of older units were traded. These new units immediately appeared at the head of the premier freight trains.

The following year, 1962, saw EMD deliver 10 GP30s and Alco another 10 RS-32 again on a trade-in basis.

The year 1963 would have been barren except for the delivery of 3 GP35s in December, the first of 31 of that model to be received between 1963-1965, including EMD's New York World's Fair exhibition unit 1964 (1965 during the second year of the fair). Except for this last unit, all of these GP35s were acquired on a trade-in basis.

The year 1964 started off with the delivery of New York Central's first General Electric U25B units, and a total of 70 of these units were received in 1964-1965. Trade-ins for the U25Bs came from the Alco 244 fleet, which began to diminish noticeably at this time.

The end of 1965 also saw delivery of the first 50 EMD GP40s. These units were also acquired on a trade-in basis, and it is interesting to note that the trade-ins for fourteen of these GP40s were ex-New York, Ontario & Western FT units which were purchased by the NYC for that purpose and which had been sitting out of service in the Jersey Meadows since since the abandonment of the NYO&W in 1957.

In 1966 NYC acquired 22 U28B units for the Pittsburgh & Lake Erie and 2 U28Bs for the Central itself. The P&LE units represented GE' s first U28B production and appeared in U25B car-bodies, while the two Central units were in the final U28B configuration. With this acquisition the P&LE traded in its Alco 539 switcher fleet, many of which were resold to the NYC proper and ended their days there. On the Indiana Harbor Belt, 1966 saw the acquisition of 8 EMD SW1500 switchers. This program was continued in 1967 with an additional 8 units, all of which were trade-in basis.

In 1966 approximately 50% of the Central's diesel fleet, was renumbered and all were reclassified in accord with a scheme developed in collaboration with the Pennsylvania Railroad in preparation of the Penn Central merger.

Which brings us to the year 1967, the last full year before the Penn Central merger. During that year EMD delivered 55 GP40s, GE 60 U30Bs, and Alco 10 C-430s, all on a trade-in basis, which further decimated the ranks of the first generation road fleet. Ironically, the Alco C-430s Central's first Alcos in five years, were also the last pre-merger units delivered, presaging the end in the coming year of the New York Central as an independent railroad and of Alco as a locomotive builder.

Continuing the policy mentioned previously, the EMD units acquired in this period were assigned to Collinwood maintenance, while the Alco and General Electric units assigned at DeWitt. In service, however, they ranged throughout the system.

Looking back, the Central's diesel fleet increased from 20 road and 250 switch units in early 1946 to 1,400 road and 881 switch units in 1957, dropping back slightly to 1,359 road and 759 switch units just before the Penn Central merger. That this abrupt change from traditional railroading took place in such a short span of time causes us to reflect upon the words spoken by F.H. Hardin, Chief Engineer of Motive Power and Rolling Stock, in a speech at Rochester, on November 12, 1925. Mr. Hardin said "The Diesel represents the most efficient method of burning fuel at the present time. It has been successfully used in marine circles for a number of years. It is being developed for railroad use, and, while there are still many problems to overcome before it can be substituted successfully for the steam locomotive in all branches of service, several locomotives have already been built and have operated successfully within their limited capacities, and there is little doubt but what the use of such a locomotive, once started, will be rapidly extended."

Explanation and Remarks

This roster of New York Central Diesel powered locomotives is based on the individual locomotive records.

The Classes are listed by type of locomotive, that is, Switchers, Road Switchers, Freight, Passenger and Freight/Passenger combination, beginning with the early experimental units. Under each type, the locomotives are listed in the numerical order of each class. Although this is generally a chronological order, it is not necessarily so, for instance, the original DES-1 Class was never built. Later Classes DES-1A etc. were assigned to some 70 Ton GE-built units. The general arrangement is similar to "Locomotives of the New York Central Lines" showing the Steam and Electric power by W. D. Edson and Edward L. May published in 1966.

The format used for this roster is to show on one line the general class designation, followed by the general data for the entire class, in the following order:

Class Designation,
Builder,
Builders Model Designation,
Locomotive Horsepower,

Abbreviations are used whenever possible. The builders are as follows:

Alco	American Locomotive Co., later Alco Products Div., Worthington Corp.
Alco-GE	per above with General Electric Co. electrical equipment as a coordinated sales effort.
BLW	Baldwin Locomotive Works.
BLH	Baldwin Lima Hamilton Corp.
EMC	Electro-Motive Corp., a division of General Motors Corp. The New York Central did not purchase any locomotives before EMC became a division of GM.
EMD	Electro-Motive Division of General Motors Corp. from 1950 onward.
GMD	General Motors of Canada Ltd. Diesel Division, London, Ontario, Canada. Canadian Subsidiary of GM.
FM	Fairbanks Morse & Co.
GE	General Electric.
IR	Ingersoll-Rand Corp.
LH	Lima Hamilton Corp.
McI&S	Mclntosh and Seymour Corp. (Diesel Engine Manufacturer, Auburn. N. Y,). Later became part of Alco.

Following the data is the NYC diagram for the class. Occasionally more than one diagram is shown to indicate special equipment or to show differences.

Below the diagram is the listing of each sub class under the general class, with the original road numbers, any re-numbering, any re-classification, builder's order number, builder's serial number, date built, and disposition. Notes below are indicated for additional detailed information. Each locomotive is listed only once in its original form. Where a locomotive is re-built as a different type of unit such as a Diesel Hump Trailer, it is so indicated, and is so listed. Only data on locomotives in service to and including January 31, 1968 is shown, as this is the end of NYC ownership. Where a number in parenthesis (1) follows the locomotive number, this indicates that this is the first (1) or second (2) etc. locomotive to be assigned that number.

The Classification scheme for Diesel-Electric locomotives was a natural development of the system used for steam power. Initially, the first letter of the steam class type, became DE for Diesel Electric followed by a smaller upper case letter denoting the type of service in which the unit was used. For the first two locomotives this became DEF with a small upper case "F" for the freight locomotive and DEP with a small upper case "P" for the passenger locomotive. When the " 3 power " switchers were contemplated a small "s" for switchers was used, and since a few more than one were expected a digit was added to denote the sub series, for example, DEs-2. An exception was DEs-A since no more were expected of that type. The DEs - (small digit) became DES - (large digit) with units acquired after DEs-4, and when units were re-painted thereafter the "s" and the digit became the larger one.

Following this a sub letter smaller than the digit was added denoting successive orders of the same model.

Beginning with the first mass-produced freight units acquired in 1944, additional letters were added to the classification scheme to further describe not only the service for which the unit was used, but also the style of unit. The "E" was dropped from the newly created classes as everyone called them diesels anyway. Thus, the following class designations were D for Diesel followed by F for Freight, or P for Passenger, or C for Combination freight and passenger, or FT for Transfer, or RS for Road Switcher. The third letter after the letters F, C, or P indicated whether the unit was an A with a cab and train operating controls, or a B unit without a cab and train operating controls.

Following the letter class designation, came the class number, and with a sub class letter following as before. Thus, when the EMC model FT's arrived they were assigned DFA-1, for the "A" units and DFB-1 for the "B" units. Three variations occurred. First DRSP was assigned to passenger equipped road switchers. Second, the DH-1 diesel hydraulic-locomotives for the "X-Plorer" train. Third, the DHT designation for "Diesel Hump Trailer", used in combination with diesel locomotives to increase tractive effort at low speed in hump yard service.

The New York Central, in anticipation of merger with the Pennsylvania Railroad, re-classified and re-numbered where necessary, all locomotives. This re-arrangement was completed and approved in early 1966, with the locomotives re-numbered and re-classified as required beginning in March, 1966, and being generally completed by the end of May, 1966. The basis for the classification is as follows, as printed in the New York Central "Locomotive Directory" of 10-1-1967.

1. First letter designates builder:

   A - Alco Products Inc. (American Locomotive Company)

   B - Baldwin-Lima-Hamilton Corporation (Baldwin Locomotive Works)

   E - Electro-Motive Division of General Motors Corporation

   F- Fairbanks-Morse & Company

   G - General Electric Company

   L - Lima-Hamilton Corporation

2. Second letter (and third letter where used) designates service:

   F - Road freight unit with streamlined ("covered wagon") carbody, low-nosed road switcher carbody or "B" unit road switcher carbody; equipped with multiple unit connections.

   P - Road passenger with streamlined ("covered wagon") carbody; equipped with multiple unit connections and steam generators.

   FP - Road passenger or road freight with streamlined ("covered wagon") carbody or low nose road switcher carbody; equipped with multiple unit connections and steam generators.

   RS - Switcher type carbody with high speed trucks; horsepower limits for four traction motors from 1000 to 2000 horsepower and six traction motors from 1500 to 2400 horsepower.

   S- Yard switcher

3. Numerals indicate engine horsepower in nearest, lowest hundred, i. e., 1750 horsepower would be 17, 2250 horsepower would be 22, and 2750 horsepower would be 27.

4. Final letter, or letters (all small letters), indicate special features as follows:

   A - Change in original design. Major modification over standard model such as six-wheel trucks or engine model change.

   M - Multiple unit equipped. Used for yard switchers only as all other locomotives, except "X" designated locomotives, are equipped.

   s - Steam generator equipped. (Used for RS only as P and FP types are all equipped with steam generators, and F and S types do not have steam generators.)

   x - Road switcher locomotives not equipped with m.u. control. (This letter would be dropped as older locomotives are phased out.)

Special Notes Regarding Locomotive Dispositions.

In the column headed "Disposition" the initials PC indicate NYC units included in the original Penn Central roster of February 1, 1968. These units retained their old NYC numbers and classification, but within several months a few switchers were rebuilt and renumbered. Many units survived into the Conrail merger of July 1, 1976, as indicated by the initials CR. Again, there were no immediate changes in numbers or classes.

The initials AM indicate units purchased by Amtrak, including several EP22 passenger units from Penn Central in 1971, and several switchers and road switchers from Conrail when Amtrak acquired the Northeast Corridor in 1976.

The Pittsburgh & Lake Erie was not included in the Penn Central merger of 1968, and for a few years the P&LE maintained a separate roster with the same old numbers. However, during the early 1970's a horsepower-related numbering scheme was adopted, and surviving switchers were renumbered into a new 1200 series, and road switchers into a 1500 series. The P&LE U-Boats retained their 2800 series numbers.

The IHB (Indiana Harbor Belt) also retained its own roster, with numbers unchanged, but the Chicago River & Indiana, the Peoria & Eastern, and the Cleveland Union Terminal units were eventually relettered Penn Central, with no number changes.

Other abbreviations in the "Disposition" column are as follows:

RB - Rebuilt, sometimes to DHT (Diesel Hump Trailers).
Rt - Retired. Usually scrapped or sold within a few months.
Sc - Scrapped or dismantled, usually by the railroad itself.
SS - Sold for scrap by dealers or salvage companies
So - Sold, often to EMD or GE as trade ins on new power.
CK&S - Carthage, Knightstown & Shirley RR
CRI&P - Chicago, Rock Island & Pacific RR
C&BL - Conemaugh & Black Lick RR
DSI - Despatch Shops, Inc. (East Rochester, NY)
GCS - Granite City Steel Co.
ICG - Illinois Central Gulf RR
LIRR - Long Island RR
L&JB - Louisville & Jeffersonville Bridge & RR Co.
L&N - Louisville & Nashville RR
Ms&SV - Mississippi & Skuna Valley RR
Monga - Monongahela RR
NJT - New Jersey Transit
PC&Y - Pittsburgh, Chartiers & Youghiogheny RR
PE - Precision Engineering
PNC - Precision National
TO&E - Texas, Oklahoma & Eastern RR
Y&A - Youngstown & Austintown RR
YS&T - Youngstown Sheet & Tube

New York Central Diesel Locomotives, 1928-1968.

The table below lists a total of 2,751 units acquired by the NYC System prior to merger into Penn Central. Included are 33 second hand units. Also included are units lettered for component lines - the Pittsburgh & Lake Erie, Indiana Harbor Belt, Chicago River & Indiana, Peoria & Eastern, Cleveland Union Terminal, Boston & Albany, Louisville & Jeffersonville Bridge & RR Co., and Michigan Central.

New York Central Diesel Locomotives, By Service

Builder	Model	HP	Built	Class	Number
Early Experimental Units					
Alco-GE	—	750	1928	DEF	1
Alco-GE	—	880	1928	DEP	1
Three-Power-Switchers					
Alco-GE-IR	—	300	1928	DES-2	1
Alco-GE-IR	—	300	1930	DES-3	41
Light Switchers					
General Electric	—	250	(1923)	DESA	1
EMD	SC	600	1936	DES-4	7
EMD	SW1	600	1939-50	DES-5,6	103
EMD	SW8	800	1950-53	DES-18	28
EMD	SW900	900	1954-55	DES-21	19
Alco-GE	HH600	600	1938-39	DES-7	11
Alco-GE	S-1,S-3	660	1940-51	DES-8,9	114
Baldwin	DS-4-4-6	660	1941-44	DES-10	12
General Electric	—	330	1940-42	DES-1	8
Lima	—	800	1951	DES-19	21
Heavy Switchers					
Alco-GE	S-2,5-4	1000	1943-53	DES-11	168
Baldwin	DS-4-4-10	1000	1944-45	DES-12	8
Baldwin	S-12	1200	1951-52	DES-20	21
EMD	NW-2	1000	1946-49	DES-13	152
EMD	SW-7,9	1200	1949-53	DES-16	174
EMD	SW1500	1500	1966-68	(DES-22)	22
F-M	LCC(H10-44)	1000	1946-50	DES-14	11
F-M	H-12-44	1200	1950-52	DES-17	27
LIMA	—	1000	1949	DES-15	6
LIMA	—	1200	1951	DES-15	6
Hump Trailers					
NYC	---	---	1945	DHT-1	4
NYC	---	---	1945-62	DHT-2	9
Passenger Units					
EMD	E7(A)	2000	1945-49	DPA-1	36
EMD	E7(8)	2000	1945-48	DPB-1	14
EMD	E8(A)	2250	1951-53	DPA-5	60
Alco-GE	PA-1	2000	1948-49	DPA-2	8
Alco-GE	PB-1	2000	1948	DPB-2	4
Alco-GE	PA-2	2250	1950-52	DPA-4	7
Alco-GE	PB-2	2250	1950	DPB-4	1
F-M	ERIE BLT.	2000	1949	DPA-3	6
F-M	CPA-24-4	2400	1952	DPA-6	8
B-L-H	Hydr. RP-20	1000	1956	DH-1	1

Builder	Model	HP	Built	Class	Number
Passenger "Combination" Units					
EMD	F-3(A)	1500	1947	DCA-1	4
EMD	F-3(B)	1500	1947	DCB-1	2
Baldwin	DR-6-4-1S	1500	1947-48	DCA-2	4
Baldwin	DR-6-4-1S	1500	1947-48	DCB-2	2
Freight Units					
EMD	FT(A)	1350	1944	DFA-1	4
EMD	FT(B)	1350	1944	DFB-1	4
EMD	F2(A)	1350	1946	DFA-1	2
EMD	F3(A)	1500	1947-48	DFA-2	30
EMD	F3(B)	1500	1947-48	DFB-2	16
EMD	F7(A)	1500	1949-52	DFA-2	238
EMD	F7(B)	1500	1949-52	DFB-2	55
Alco-GE	FA-1	1500	1947-49	DFA-3	44
Alco-GE	FB-1	1500	1947-49	DFB-3	23
Alco-GE	FA-2	1600	1951-52	DFA-7	80
Alco-GE	FB-2	1600	1951-52	DFB-7	50
Baldwin	DR-4-4-15	1500	1948	DFA-4	4
Baldwin	DR-4-4-15	1500	1948	DFB-4	2
Baldwin	RF-16	1600	1951-52	DFA-8	18
Baldwin	RF-16	1600	1951-52	DFB-8	8
F-M	ERIE BLT.	2000	1947-49	DFA-5	6
F-M	ERIE BLT.	2000	1948-49	DFA-5	2
F-M	CFA- 20-4	2000	1950	DFA-6	12
F-M	CFB-20-4	2000	1950	DFB-6	3
F-M	CFA-16-4	1600	1952	DFA-9	8
F-M	CFB-16-4	1600	1952	DFB-9	4
Road Switchers					
Alco-GE	RS-1	1000	1948-50	DRS-1	14
Lima	---	1200	1950	DRS-5	16
B-L-H	RS-12	1200	1951-52	DRS-8	17
Baldwin	RS-4-4-15	1500	1948	DRS-3	2
Alco-GE	RS-2	1500	1948-50	DRS-2	23
Alco-GE	RS-3	1600	1950-53	DRS-6	135
Alco	RS-11	1800	1957	DRS-10	9
EMD	GP7	1500	1950-53	DRS-4	228
EMD	GP9	1750	1954-57	DRS-9	176
F-M	H-16-44	1600	1951	DRS-7	13
F-M	H-20-44	2000	1948-49	DFT-1	19
Alco	RS-32	2000	1961-62	DRS-12	25
EMD	GP20	2000	1961	DRS-11	15
EMD	GP30	2250	1962	DRS-13	10
EMD	GP35	2500	1963-65	DRS-14	31
EMD	GP40	3000	1965-67	DRS-16	105
General Electric	U-25B	2500	1964-65	DRS-15	70
General Electric	U-28B	2800	1966	DRS-17	24
General Electric	U-30B	3000	1967	---	60
Alco	C-430	3000	1967	---	10

This table was originally prepared in 1979 by W. D. Edson for the book *New York Central's Later Power*, by Alvin F. Staufer and Edward L. May.

CLASS DEp 2-D-2: Alco-GE-McI&S Diesel Electric - 900HP-12 Cyl. - 60MPH - 57000-359, 500

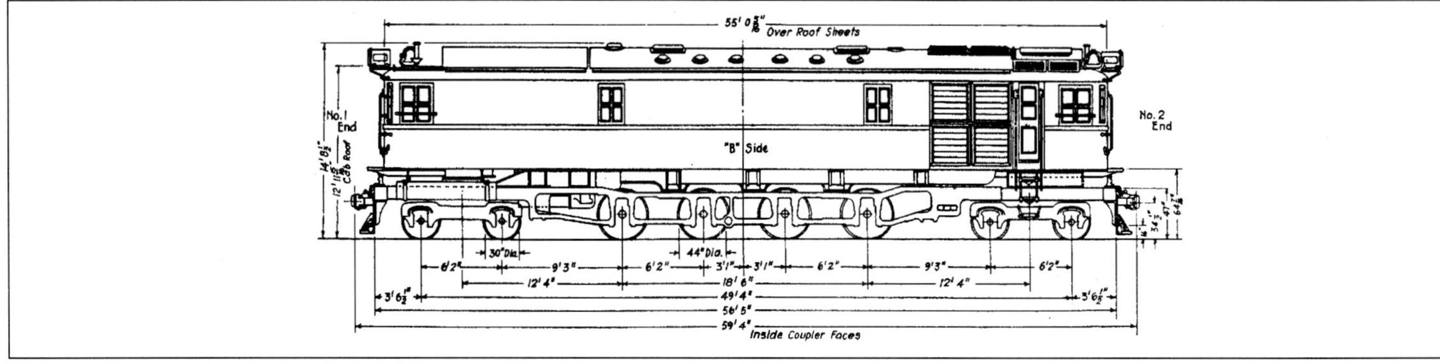

Class	Road Number	Builder Order No.	c/n	Date	Disposition
DEp	1500	Alco S-1537	66715	3/1928	Note

Note: First Road Passenger Diesel Electric Locomotive built in U. S. A. Locomotive did not meet NYC specification, was not officially accepted, and was returned to Alco 2/1936. Scrapped by Alco. Diagram never appeared in NYC Diagram book. Purchase price $192,000.

CLASS DEf 2-D-2: Alco-GE-IR Diesel Electric - 750HP-6 Cyl. (in Line)-50MPH -60, 000 - 301, 000

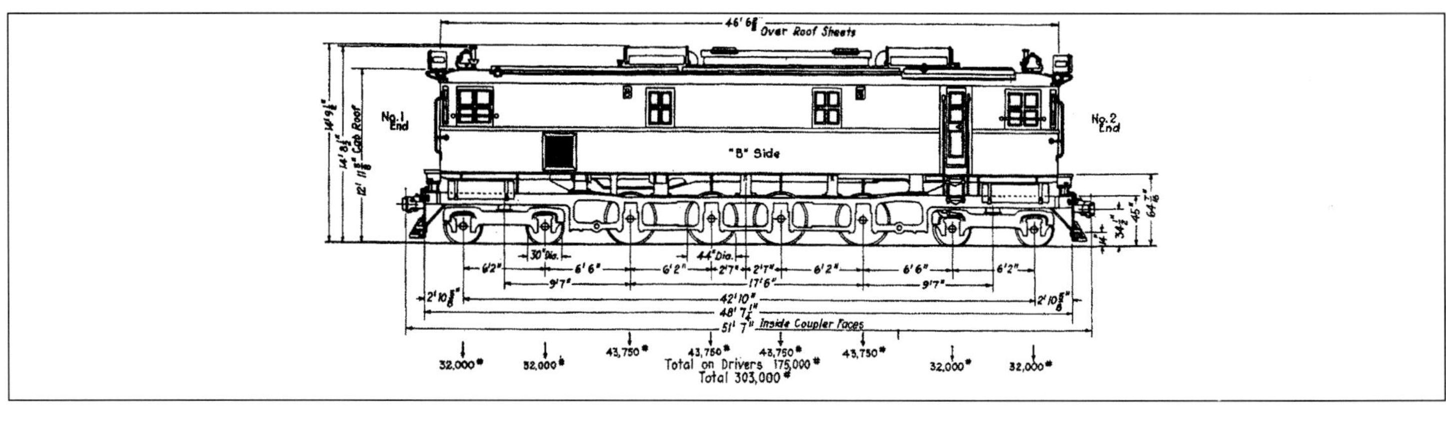

Class	Road No.	Re 1929	Re. 1936	Re 7/1941	Bldr. Order	Bldr. Ser. No.	Date	Disposition
DEF	1550	1510	510	500	Alco 5-1533	66704	6-1928	Note

Note: Purchase price $177, 000. Generally regarded as first successful Diesel Electric Road Freight Locomotive built in United States; Re-built 12/1946 into Diesel Hump Trailer No. 469.

Class DEs-I

DEs-1 (1520) Class and Number assigned but Locomotive not built.

NYCSHS Collection

No. 1500 Class DEP Built by Alco in March 1928 for passenger service. After eight years of trial and error it was returned to the builder.

George Votava

No. 510 Class DEF Built by Alco-GE-IR in June 1928 for experimental freight service on the NYC at a cost of $177,000. In 1929, the locomotive was renumbered 1510; in 1936 to 510; and in 1941 to 500, which it kept along with its 750 HP engine until December 1948 when it was rebuilt into a diesel hump trailer (slug) and numbered 469. It was finally scrapped in November 1953. This photo was made May 30, 1938 at Harmon, NY after occasional use on the Putnam Division.

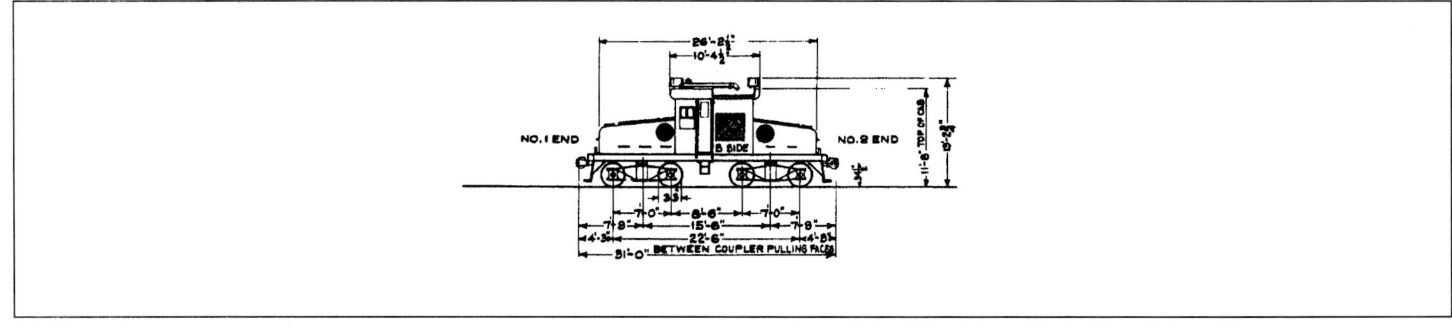

Class	Road No.	Re 1936	Bldr. Ser. No.	Date	Disposition
DEs-A	1505	505	8754	1923 (Acq. 6/1933)	Note

NOTE: Built for Bethlehem Steel Co. as battery switcher. Weight as built 80,000. Buda Engine and Generator added about 1930. Purchased by NYC 6/1933. Sold 12/1944 to Eastman Kodak Co. No. 5.

Three Power Switcher -- Diesel -Battery-Electric

Class DEs-2 B-B Alco-GE-IR Diesel-Battery-Electric 300 HP (Diesel) 1665 (Electric) 40 MPH - 64375 - 250, 700

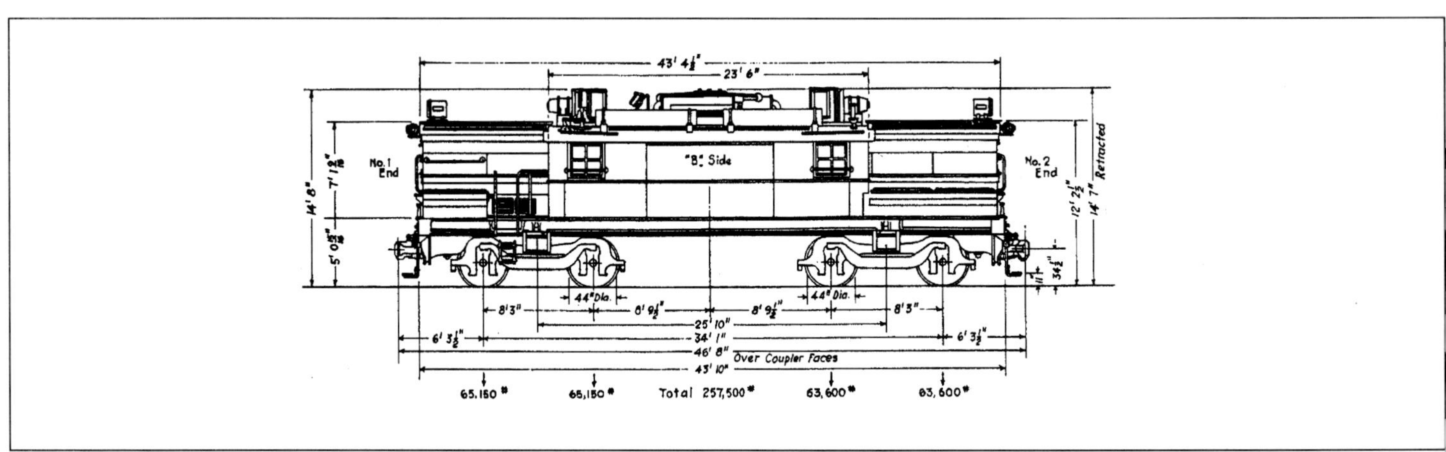

Class	Road No.	Re 1936	Bldr. Order	Bldr. Ser. No.	Date	Disposition
DEs-2	1525	525	Alco S-1566 GE 47852 IR 19-2055 ESB 18127	67101	2/1928	Rebuilt 12/45 to DHT No. 470

No. 1505 Class DES-A Built by General Electric in 1923 for Bethlehem Steel Corporation was purchased by the NYC in 1933.

Both: NYCSHS Collection

No. 1525 Class DES-2. Built by Alco-GE-IR in February 1928 at a cost of $136,000. This Diesel-Electric-Battery "3 power" locomotive was renumbered 525 in 1936, rebuilt into Diesel Hump Trailer No. 470 in December 1945 and finally scrapped in December 1963.

CLASS DES-3 Alco-GE-IR Three-Power Diesel-Battery-Electric

Class	Original Number	Re '36	Builder	c/n	Builder	c/n	Date	Disposition
DES-3	1526	526	Alco	68359	GE	11111	7/1930	Rt 8/54 Sc 1/56
"	1527	527	"	68360	"	11112	"	Rt 6/57 Sc 8/57
"	1528	528	"	68361	"	11113	"	Rt 7/57 Sc 5/58
"	1529	529	"	68362	"	11114	"	Rt 8/56 Sc /57
"	1530	530	"	68363	"	11115	"	Rt 8/54 Sc 12/55
"	1531	531	"	68364	"	11116	8/1930	Rt 11/56 Sc 1/57
"	1532	532	"	68365	"	11117	"	Rt 8/54 Sc 11/55
"	1533	533	"	68366	"	11118	"	Rt 7/55 Sc 8/55
"	1534	534	"	68367	"	11119	"	Rt 7/57 Sc 6/58
"	1535	535	"	68368	"	11120	"	RB 11/53 to DHT 476
"	1536	536	"	68369	"	11121	"	Rt 6/57 Sc 7/58
"	1537	537	"	68370	"	11122	"	Rt 7/55 Sc10/55
"	1538	538	"	68371	"	11123	11/1930	Rt 1/57 Sc /57
"	1539	539	"	68372	"	11124	"	Rt 10/55 Sc 12/55
"	1540	540	"	68373	"	11125	"	Rt 7/57 Sc 7/58
"	1541	541	"	68374	"	11126	"	Rt 7/57 Sc 6/58
"	1542	542	"	68375	"	11127	"	RB 8/50 to DHT 473
"	1543	543	"	68376	"	11128	"	Rt 8/54 Sc 10/55
"	1544	544	"	68377	"	11129	"	Rt 2/56 Sc 5/56
"	1545	545	"	68378	"	11130	"	Rt 1/57 Sc /57
"	1546	546	"	68379	"	11131	12/1930	Rt 8/54 Sc 10/55
"	1547	547	"	68380	"	11132	11/1930	Rt 7/55 Sc 10/55
"	1548	548	"	68381	"	11133	12/1930	Rt 7/55 Sc 11/55
"	1549	549	"	68382	"	11134	"	Rt 8/56 Sc /57
"	1550	550	"	68383	"	11135	"	Rt 2/56 Sc 5/56
"	1551	551	"	68384	"	11136	"	RB 3/54 to DHT 475
"	1552	552	"	68385	"	11137	"	Rt 7/55 Sc /56
"	1553	553	"	68386	"	11138	11/1930	Rt 1/57 Sc /57
"	1554	554	"	68387	"	11139	"	Rt 3/56 Sc /57
"	1555	555	"	68388	"	11140	"	Rt 7/55 Sc 10/55
"	1556	556	"	68389	"	11141	12/1930	Rt 7/55 Sc 1/56
"	1557	557	"	68390	"	11142	"	Rt 7/57 Sc 6/58
"	1558	558	"	68391	"	11143	"	Rt 2/56 Sc 6/56
"	1559	559	"	68392	"	11144	"	Rt 8/54 Sc 10/55
"	1560	560	"	68393	"	11145	"	Rt 7/57 Sc 7/58
"	1561	561	"	68397	"	11230	7/1930	RB 7/48 to DHT 472
"	1562	562	"	68398	"	11231	6/1930	RB 8/46 to DHT 471
"	MC 7530	563	"	68355	"	11210	5/1930	RB 10/50 to DHT 474
"	MC 7531	564	"	68356	"	11211	"	Rt 7/57 Sc 8/58
"	MC 7532	565	"	68357	"	11212	6/1930	Rt 7/57 Sc 7/58
"	MC 7533	566	"	68358	"	11213	"	Rt 8/54 Sc 9/55

Order Nos.:			
1526-1560	Alco S-1690	GE N-369990	IR 31-587
1561-1562	Alco S-1691	GE N-392689	IR 31-587
7530-7533	Alco S-1689	GE N-384854	IR 19-3113

Note: 1561-1562 built without third rail equipment for service at La Salle Street Station, Chicago.

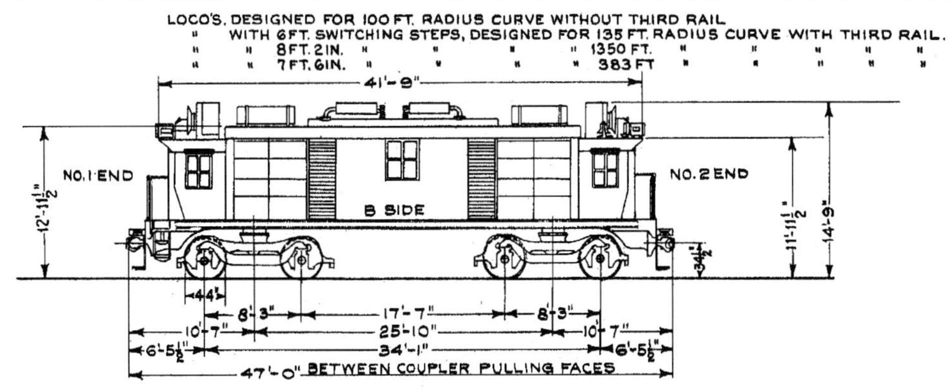

Weight 252400 to 257300

OIL ENGINE ● INGERSOLL-RAND, FOUR CYCLE, SOLID INJECTION, WATER COOLED
H.P. OF ENGINE 300
NUMBER OF CYLINDERS 6 IN LINE
BORE AND STROKE 10" × 12"
SPEED NO LOAD - 573 R.P.M.; FULL LOAD - 550 R.P.M.
MAIN GENERATOR G.E.Co. DT-523-A1 DIRECT CONNECTED
VOLTAGE OF GENERATOR MAXIMUM - 575 V.; FULL LOAD - 500V.
CAPACITY OF GENERATOR 200 KW
CAPACITY OF FUEL OIL TANK 255 GALS.
FUEL CAPACITY (IN OPERATING HOURS) 25 APPROX.
NUMBER AND TYPE OF TRACTION MOTORS FOUR GE-286-B
NOMINAL VOLTAGE OF MOTORS 600/1200
GEAR RATIO 72/17 (4.235)
CONTROL - TYPE AND VOLTAGE PCL (S.U) - 32V.
FUSE CUTTERS ■ THIRD RAIL SHOE AND BATTERY FUSE BOXES
TYPE OF CIRCUIT BREAKER JR-22-E1
MAXIMUM SPEED 40 M.P.H.
NUMBER OF RUNNING SPEEDS (EXTERNAL POWER) FS-1-3; TOTAL - 3
NUMBER OF RUNNING SPEEDS (INTERNAL POWER) FS-1-2; TOTAL - 2
AIR BRAKE SCHEDULE ±14 EL DOUBLE END WITH K-14-BP BRAKE VALVE
TRAIN CONTROL NONE
NUMBER AND TYPE OF AIR COMPRESSORS ONE CP-26-C6
AIR SIGNAL YES

PRINTED 3-1-41

		FS-1	
CONTINUOUS RATING - (EXTERNAL POWER) (600 V.)	TRACTIVE EFFORT	24600 LBS.	
	SPEED	19.8 M.P.H.	
	HORSEPOWER	1300	
	VENTILATION	FORCED	
		FS-1	
		30 MIN.	60 MIN.
RATING (INTERNAL POWER) (SERIES PARALLEL)	TRACTIVE EFFORT	20800 LBS.	16000 LBS.
	SPEED	7.5 M.P.H.	8.3 M.P.H.
	HORSEPOWER	417	358
	VENTILATION	FORCED	FORCED

MAXIMUM TRACTIVE EFFORT (AT 25% ADHESION) ✱62,375, ▲63,100 LBS.

▲ WITH THIRD RAIL EQUIPMENT.
✱ WITHOUT THIRD RAIL EQUIPMENT.

● ONE LOCO. EQUIPPED WITH COOPER-BESSEMER, FOUR CYCLE, SOLID INJECTION, WATER COOLED ENGINE.

■ LOCO'S. OPERATING IN DETROIT TERRITORY ALSO HAVE OVERHEAD SHOE WITH FUSE CUTTERS IN FUSE BOXES.

RATING - ✱ 62.4%, ▲63.1%

CLASS DES-3 (WITH 400 A.H. BATTERY)

NYCSHS Collection

No. 1543 Class DES-3. Built by Alco-GE-IR in November 1930, this "3 power" locomotive was rated at 300 HP when used as as diesel-electric and 1,665 HP when used as a "straight" electric. It is shown here shortly after delivery at Harmon, New York. It was renumbered 543 in 1936 and withdrawn from service in 1954 and scrapped about a year later. Note the narrow footboard needed to clear the third rail. The lettering was aluminum as on all the GCT electrics.

Class DES-1, General Electric 70-Ton 350 HP

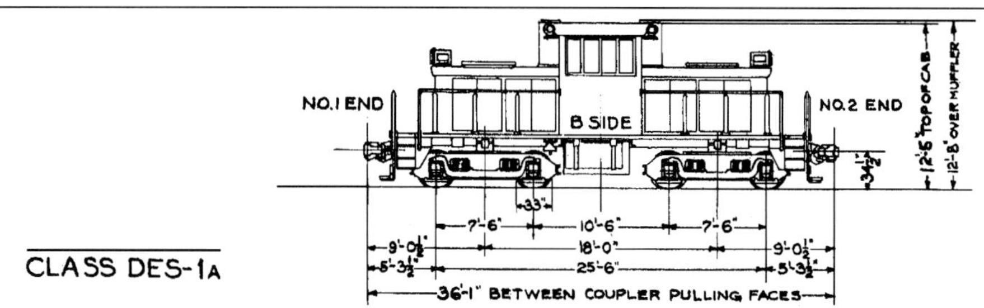

OIL ENGINES — TWO CUMMINS, FOUR CYCLE, SUPERCHARGED, SOLID INJECTION, WATER COOLED.
H.P. ENGINES (TOTAL) — 380(350 FOR TRACTION)✻
NUMBER OF CYLINDERS — 6 IN LINE
BORE AND STROKE — 4⅞" × 6"
SPEEDS — IDLING 500 R.P.M. FULL LOAD 1800 R.P.M.
MAIN GENERATORS — GE.Co. GT-550-B-1 DIRECT CONNECTED
VOLTAGE OF GENERATORS — MAXIMUM 570-V FULL-LOAD - 400V.
CAPACITY OF GENERATORS (TOTAL) — 260 K.W.
CAPACITY OF FUEL OIL TANK — 300 GALS.
FUEL CAPACITY (IN OPERATING HOURS) — 50 HOURS
NUMBER AND TYPE OF TRACTION MOTORS — FOUR GE 1204-T
NOMINAL VOLTAGE OF MOTORS — 250
GEAR RATIO (DOUBLE REDUCTION GEARING) — 58/18 X 76/14 (17.492)
CONTROL-TYPE AND VOLTAGE — M(S.U.) 32V.
FUSE CUTTERS — NONE
TYPE OF CIRCUIT BREAKER — NONE
MAXIMUM SPEED — 25 M.P.H.
NUMBER OF RUNNING SPEEDS — TOTAL 7
AIR BRAKE SCHEDULE — #14 EL SINGLE END WITH K 14-B BRAKE VALVE
TRAIN CONTROL — NONE
Nº & TYPE AIR COMPRESSORS - TWO GARDNER-DENVER TYPE ACM-1000 BELT DRIVEN
AIR SIGNAL — NONE

		FS-1	FS-2
CONTINUOUS RATING -	TRACTIVE EFFORT	14600 LBS	8600 LBS.
	SPEED	7.1 M.P.H.	11.9 M.P.H.
	HORSEPOWER	276	273
	VENTILATION	NATURAL	NATURAL

MAXIMUM TRACTIVE EFFORT (AT 25% ADHESION) — 35000 LBS.

✻ WITH COMPRESSORS UNLOADED.

NOTE: LOCOMOTIVE Nº 506 EQUIPPED WITH CLASSIFICATION LIGHTS AND IMMERSION HEATERS.

RATING - 35%

1-1-46

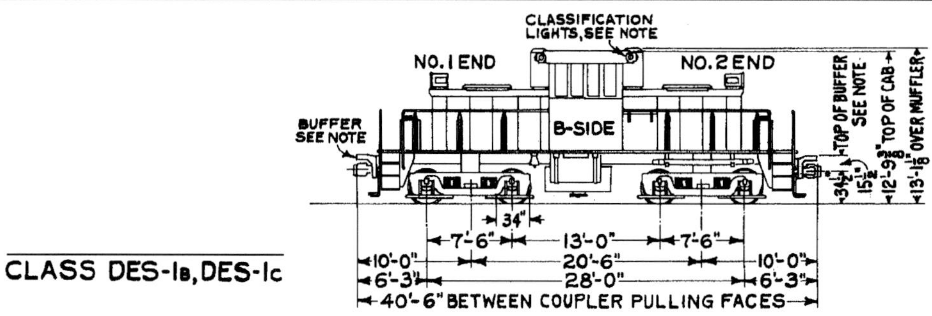

OIL ENGINES - TWO CUMMINS, FOUR CYCLE, SUPERCHARGED, SOLID INJECTION, WATER COOLED.
H.P. ENGINES (TOTAL) — 380(350 FOR TRACTION)✻
NUMBER OF CYLINDERS — 6 IN LINE
BORE AND STROKE — 4⅞" × 6"
SPEEDS — IDLING 500 R.P.M. FULL LOAD 1800 R.P.M.
MAIN GENERATORS — G.E.CO. GT-558-K-1 DIRECT CONNECTED
VOLTAGE OF GENERATORS — MAXIMUM 300-V FULL LOAD 225-V.
CAPACITY OF GENERATORS (TOTAL) — 270 K.W.
CAPACITY OF FUEL OIL TANK — 360 GALS.
FUEL CAPACITY (IN OPERATING HOURS) — 60 HOURS
NUMBER AND TYPE OF TRACTION MOTORS — FOUR GE-733-H-2.
NOMINAL VOLTAGE OF MOTORS — 250.
GEAR RATIO (DOUBLE REDUCTION GEARING) — 56/18 × 76/15 (15.75).
CONTROL-TYPE AND VOLTAGE — M (S.U.) 32V.
FUSE CUTTERS — NONE
TYPE OF CIRCUIT BREAKER — NONE
MAXIMUM SPEED — 25 M.P.H. ■
NUMBER OF RUNNING SPEEDS — TOTAL 7
AIR BRAKE SCHEDULE — #14 EL SINGLE END WITH K14-F BRAKE VALVE
TRAIN CONTROL — NONE
Nº & TYPE AIR COMPR. 2 GARDNER-DENVER — ▲ACM-1000, ●ADR-9001, BELT DRIVEN
AIR SIGNAL — ▲NONE, ●YES

		FS-1	FS-2
CONTINUOUS RATING -	TRACTIVE EFFORT	17000 LBS.	10860 LBS.
	SPEED	5.0 M.P.H.	9.4 M.P.H.
	HORSEPOWER	227	259
	VENTILATION	NATURAL	NATURAL

MAXIMUM TRACTIVE EFFORT (AT 25% ADHESION) ▲35800, ●36125 LBS.

✻ WITH COMPRESSORS UNLOADED.
▲ REFERS TO CLASS DES-1B.
● REFERS TO CLASS DES-1C.
■ 40 M.P.H. WITH TRACTION MOTOR PINIONS REMOVED.

NOTE: CLASS DES-1B NOT EQUIPPED WITH BUFFERS. LOCOMOTIVE Nº 513 EQUIPPED WITH CLASSIFICATION LIGHTS. LOCOMOTIVE Nº'S 507, 508 & 513 EQUIPPED WITH IMMERSION HEATERS.

RATING ▲35.8%, ●36.1%

Class	Original No.	Renumbered	Builder	c/n	New	Disposition
DES-1A	506	X506 (2/52)	GE	12592	7/40	So 9/54 DSI 3
DES-1B	507	X507 (4/54)	GE	15168	11/42	So 7/54 DSI 1
DES-1B	508	X508 (12/53)	GE	15169	11/42	So 7/54 DSI 2, PC 2
DES-1C	509	X509 (4/54)	GE	15170	11/42	Rt 7/64, SS 1/65
DES-1C	510	X510 (4/54)	GE	15171	12/42	Rt 12/60, Sc 9/62
DES-1C	511	—	GE	15172	12/42	So 12/52 Ortner Slag
DES-1C	512	—	GE	15173	12/42	So 10/52 Ortner Slag
DES-1C	513	—	GE	15174	11/42	So 11/52 Ortner Slag

Notes:
Order Nos.: 506 GE N-837725; 507-513 GE N-90310
506 and 513 equipped with classification lights.
All except 507 and 508 equipped with buffers.

CLASS DES-4 Electro-Motive 600HP Model SC

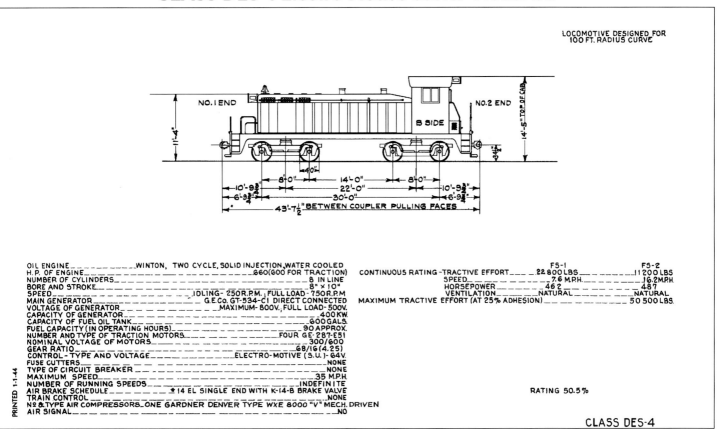

LOCOMOTIVE DESIGNED FOR 100 FT. RADIUS CURVE

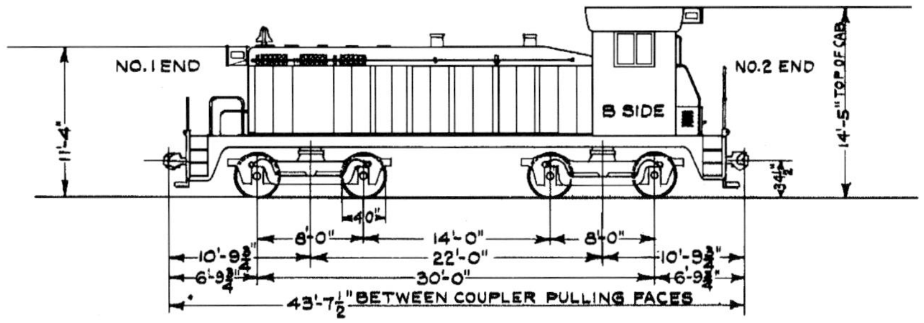

NO. 1 END
NO. 2 END
B SIDE
11'-4"
14'-5" TOP OF CAB
34½"
4'0"
8'0"
14'-0"
8'0"
10'-9¾"
22'-0"
10'-9¾"
6'-9¾"
30'-0"
6'-9¾"
43'-7½" BETWEEN COUPLER PULLING FACES

OIL ENGINE	WINTON, TWO CYCLE, SOLID INJECTION, WATER COOLED
H. P. OF ENGINE	660 (600 FOR TRACTION)
NUMBER OF CYLINDERS	8 IN LINE
BORE AND STROKE	8" × 10"
SPEED	IDLING - 250 R.P.M.; FULL LOAD - 750 R.P.M
MAIN GENERATOR	G.E.Co. GT-534-C1 DIRECT CONNECTED
VOLTAGE OF GENERATOR	MAXIMUM - 800V.; FULL LOAD - 500V.
CAPACITY OF GENERATOR	400 KW.
CAPACITY OF FUEL OIL TANK	600 GALS.
FUEL CAPACITY (IN OPERATING HOURS)	90 APPROX.
NUMBER AND TYPE OF TRACTION MOTORS	FOUR GE-287-E51
NOMINAL VOLTAGE OF MOTORS	300/600
GEAR RATIO	68/16 (4.25)
CONTROL - TYPE AND VOLTAGE	ELECTRO-MOTIVE (S.U.) - 64V.
FUSE CUTTERS	NONE
TYPE OF CIRCUIT BREAKER	NONE
MAXIMUM SPEED	35 M.P.H.
NUMBER OF RUNNING SPEEDS	INDEFINITE
AIR BRAKE SCHEDULE	* 14 EL SINGLE END WITH K-14-B BRAKE VALVE
TRAIN CONTROL	NONE
Nº & TYPE AIR COMPRESSORS	ONE GARDNER DENVER TYPE WXE 8000 "V" MECH. DRIVEN
AIR SIGNAL	NO

		FS-1	FS-2
CONTINUOUS RATING	TRACTIVE EFFORT	22 800 LBS	11 200 LBS
	SPEED	7.6 M.P.H.	16.2 M.P.H.
	HORSEPOWER	462	487
	VENTILATION	NATURAL	NATURAL
MAXIMUM TRACTIVE EFFORT (AT 25% ADHESION)			50 500 LBS.

RATING 50.5%

PRINTED 1-1-44

CLASS DES-4

Road	Number		Builder	c/n	Date	Disposition
CR&I	567	(to NYC in 1951)	EMC	604	7/1936	Rt 12/60, Sc 1/63
CR&I	568	"	"	605	"	Rt 12/60, Sc 4/63
CR&I	569	"	"	606	"	Rt 12/60, Sc 5/63
CR&I	570	"	"	607	"	Rt 12/60, So 3/62 (Note)
CR&I	571	"	"	608	"	Rt 12/60, Sc 3/63
CR&I	572	"	"	609	"	Rt 12/60, Sc 2/63
CR&I	573	"	"	610	"	Rt 12/60, Sc 1/62

Note: EMD order no. E-139. No.570 to Empire Coke Co., Holt, Ala. through Birmingham Rail & Equipment Co.

NYCSHS Collection

No. 573 Class DES-4. (Chicago River & Indiana). This EMC model "SC" was built in July 1936. The 600 HP switcher was painted gray instead of the usual black and was scrapped in January 1962.

CLASS DES-5 (ES-6) ELECTRO-MOTIVE 600HP Model SW1 (Light)

LOCOMOTIVE DESIGNED FOR 100 FT. RADIUS CURVE

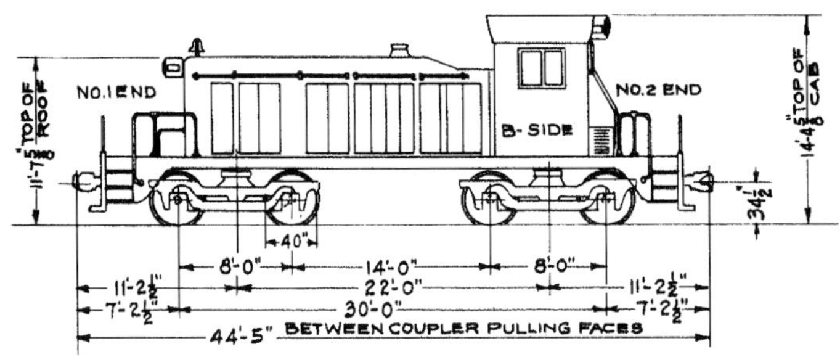

OIL ENGINE — GENERAL MOTORS, TWO CYCLE, SOLID INJECTION, WATER COOLED
H.P. OF ENGINE — 660 (600 FOR TRACTION)
NUMBER OF CYLINDERS — 6-V TYPE
BORE AND STROKE — 8 1/2" x 10"
SPEED — IDLING 275 R.P.M; FULL LOAD 800 R.P.M.
MAIN GENERATOR — E.M.CO. D-4-D DIRECT CONNECTED
VOLTAGE OF GENERATOR — MAXIMUM 800V., FULL LOAD 600V.
CAPACITY OF GENERATOR — 400 KW
CAPACITY OF FUEL OIL TANK — 600 GALS.
FUEL CAPACITY (IN OPERATING HOURS) — 90 HOURS
NUMBER AND TYPE OF TRACTION MOTORS — FOUR E.M.CO. D-7-A1
NOMINAL VOLTAGE OF MOTORS — 300/600
GEAR RATIO — 62/15 (4.133)
CONTROL-TYPE AND VOLTAGE — ELECTRO-MOTIVE (S.U.) 64 V.
FUSE CUTTERS — NONE
TYPE OF CIRCUIT BREAKER — NONE
MAXIMUM SPEED — 45 M.P.H.
NUMBER OF RUNNING SPEEDS — INDEFINITE
AIR BRAKE SCHEDULE — #14 EL SINGLE END WITH K-14-B BRAKE VALVE
TRAIN CONTROL — NONE
Nº & TYPE AIR COMPRESSORS — ONE GARDNER DENVER TYPE WXE-8013 "V" MECH. DRIVEN
AIR SIGNAL — NONE

CONTINUOUS RATING - TRACTIVE EFFORT — 23,400 LBS.
SPEED — 7.5 M.P.H.
HORSEPOWER — 468
VENTILATION — NATURAL
MAXIMUM TRACTIVE EFFORT (AT 25% ADHESION) — 48,925 LBS.

RATING: 48.9%

PRINTED 1-1-44

CLASS DES-5B

Class	Number	Re '66		Builder	c/n	Date	Disposition
DES-5A	574	*8400		EMC	853	2/39	PC, CR
"	575	8401		"	854	"	PC, CR
"	576	8402		"	855	"	PC, CR
"	577	*8403	8415 (1/67)	"	856	"	Rt 1/67
"	578	8404		"	857	"	PC Rt 6/68
"	579	8405		"	858	"	PC, CR
DES-5B	580	*8406		"	1878	1/43	PC, CR
"	581	8407		"	1879	12/42	Rt 2/67 EMD
"	582	8408		"	1880	3/43	PC
"	583	8409		"	1881	"	PC, CR
"	584	8410		"	1882	"	PC, CR
DES-5C	585	8411		EMD	6391	4/49	PC, CR
"	586	8412		"	6392	"	PC, CR
"	587	8413		"	6393	"	PC, CR
"	588	8414		"	6394	"	PC, CR
"	589	8415	8403 (1/67)	"	6395	"	PC, CR
"	590	8416		"	6396	"	PC, CR
"	591	8417		"	6397	"	PC, CR
"	592	8418		"	6398	"	PC Rt 6/68
"	593	8419		"	6399	"	PC
"	594	*8420		"	6400	"	PC, CR
"	595	8421		"	6401	6/49	PC, CR

Class	Number	Re '66	Builder	c/n	Date	Disposition
DES-5c	596	(8422)	EMD	6402	6/49	Rt 4/66 EMD
"	597	8423	"	6403	"	PC, CR
"	598	8424	"	6404	"	PC, CR
"	599	8425	"	6405	"	PC, AM 243
"	600	8426	"	6406	"	PC Rt 6/68
"	601	8427	"	6407	"	PC, CR
"	602	8428	"	6408	"	PC, AM 244
"	603	8429	"	6409	"	PC, CR
"	604	*8430 8474 (1/67)	"	6410	"	Rt 1/67
"	605	8431	"	6411	"	PC, AM 245
"	606	8432	"	6412	"	PC, CR
"	607	8433	"	6413	"	PC, CR
"	608	8434	"	6414	"	PC, CR
"	609	8435	"	6415	"	PC, CR
DES-5d	610	8436	"	11767	10/50	PC, CR
"	611	*8437	"	11768	"	PC, CR
"	612	8438	"	11769	"	PC, CR
"	613	8439	"	11770	"	PC, CR
"	614	8440	"	11771	"	PC, CR
DES-5e	615	8441	"	11782	6/50	PC, CR
"	616	8442	"	11783	"	PC, CR
"	617	8443	"	11784	"	PC Rt 6/68
"	618	*8444	"	11785	"	PC, CR
"	619	8445	"	11786	"	Rt 4/66 EMD
"	620	8446	"	11787	10/50	PC, CR
"	621	8447	"	11788	"	PC, CR

Note: * re 10/64 to CR&I same nos. Order Nos.: DES-5a E-217; DES-5b E-521; DES-5c E-999; DES-5d 6115; DES-5e 6116 DES-5e lettered for CR&I until 1951.

NYCSHS Collection

No. 588 Class DES-5c. One of more than a hundred EMD SW1 units on the NYC system.

Class DES-6 (ES-6,m) Electro-Motive 600 HP Model SW1 (Heavy)

Class	Number	Re'49	Re'66	Builder	Order Number	c/n	Date	Disposition
DES-6A	600	650	8448	EMC	(E-217)	808	2/39	Rt 4/66 EMD
"	601	651	8449	"	"	809	"	PC, CR
"	602	652	8450	"	"	810	"	PC, CR
"	603	653	8451	"	"	811	"	PC, CR
DES-6B	@604	654	8452	"	"	812	"	PC
"	@605	655	*8453	"	"	813	3/39	PC, CR
"	@606	656	8454	"	"	814	"	PC, CR
"	@607	657	8455	"	"	815	4/39	PC
"	@608	658	(8456)	"	"	816	"	Rt 4/66 EMD
"	609	659	8457	"	"	817	"	PC, CR
"	610	660	8458	"	"	818	"	PC
"	611	661	*8459	"	"	819	"	PC, CR
"	612	662	8460	"	"	820	"	PC, CR
"	613	663	8461	"	"	821	"	PC, CR
DES-6C	614	664	8462	"	(E-239)	875	5/39	PC, CR
"	615	665	8463	"	"	876	"	PC, CR
"	616	666	8464	"	"	877	"	PC, AM 246
"	617	667		"	(E-282)	1010	12/39	SS 10/63
"	618	668	8465	"	"	1011	"	PC, CR
"	619	669	8466	"	"	1012	1/40	PC, CR
"	620	670	8467	"	"	1013	"	PC
"	621	671	8468	"	"	1014	"	PC, CR
DES-6D	622	672	8469	"	(E-372)	1254	3/41	PC Rt 6/68
"	623	673	8470	"	"	1255	"	PC, CR
"	624	674	(8471)	"	"	1256	"	Rt 4/66 EMD
"	625	675	8472	"	"	1257	4/41	PC, CR
"	626	676	8473	"	"	1258	"	Rt 1/67
"	627	677	8474-8430	"	"	1259	5/41	PC, CR (Re 1/67)
"	628	678	8475	"	"	1260	"	PC, AM 247
"	629	679	8476	"	"	1261	6/41	PC, AM 248
"	630	680	8477	"	"	1262	"	PC, CR
"	631	681	8478	"	"	1263	"	PC, CR
"	632	682	(8479)	"	"	1264	7/41	Rt 4/66 EMD
"	633	683	8480	"	"	1265	"	PC, CR
"	634	684*	8481	"	"	1266	"	PC Rt 9/69
"	635	685	8482	"	"	1267	8/41	PC Rt 6/68
"	636	686	8483	"	"	1268	"	PC, CR
"	637	687	8484	"	"	1269	"	PC, CR
"	638	688	8485	"	"	1270	"	PC, CR
"	639	689	8486	"	"	1271	"	PC, CR
"	640	690	8487	"	"	1272	9/41	PC, CR
"	641	691	8488	"	"	1273	"	PC, CR
DES-6E	642	692	8489	"	(E-373)	1274	4/41	PC
"	643	693	8490	"	"	1275	"	PC So P-N
"	644	694	8491	"	"	1276	"	PC, CR
DES-6F	645	695	8492 mu	"	(E-374)	1277	7/41	PC, CR
"	646	696	mu	"	"	1278	"	Sc 2/59
"	647	697	8493 mu	"	"	1279	"	PC, CR
DES-6G	648	698	8494	"	(E-456)	1582	12/41	PC
"	649	699	8495	"	"	1583	"	PC Rt 6/68
"	650	700	8496	"	"	1584	1/42	PC, CR
"	651	701	8497	"	"	1589	"	PC, AM 249
"	652	702	*8498	"	"	1590	"	PC, CR
"	653	703	8499	"	"	1591	2/42	PC, AM 250
"	654	704	8500	"	"	1592	"	PC, CR

Note @ CR&I 1941 to 1950.
* Re 10/64 CR&I same nos.
All DES-6 Units had air whistle and short exhaust stacks. DES-6a,e equipped with buffers and air signal.
671,690,696 double end train control.

LOCOMOTIVE DESIGNED FOR
100 FT. RADIUS CURVE

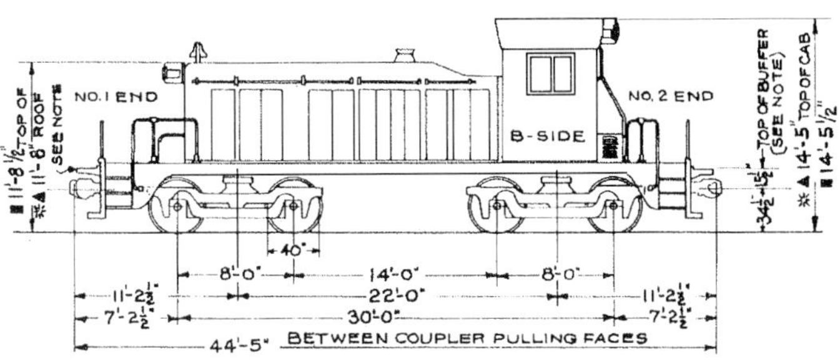

OIL ENGINE	GENERAL MOTORS, TWO CYCLE, SOLID INJECTION, WATER COOLED
H.P. OF ENGINE	660 (600 FOR TRACTION)
NUMBER OF CYLINDERS	6-V TYPE
BORE AND STROKE	8½" x 10"
SPEED	IDLING 275 R.P.M; FULL LOAD 800 R.P.M
MAIN GENERATOR	E.M.CO. D-4-D DIRECT CONNECTED
VOLTAGE OF GENERATOR	MAXIMUM 800V., FULL LOAD 600V.
CAPACITY OF GENERATOR	400 KW
CAPACITY OF FUEL OIL TANK	600 GALS.
FUEL CAPACITY (IN OPERATING HOURS)	90 HOURS
NUMBER AND TYPE OF TRACTION MOTORS	FOUR E.M.CO. D-7-A
NOMINAL VOLTAGE OF MOTORS	300/600
GEAR RATIO	62/15 (4.133)
CONTROL-TYPE AND VOLTAGE	ELECTRO-MOTIVE (S.U.) 64V.
FUSE CUTTERS	NONE
TYPE OF CIRCUIT BREAKER	NONE
MAXIMUM SPEED	45 M.P.H.
NUMBER OF RUNNING SPEEDS	INDEFINITE
AIR BRAKE SCHEDULE	#14 EL SINGLE END WITH K-14-B BRAKE VALVE
TRAIN CONTROL	NONE
Nº & TYPE AIR COMPRESSORS	ONE GARDNER DENVER TYPE WXE-8009"V" MECH. DRIVEN OR ONE GARDNER DENVER TYPE WXE-8013"V" MECH. DRIVEN
AIR SIGNAL	▲YES, ✻■NONE

PRINTED 1-1-44

CONTINUOUS RATING - TRACTIVE EFFORT	23,400 LBS.
SPEED	7.5 M.P.H.
HORSEPOWER	468
VENTILATION	NATURAL
MAXIMUM TRACTIVE EFFORT (AT 25% ADHESION)	✻55,775, ▲56,125, ■55,875 LBS.

✻ REFERS TO CLASS DES-6D
▲ REFERS TO CLASS DES-6E
■ REFERS TO CLASS DES-6G

NOTE: CLASS DES-6D & DES-6G NOT EQUIPPED WITH BUFFERS

RATING: ✻55.8%, ▲56.1%, ■55.9%

CLASS DES-6D, DES-6E, DES-6G

Collection of H.L. Vail

No. 607 Class DES-6B. One of five EMD SW1 units lettered for Chicago River & Indiana from 1941 to 1950. Photograph made at the Chicago stockyards.

CLASS DES-7 ALCO-GE "HIGH HOOD" 600 HP

LOCOMOTIVE DESIGNED FOR
100 FT. RADIUS CURVE

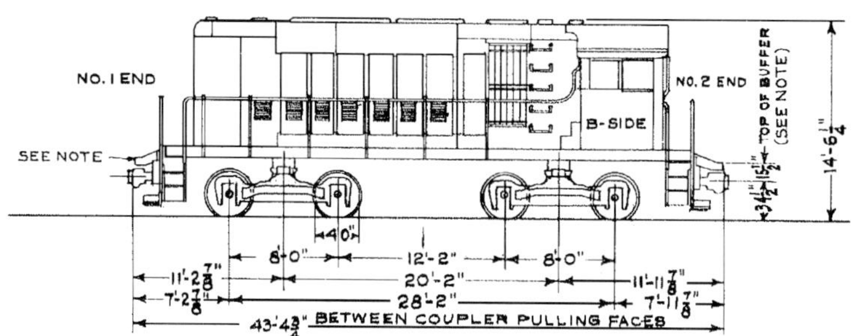

OIL ENGINE McINTOSH-SEYMOUR, A.L.CO. FOUR CYCLE, SOLID INJECTION, WATER COOLED
H.P. OF ENGINE — 660 (600 FOR TRACTION)
NUMBER OF CYLINDERS — 6 IN LINE
BORE AND STROKE — 12½" × 13"
SPEED — IDLING - 350 R.P.M. ; FULL LOAD - 700 R.P.M.
MAIN GENERATOR — G.E.CO ; GT 551 B1 DIRECT CONNECTED
VOLTAGE OF GENERATOR — MAXIMUM - 600V. FULL LOAD - 500V.
CAPACITY OF GENERATOR — 415 K.W.
CAPACITY OF FUEL OIL TANK — 625 GALS.
FUEL CAPACITY (IN OPERATING HOURS) — 75 HOURS
NUMBER AND TYPE OF TRACTION MOTORS — FOUR G.E.-287-E51
NOMINAL VOLTAGE OF MOTORS — 300/600
GEAR RATIO — 68/16 (4.25)
CONTROL - TYPE AND VOLTAGE — G.E.CO. (S.U.) - 125V.
FUSE CUTTERS — NONE
TYPE OF CIRCUIT BREAKER — NONE
MAXIMUM SPEED — 40 M.P.H.
NUMBER OF RUNNING SPEEDS — INDEFINITE
AIR BRAKE SCHEDULE — * 14 EL SINGLE END WITH K-14-E BRAKE VALVE
TRAIN CONTROL — NONE
NUMBER AND TYPE OF AIR COMPRESSORS — ONE G.E.CO. CP-26-E-4
AIR SIGNAL — NONE & ▲YES

PRINTED 1-1-44

CONTINUOUS RATING - TRACTIVE EFFORT — 28,000 LBS.
SPEED — 6 M.P.H.
HORSEPOWER — 450
VENTILATION — FORCED
MAXIMUM TRACTIVE EFFORT (AT 25% ADHESION) * 53950, ▲ 54375 LBS.

* REFERS TO CLASS DES-7A
▲ REFERS TO CLASS DES-7B

NOTE: CLASS DES-7A NOT EQUIPPED WITH BUFFERS.
LOCOMOTIVE Nº'S 674, 677 & 679 EQUIPPED WITH IMMERSION HEATERS.

RATING - * 54 %, ▲ 54.4 %

CLASS DES-7A, DES-7B

Class	Original No.	Re'39	Re'48	Builder	c/n	Date	Disposition
DES-7A	614	674	800	Alco	69127	12/38	Rt 12/62 So 2/63
"	615	675	801	"	69128	"	Rt 12/62 SS 9/63
"	616	676	802	"	69129	1/39	Rt /63 So 12/63
"	617	677	803	"	69130	"	Rt 12/62 SS 9/63
"	618	678	804	"	69131	3/39	Rt /63 Sc 9/63
"	(619)	679	805	"	69132	"	Rt /63 So 12/63
DES-7B	B&A	680	806	"	69133	"	Rt /63 So 12/63
"	"	681	807	"	69134	"	Rt 12/62 SS 9/63
"	"	682	808	"	69135	5/39	So 12/63
"	"	683	809	"	69151	"	So 12/63
"	"	684	810	"	69152	"	So 12/63

Order No. S-1806.
DES-7b built with buffers and air signal. 801 later equipped.
806-810 lettered NYC in 1952.

NYCSHS Collection

No 682 Class DES-7B. (Boston & Albany) Model HH-600 switcher was built by Alco in May 1939. B&A steam power of that era was numbered in its own series, but these five switchers retained NYC numbering with B&A lettering until 1952.

Norton D. Clark

Probably the most unique New York Central paint scheme was applied to the only Class DES-8A numbered 590. Alco displayed the S-1 at the 1940 World's Fair in New York numbered 660 (representing the HP). It was delivered to the NYC in March 1941. It was renumbered to 811 in 1948 and again to 9300 in 1966. The paint appeared to be black and silver or gray with gray lettering outlined in white with a cast Alco logo on the cab.

CLASS DES-8A to 8D (AS-6,m) ALCO-GE 660 HP Model S-1(Light)

LOCOMOTIVE DESIGNED FOR
100 FT. RADIUS CURVE

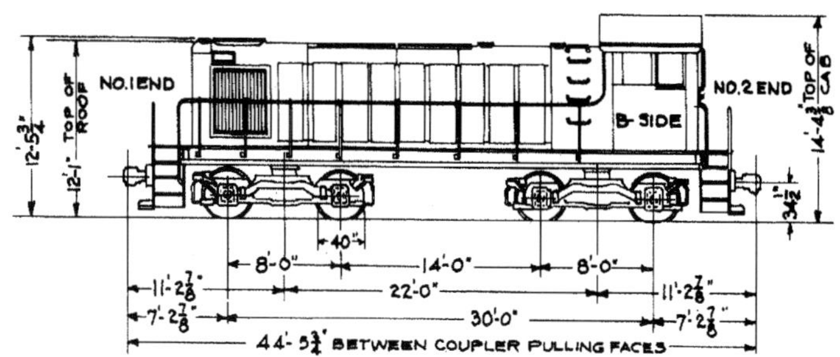

OIL ENGINE __ McINTOSH-SEYMOUR, A.L.CO. FOUR CYCLE, SOLID INJECTION, WATER COOLED
H.P. OF ENGINE __ 600 (550 FOR TRACTION)
NUMBER OF CYLINDERS __ 6 IN LINE
BORE AND STROKE __ 12½" x 13"
SPEED __ IDLING 270 R.P.M., FULL LOAD 700 R.P.M.
MAIN GENERATOR __ G.E.CO. GT-552-A3 OR A4 DIRECT CONNECTED
VOLTAGE OF GENERATOR __ MAXIMUM-700V., FULL LOAD 600 V.
CAPACITY OF GENERATOR __ 435 KW
CAPACITY OF FUEL OIL TANK __ 635 GALS.
FUEL CAPACITY (IN OPERATING HOURS) __ 75 HOURS
NUMBER AND TYPE OF TRACTION MOTORS __ FOUR GE-731-C2 OR D2
NOMINAL VOLTAGE OF MOTORS __ 300/600
GEAR RATIO __ 75/16 (4.69)
CONTROL-TYPE AND VOLTAGE __ G.E.CO. (SU) 64V.
FUSE CUTTERS __ NONE
TYPE OF CIRCUIT BREAKER __ NONE
MAXIMUM SPEED __ 60 M.P.H.
NUMBER OF RUNNING SPEEDS __ INDEFINITE
AIR BRAKE SCHEDULE __ #14 EL SINGLE END WITH K-14-F BRAKE VALVE
TRAIN CONTROL __ NONE
Nº & TYPE AIR COMPRESSORS __ ONE W.A.B.CO. TYPE 3-CD "V" MECH. DRIVEN
AIR SIGNAL __ NONE

PRINTED 1-1-44

CONTINUOUS RATING - TRACTIVE EFFORT __ 29,200 LBS.
SPEED __ 5.3 M.P.H.
HORSEPOWER __ 413
VENTILATION __ FORCED
MAXIMUM TRACTIVE EFFORT (AT 25% ADHESION) __ 50,125 LBS. (APPROX.)

RATING 50.1% APPROX.

CLASS DES-8B

Class	Original No.	Re '48	Re '66	Builder	Builder Order Number	c/n	Date	Disposition
DES-8A	590	811	9300	Alco	(S-1816)	69193	5/40*	PC
DES-8B	693	812	9301	"	(S-1857)	69825	3/41	PC
"	694	813	9302	"	"	69826	9/42	Rt 5/67 GE
"	695	814	9303	"	(S-1858)	69830	"	PC
"	696	815	9304	"	"	69831	10/42	Rt 5/67 GE
"	697	816	9305	"	"	69832	"	PC
"	698	817	9306	"	"	69833	"	Rt 9/67
"	699	818	9383 mu	"	"	69834	"	PC
"	700	819	9307	"	"	69835	7/43	PC
"	701	820	9308	"	"	69836	"	Rt 5/67 GE
"	702	821	9309	"	"	69837	8/43	PC
"	703	822	9384 mu	"	"	69838	"	PC
"	704	823	9310 mu	"	"	69838	"	PC Rt EMD
"	705	824	9311	"	"	69840	"	PC
"	706	825	9385 mu	"	"	69841	"	PC
"	707	826	9312	"	"	69842	"	PC
"	708	827	9313	"	(S-1913)	71262	1/44	PC Rt 7/68
"	709	828	9314	"	"	71263	"	Rt 5/67 GE
"	710	829	9315	"	"	71266	2/44	Rt 12/67
"	711	830	9316	"	"	71267	"	Rt 5/67 GE
"	712	831	9317	"		71268	4/44	Rt 8/67

* 590 exhibited by Alco at 1940 New York Worlds Fair, not received until 3/41
710 and 711 not renumbered until 1950.

No. 700 Class DES-8B built by Alco-GE in July 1943 was a 660 HP model S-1 switcher.

Both: NYCSHS Collection

No. 865 Class DES-8D was another model S-1 switcher, built by Alco in March 1950.

Class	Original No.	Re '48	Re '66	Builder	Builder Order Number	c/n	Date	Disposition
DES-8b	713	832	9386 mu	Alco	(S-1913)	71272	4/44	Rt 5/67 GE
"	714	833	9387 mu	"	"	71273	5/44	Rt 5/67 GE
"	715	834	9318	"	"	71270	2/44	PC
"	716	835	9319	"	(S-1929)	71990	5/44	Rt 5/67 GE
"	717	836	9320	"	"	71993	6/44	Rt 12/67
"	718	837	9321	"	"	71994	"	Rt 8/67
"	719	838	9388 mu	"	"	71995	"	PC Rt 7/68
"	720	839	9389 mu	"	"	70042	7/44	PC SS Luntz
"	721	840	9390 mu	"	"	70043	"	PC, Rt 2/68
"	722	841	9322	"	"	70044	"	5/67 GE
"	723	842	9323	"	"	70045	"	PC
"	724	843	9391 mu	"	"	70046	"	PC, Rt 7/68
"	725	844	9324	"	"	70052	8/44	PC
"	726	845	9325	"	"	70053	"	PC
"	727	846	9326	"	"	70054	"	PC
"	728	847	9327	"	"	70055	"	Rt 5/67 GE
"	729	848	9328	"	"	70056	"	PC
DES-8c	730	849	9329	"	(S-1953)	73082	1/45	PC
"	731	850	9330	"	"	73087	2/45	PC
"	732	851		"	"	73088	"	Rt C/65
"	733	852	9392 mu	"	"	73089	3/45	PC
"	734	853	9331	"	"	73090	"	Rt 8/67
"	735	854	9332	"	"	73091	"	Rt 5/67 GE
"	736	855	9333	"	"	73092	"	PC
"	737	856	9393 mu	"	(S-1964)	73338	4/45	PC
"	738	857	9334	"	"	73339	"	PC
"	739	858	9394 mu	"	"	73340	"	PC
"	740	859	9335	"	"	73341	"	PC, SS, Luntz
"	741	860	9336	"	"	73342	"	PC, SS, Luntz
"	742	861	9337	"	"	73348	5/45	PC
"	743	862	9338	"	"	73349	"	PC
"	744	863	(9339)	"	"	73350	"	Rt 3/66 Sc

Class	Original No.	Re'66	Builder	Order Number	c/n	Date	Disposition
DES-8d	864	9340	Alco	(S-3119)	77791	3/50	PC
"	865	9341	"	"	77792	"	Rt 5/67 GE
"	866	9342	"	"	77793	"	Rt 8/67
"	867	9343	"	"	77794	"	Rt 8/67
"	868	9344	"	"	77795	"	Rt 5/67 GE
"	869		"	"	77074	"	Rt c/65
"	870	9345	"	"	77075	"	PC
"	871	9346	"	"	77076	"	PC
"	872		"	"	77077	"	So /65 DSI 5
"	873	9347	"	"	77078	"	PC

LOCOMOTIVE DESIGNED FOR
57.5° CURVE

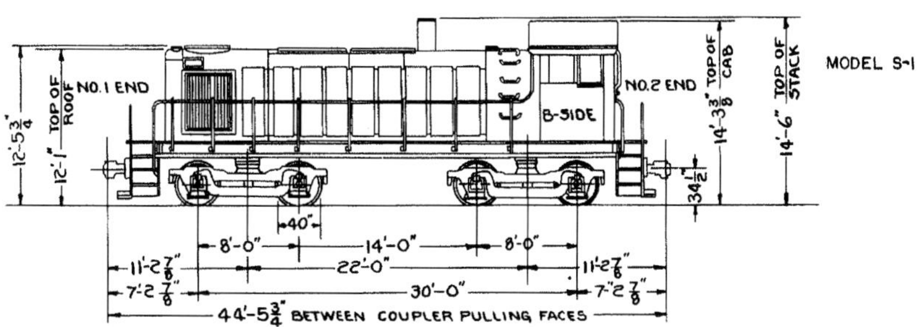

DIESEL ENGINE .... ALCO MODEL 539
DIESEL ENGINE H.P. .... 600 FOR TRACTION
NUMBER OF CYLINDERS .... 6 IN LINE
BORE AND STROKE .... 12½" X 13"
ENGINE SPEED R.P.M. .... IDLING 315, FULL LOAD 740
MAIN GENERATOR .... G.E.CO. TYPE GT-554-A3 DIRECT DRIVEN
MAIN GENERATOR VOLTAGE .... MAX. 775V. FULL LOAD 660V
MAIN GENERATOR CAPACITY .... 435 K.W.
NUMBER AND TYPE OF TRACTION MOTORS .... FOUR GE-731-D3
TRACTION MOTOR VENTILATION .... FORCED
GEAR RATIO 75/16 (4.69)
CONTROL VOLTAGE 75V

MAXIMUM SPEED OF LOCOMOTIVE .... ✲ 60 M.P.H.
CONTINUOUS RATING - TRACTIVE EFFORT .... 29,200 LBS.

✲ 75/16 GEAR RATIO SPEED. LOCOMOTIVE RESTRICTED TO 45 MPH.

PRINTED 4-15-57

CLASS DES-8E, 8F

NYCSHS Collection

No. 880 Class DES-8E one of 43 Alco S-3 switchers.

CLASS DES-8E to 8F (AS-6,m) ALCO-GE 660 HP Model S-3(Light)

Class	Original No.	Re'66	Builder	Order Number	c/n	Date	Disposition
DES-8E	874	9348	Alco	(S-3143)	78141	6/50	PC
"	875	9349	"	"	78142	"	PC
"	876	9350	"	"	78143	"	PC
"	877	9351	"	"	78144	"	PC Rt 4/68
"	878	9352	"	"	78145	7/50	PC
"	879	9395 mu	"	"	78146	"	PC
"	880	9396 mu	"	"	78147	"	PC
"	881	9353	Alco	(S-3153)	78148	8/50	PC
"	882	9354	"	"	78149	"	PC
"	883	9355	"	"	78150	"	PC Rt 4/68
"	884	9356	"	"	78151	"	PC 7/68
"	885	9357	"	"	78152	"	PC
"	886	9358	"	"	78153	"	PC
"	887	9397 mu	"	"	78154	"	PC
"	888	9359	"	"	78155	"	PC Rt 7/68
"	889	9360	"	"	78156	"	PC
"	890	9361	"	"	78157	"	PC
"	891	9362	"	"	78158	"	PC Rt 4/68
"	892	9363	"	"	78221	"	PC
"	893	9398 mu	"	"	78222	"	PC Rt EMD
"	894	9364	"	"	78223	"	Rt 9/67
"	895	9365	"	"	78224	"	PC
"	896	(9399)mu	"	"	78225	"	Rt 2/66 Sc
"	897	9366	"	"	78226	"	PC
"	898	9400 mu	"	"	78227	"	PC
"	899	(9367)	"	"	78228	9/50	Rt 2/66 Sc
"	900	9368	"	"	78229	"	PC
"	901	9369	"	"	78230	"	PC Rt EMD
"	902	9370	"	"	78315	"	PC
"	903	9371	"	"	78316	"	PC
DES-8F	904	9372	"	(S-3166)	78787	9/51	PC
"	905	9373	"	"	78788	"	PC
"	906	9401 mu	"	"	78789	"	PC
"	907	9374	"	"	78791	10/51	PC
"	908	9402 mu	"	"	78792	"	PC
"	909	9403 mu	"	"	78793	"	PC Rt 7/68
"	910	9375	"	"	78794	"	PC
"	911	9376	"	"	78795	"	PC
"	912	9377	"	"	79351	11/51	PC
"	913	9378	"	"	79352	"	PC
"	914	9379	"	"	79353	"	PC
"	915	9380	"	"	79355	"	PC
"	916	9381	"	"	79356	"	Rt 8/67

Class DES-9 (AS-6,m) ALCO-GE 660 HP Model S-1 (Heavy)

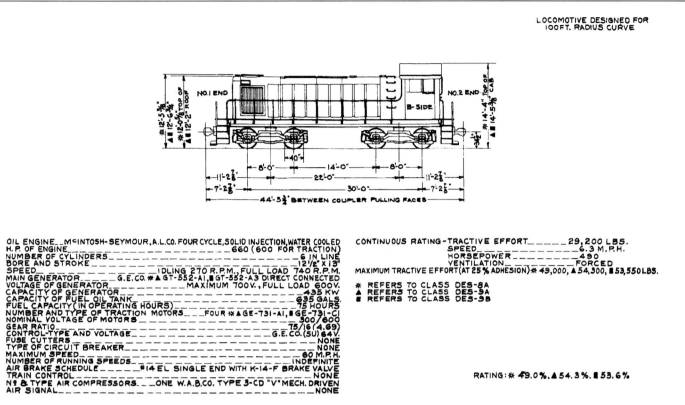

LOCOMOTIVE DESIGNED FOR 100FT. RADIUS CURVE

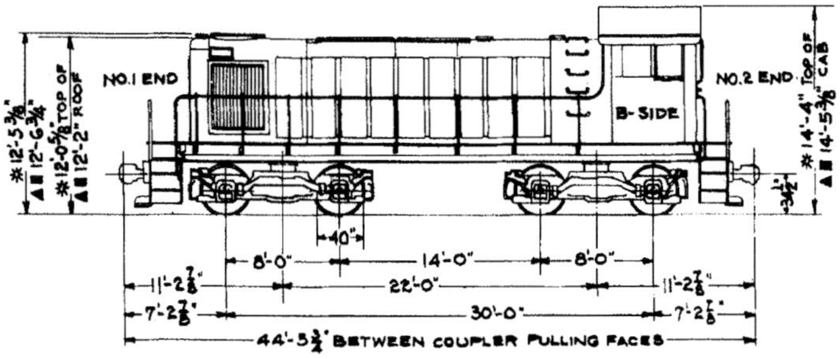

NO.1 END — B-SIDE — NO.2 END

8'-0" — 40" — 14'-0" — 8'-0"

11'-2⅞" — 22'-0" — 11'-2⅞"

7'-2⅞" — 30'-0" — 7'-2⅞"

44'-5¾" BETWEEN COUPLER PULLING FACES

OIL ENGINE — McINTOSH-SEYMOUR, A.L.CO. FOUR CYCLE, SOLID INJECTION, WATER COOLED
H.P. OF ENGINE — 660 (600 FOR TRACTION)
NUMBER OF CYLINDERS — 6 IN LINE
BORE AND STROKE — 12½" X 13"
SPEED — IDLING 270 R.P.M., FULL LOAD 740 R.P.M.
MAIN GENERATOR — G.E.CO. ✱▲ GT-552-A1, ■ GT-552-A3 DIRECT CONNECTED
VOLTAGE OF GENERATOR — MAXIMUM 700V., FULL LOAD 600V.
CAPACITY OF GENERATOR — 435 KW
CAPACITY OF FUEL OIL TANK — 635 GALS.
FUEL CAPACITY (IN OPERATING HOURS) — 75 HOURS
NUMBER AND TYPE OF TRACTION MOTORS — FOUR ✱▲ GE-731-A1, ■ GE-731-C1
NOMINAL VOLTAGE OF MOTORS — 300/600
GEAR RATIO — 75/16 (4.69)
CONTROL-TYPE AND VOLTAGE — G.E.CO. (SU) 64V.
FUSE CUTTERS — NONE
TYPE OF CIRCUIT BREAKER — NONE
MAXIMUM SPEED — 60 M.P.H.
NUMBER OF RUNNING SPEEDS — INDEFINITE
AIR BRAKE SCHEDULE — #14 EL SINGLE END WITH K-14-F BRAKE VALVE
TRAIN CONTROL — NONE
No. & TYPE AIR COMPRESSORS — ONE W.A.B.CO. TYPE 3-CD "V" MECH. DRIVEN
AIR SIGNAL — NONE

CONTINUOUS RATING - TRACTIVE EFFORT — 29,200 LBS.
SPEED — 6.3 M.P.H.
HORSEPOWER — 490
VENTILATION — FORCED
MAXIMUM TRACTIVE EFFORT (AT 25% ADHESION) ✱ 49,000, ▲ 54,300, ■ 53,550 LBS.

✱ REFERS TO CLASS DES-8A
▲ REFERS TO CLASS DES-9A
■ REFERS TO CLASS DES-9B

RATING: ✱ 49.0%. ▲ 54.3%. ■ 53.6%

PRINTED 1-1-44

CLASS DES-8A, DES-9A, DES-9B

Class	Original No.	Re '48	Re '50	Re '66	Builder	c/n	Date	Disposition
DES-9A	685	900	950	9404 mu	Alco	69200	8/40	PC
DES-9B	686	901	951	9405 mu	"	69458	5/41	PC
"	687	902	952	9406 mu	"	69459	"	PC
"	688	903	953	9407 mu	"	69462	"	PC
"	689	904	954	9408 mu	"	69463	"	PC
"	690	905	955	9409 mu	"	69466	6/41	PC
"	691	906	956	9382	"	69467	"	PC
"	692	907	957	9410 mu	"	69468	"	PC

Order Nos.: DES-9A Alco S-1816 DES-9b Alco S-1839.

No. 687 Class DES-9B was a model S-1 switcher built by Alco in May 1941. The eight units in classes DES-9A and weighed almost 9 tons more than the DES-8's.

NYCSHS Collection

Class DES-10 Baldwin-Westinghouse 660HP Model DS-4-4-6

LOCOMOTIVE DESIGNED FOR 57.5° CURVE

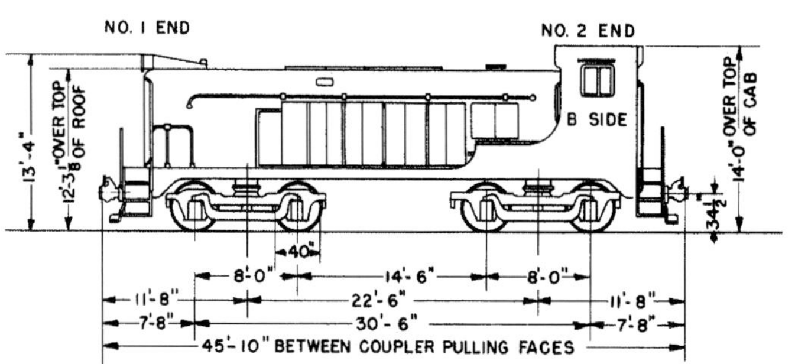

DIESEL ENGINE — DE LA VERGNE — MODEL — VO
DIESEL ENGINE H.P. — 660 (600 FOR TRACTION)
NUMBER OF CYLINDERS — 6 IN LINE
BORE AND STROKE — 12¾"x 15½"
ENGINE SPEED R.P.M. — IDLING 315, FULL LOAD 625
MAIN GENERATOR — W.E. CORP. TYPE 485-H-4 OR K-4 DIRECT DRIVEN
MAIN GENERATOR VOLTAGE — MAX. 660V., FULL LOAD 600V.
MAIN GENERATOR CAPACITY — 420 K.W.
NUMBER AND TYPE OF TRACTION MOTORS — FOUR W.E. CORP. 362-B
TRACTION MOTOR VENTILATION — FORCED
GEAR RATIO — 76/16 (4.75)
CONTROL VOLTAGE — 130 V.

MAXIMUM SPEED OF LOCOMOTIVE — ☆ 60 M.P.H.
CONTINUOUS RATING - TRACTIVE EFFORT — 29,200 LBS.
SPEED — 6.3 M.P.H.
HORSEPOWER — 490

☆ 76/16 GEAR RATIO SPEED. LOCOMOTIVE RESTRICTED TO 45 M.P.H.

PRINTED 4-15-57

CLASS DES-10A, DES-10B, DES-10C

Class	Original No.	Renumber 1943	Builder	Order Number	c/n	Date	Disposition
DES-10A	501	750	BLW	(40510D)	62494	4/41	Rt 12/62, SS 9/63
DES-10B	502	751	"	(41505B)	64234	1/42	Rt 12/62, SS 9/63
DES-10C		752	"	(41518A)	64396	10/42	Rt 12/62, SS 10/63
"		753	"	"	64397	"	Rt 12/62, SS 9/63
"		754	"	"	64398	"	Rt 12/62, SS 10/63
DES-10D		755	"	(44502)	70327	12/44	Rt 12/62, SS 9/63
"		756	"	"	70328	"	Rt 12/62, SS 9/63
"		757	"	"	70329	"	Rt 12/62, SS 9/63
"		758	"	"	70330	"	Rt 12/62, SS 9/63
"		759	"	"	70331	"	Rt 12/62, SS 9/63
"		760	"	"	70332	"	Rt 12/62, SS 9/63
"		761	"	"	70333	"	Rt 12/62, SS 9/63

NYCSHS Collection

No. 501 Class DES-10A was a model DS-4-4-6 (VO-660) switcher built by Baldwin in April 1941. It was renumbered 750 in April 1943 and sold for scrap in September 1963.

No. 501 Class DES-10A. Built by Baldwin in April 1941 shows off the 6 cylinder normally aspirated engine in this view at Baldwin. Unusual is the air compressor location, behind the generator towards the cab.

Both: NYCSHS Collection

No. 502 Class DES-10B. Built by Baldwin in January 1942 was renumbered in 1943 to 751 and served on through retirement at the end of 1962.

Class DES-11A TO DES-11J(AS-10, m) Alco-GE 1000HP Model S-2

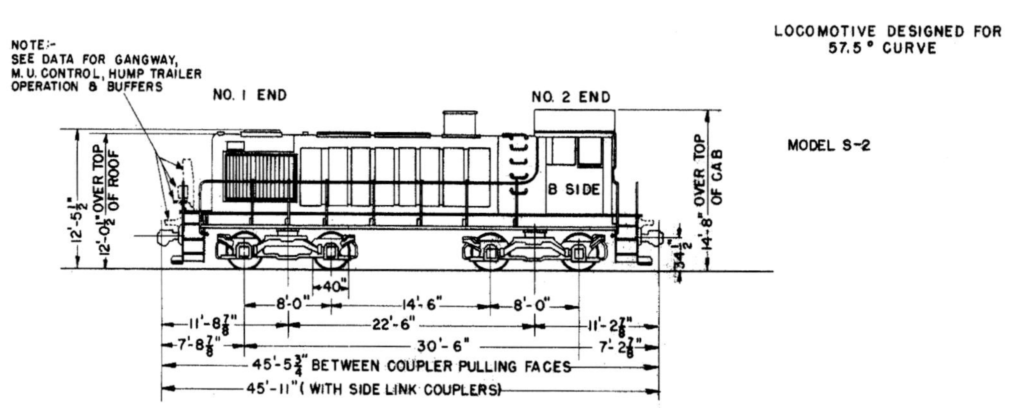

DIESEL ENGINE — ALCO MODEL 539
DIESEL ENGINE H.P. — 1000 (950 FOR TRACTION)
NUMBER OF CYLINDERS — 6 IN LINE
BORE AND STROKE — 12 1/2"X13"
ENGINE SPEED R.P.M. — ▲270, ■315, FULL LOAD 740
MAIN GENERATOR — G.E. CO. TYPE GT-553-C3 DIRECT DRIVEN
MAIN GENERATOR VOLTAGE — MAX. 900V, FULL LOAD 750V
MAIN GENERATOR CAPACITY — 640 K.W.
NUMBER AND TYPE OF TRACTION MOTORS — FOUR GE-731-D2 OR D3
TRACTION MOTOR VENTILATION — FORCED
GEAR RATIO — 75/16 (4.69)
CONTROL VOLTAGE — 75V

MAXIMUM SPEED OF LOCOMOTIVE — ☆60 M.P.H.
CONTINUOUS RATING - TRACTIVE EFFORT — 34,000 LBS.
SPEED — 8.0 M.P.H.

▲ APPLIES TO LOCOS. 8537 - 8549
■ " " " 8500 - 8536, 8550 - 8589
☆ 75/16 GEAR RATIO SPEED. LOCOMOTIVE RESTRICTED TO 45 MPH

PRINTED 4-15-57

CLASS DES-11A, 11B, 11C, 11D, 11E, 11F, 11G, 11H, 11J

Class	Original No.	Re '44	Re '66	Builder	Order Number	c/n	Date	Disposition
DES-11A	780	8500	9600	Alco	(S-1892)	70946	9/43	PC, CR re 9662
"	781	8501	9601	"	"	70947	"	PC
"	782	8502	9602	"	"	70948	"	PC
"	783	8503	9603	"	"	70949	"	PC
"	784	8504	9604	"	(S-1915)	71294	12/43	PC
"	785	8505		"	"	71295	"	Rt c/64
"	786	8506	9606	"	"	71296	"	PC
"	787	8507	9706 mu	"	(S-1930)	72010	2/44	PC
"	788	8508	9607	"	"	72011	"	PC
"	789	8509	9608	"	"	72012	"	PC, CR re 9663
DES-11B		8510	9707 mu	"	(S-1941)	72831	9/44	PC Rt Luntz
"		8511	9609	"	"	72832	"	PC Rt EMD
"		8512	9708 mu	"	"	72833	"	PC
"		8513	9610	"	(S-1943)	72860	11/44	PC
"		8514	9709 mu	"	"	72861	"	PC
"		8515	9710 mu	"	"	72862	"	PC
"		8516	9711 mu	"	"	72863	"	PC
"		8517	9611	"	"	72864	"	PC
"		8518	9712 mu	"	"	72865	"	PC
"		8519	9713 mu	"	"	72866	"	PC
"		8520	9612	"	"	72867	"	Rt /67
"		8521	9613	"	"	72875	"	PC
"		8522	9714 mu	"	"	72876	"	PC Rt 6/68
"		8523	9715 mu	"	"	72877	"	PC
"		8524	9614	"	"	72878	12/44	PC

Class	Original No.	Re '44	Re '66	Builder	Order Number	c/n	Date	Disposition
DES-11C		8525	9615	Alco	(S-1943)	72891	"	PC
"		8526	9716 mu	"	"	72895	"	PC
"		8527	9717 mu	"	"	72896	"	PC
"		8528	9718 mu	"	"	72897	2/45	PC
"		8529	9616	"	"	72898	"	PC
"		8530	9617	"	"	72899	"	PC
"		8531	9719 mu	"	"	72900	"	PC
"		8532	9618	"	"	72901	2/45	PC
"		8533	9720 mu	"	"	72910	3/45	PC
"		8534	9721 mu	"	"	72911	"	PC
DES-11D		8535	9722 mu	"	(S-3016)	73903	1/47	PC
"		8536	9723 mu	"	"	73918	"	PC
DES-11E	P&LE	* 8537	9619	"	(S-3061)	75904	6/48	PC Rt 4/73 SS
"	"	* 8538	9620	"	"	75905	"	PC Rt 12/69 SS
"	"	* 8539	9621	"	"	75906	"	PC Rt 12/71 SS
DES-11F	"	* 8540	9622	"	(S-3105)	76960	8/49	PC Rt 4/72 SS
"	"	* 8541	9731 mu	"	"	76961	"	PC,CR Rt 3/78 SS
"	"	* 8542	9623	"	"	76962	9/49	PC Rt 12/69 GE
"	"	* 8543	9624	"	"	76963	"	PC Rt /72 Luntz
"	"	* 8544	9625	"	"	76964	"	PC Rt 6/68 SS
"	"	* 8545	9626	"	"	76965	"	PC Rt 7/72 SS
"	"	8546		"	"	76966	"	So 10/59 (a)
"	"	8547		"	"	76967	"	So 8/59 (b)
"	"	* 8548	9732 mu	"	"	76968	"	PC,CR Rt 4/77 EMD
"	"	* 8549	9627	"	"	76969	"	PC Rt 6/68 SS

Notes: * Acquired. 2/66 by NYC.

(a) re U.S.Steel 110, Braddock, Pa. (b) re A.Hornos de Mex. 100.

NYCSHS Collection

No. 780 Class DES-11A was built by Alco-GE in September 1943; the first of NYC's S-2 model switchers, rated at 1000 HP with a turbocharged 539 engine. It was renumbered to 8500 in November 1944, then to 9600 in May 1966.

Class		No.	Re '66	Builder	Order Number	c/n	Date	Disposition
DES-11G		8550	9628	Alco	(S-3105)	76942	8/49	PC
"		8551	9629	"	"	76943	"	PC
"		8552	9630	"	"	76944	"	PC Rt 12/67
"		8553	9724 mu	"	"	76945	"	PC
"		8554	9725 mu	"	"	76946	"	PC
"		8555	9726 mu	"	"	76947	"	PC Rt 6/68
"		8556	9631	"	"	76948	"	PC
"		8557	9632	"	"	76949	"	PC
"		8558	9633	"	"	76950	"	PC,CR
"		8559	9634	"	"	76951	"	PC
"		8560	9635	"	"	76952	"	PC,CR
"		8561	9636	"	"	76953	"	PC Rt Luntz
"		8562	9637	"	"	76954	"	PC
"		8563	9638	"	"	76955	"	PC
"		8564	9639	"	"	76956	"	PC
"		8565	9640	"	"	76957	"	PC,CR
DES-11H		8566	9641	"	(S-3129)	77464	4/50	PC,CR
"		8567	9642	"	"	77465	"	PC
"		8568	9643	"	"	77466	"	PC
"		8569	9644	"	"	77467	"	PC Rt Luntz
"		8570	9645	"	"	77468	"	PC
DES-11J		8571	9646	"	(S-3132)	77522	5/50	PC
"		8572	9647	"	"	77523	"	PC
"		8573	9648	"	"	77524	"	PC
"		8574	9649	"	"	77525	"	PC
"		8575	9650	"	"	77526	"	PC,CR
"		8576	9651	"	"	77527	"	PC,CR
"		8577	9652	"	"	77528	"	PC Rt Luntz
"		8578	9653	"	"	77529	"	PC
"		8579	9654	"	"	77530	"	PC
"		8580	9655	"	"	77531	"	PC
"		8581	9727 mu	"	"	77532	"	PC
"		8582	9656	"	"	77533	"	PC,CR
"		8583	9657	"	"	77534	"	PC re 9157
"		8584	9658	"	"	77535	6/50	PC,CR
"		8585	9659	"	(S-3137)	78003	"	Rt 12/67
"		8586	9660	"	"	78004	"	PC,CR re 9155
"		8587	9728 mu	"	"	78005	"	PC
"		8588	9661	"	"	78006	"	PC
"		8589	9662	"	"	78007	"	PC
Ex D&H	3024@	8505	9605	"	(S-3080)	76513	12/48	PC Rt Luntz
Ex D&H	3031@	851	9704	"	(S-3120)	77819	11/49	PC
Ex D&H	3032@	869	9705	"	"	77820	"	PC,CR

Note: @ Acquired 5/65 by New York Central, re second 8505, 851, 869.

No. 8569 Class DES-11H built by Alco-GE in April 1950 was a 1000 HP model S-2 switcher. It was renumbered 9644 in June 1966.

Both: NYCSHS Collection

No. 8667 Class DES-11L. Built by Alco-GE for the P&LE in November 1953. This 1000 HP S-4 was painted "Pacemaker" green with black trucks. Note the older type headlight is replaced with a Pyle-National twin sealed beam unit. All P&LE switchers were painted green.

Class DES-11K and DES-11L (AS-10, m) Alco-GE 1000HP Model S-4

Class		No.	Re '66	Builder	Order Number	c/n	Date	Disposition
DES-11K		8590	9663	Alco	(S-3175)	79531	2/52	PC
"		8591	9664	"	(S-3187)	79542	"	PC
"		8592	9665	"	"	79543	"	PC
"		8593	9666	"	"	79544	"	PC
"		8594	9667	"	"	79545	"	PC
"		8595	9668	"	"	79546	"	PC
"		8596	9669	"	"	79547	"	PC
"		8597	9670	"	"	79548	"	PC
"		8598	9729 mu	"	"	79549	"	PC,CR
"		8599	9671	"	"	79550	"	PC
"		8600	9672	"	"	79551	"	PC
"		8601	9673	"	"	79552	"	PC
"		8602	9674	"	"	79553	"	PC, Rt EMD
"		8603	9675	"	"	79554	"	PC
"		8604	9676	"	"	79555	"	PC
"		8605	9677	"	"	79556	"	PC
"		8606	9678	"	"	79557	3/52	PC
"		8607	9679	"	"	79558	"	PC
"		8608	9680	"	"	79561	"	PC, Rt, EMD
"		8609	9681	"	"	79562	"	PC
"		8610	9682	"	"	79563	"	PC
"		8611	9683	"	"	79564	"	Rt /67
"		8612	9684	"	"	79565	"	PC
"		8613	9685	"	"	79566	"	PC
"		8614	9686	"	"	79567	"	PC
"		8615	9687	"	"	79568	"	PC
"		8616	9688	"	"	79569	"	PC
"		8617	9689	"	"	79570	"	PC
"		8618	9690	"	"	79571	"	PC, Rt EMD
"		8619	9691	"	(S-3195)	79775	"	PC
"		8620	9692	"	"	79776	"	PC
"		8621	9693	"	"	79777	4/52	PC
"		8622	9694	"	"	79778	"	PC
"		8623	9730 mu	"	"	79779	"	PC
"		8624	9695	"	"	79780	"	PC,CR
"		8625	9696	"	"	79781	"	PC,CR
"		8626	9697	"	"	79782	"	PC
"		8627	9698	"	"	79783	"	PC,CR
"		8628	9699	"	"	79784	"	PC,CR
"		8629	9700	"	"	79785	"	PC
"		8630	9701	"	"	79788	5/52	PC,CR
"		8631	9702	"	"	79789	"	PC
"		8632	9703	"	"	79790	"	PC
DES-11L	P&LE	* 8633	9733 mu	"	(S-3221)	80639	9/53	PC,CR Rt 77 EMD
"	"	* 8634	9734 mu	"	"	80640	"	PC Rt/72 SS
"	"	* 8635	9735 mu	"	"	80641	"	PC,CR Rt 10/78
"	"	* 8636	9736 mu	"	"	80642	"	PC Rt 2/70 SS
"	"	* 8637	9737 mu	"	"	80643	"	PC,CR Rt /77 EMD
"	"	8638	(9738)mu	"	"	80644	"	So'66 to Sabine Riv. & No.
"	"	* 8639	9739 mu	"	"	80645	10/53	PC,CR Rt 11/77
"	"	* 8640	9740 mu	"	"	80646	"	PC,CR Rt 11/77
"	"	* 8641	9741 mu	"	"	80647	"	PC Rt/74 SS
"	"	* 8642	9742 mu	"	"	80648	"	PC Rt 8/68 SS
"	"	* 8643	9743 mu	"	"	80649	"	PC Rt /76 EMD
"	"	* 8644	9744 mu	"	(S-3231)	80930	"	PC,CR Rt 11/77
"	"	* 8645	9745 mu	"	"	80931	"	PC,CR Rt 4/77

NYCSHS Collection

No. 8611 Class DES-11K was a model S-4 switcher built by Alco in March 1952.

Louis A. Marre

No. 8660 Class DES-11L a model S-4 switcher built by Alco for the P&LE in November 1953. Shown here at Youngstown, Ohio in October 1965, it would lose it's P&LE lettering only six months later.

LOCOMOTIVE DESIGNED FOR
57.5° CURVE

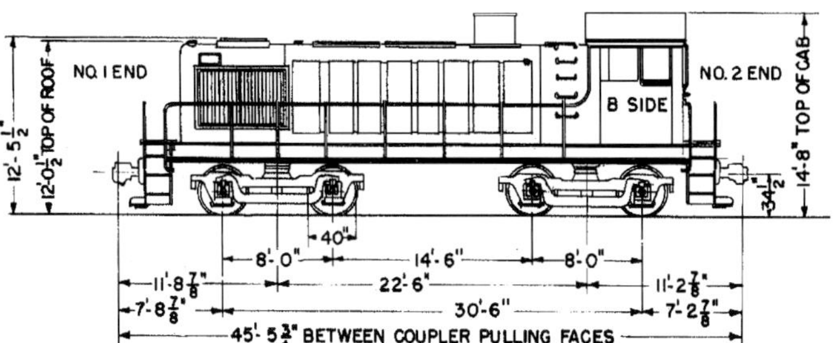

MODEL S-4

DIESEL ENGINE — ALCO MODEL 539
DIESEL ENGINE H.P. — 1000 (950 FOR TRACTION)
NUMBER OF CYLINDERS — 6 IN LINE
BORE AND STROKE — 12½" X 13"
ENGINE SPEED R.P.M. — IDLING ▲270, ■315, FULL LOAD 740
MAIN GENERATOR — G.E.CO. TYPE GT-553-C3 DIRECT DRIVEN
MAIN GENERATOR VOLTAGE — MAX. 900V, FULL LOAD 750V
MAIN GENERATOR CAPACITY — 640 K.W.
NUMBER AND TYPE OF TRACTION MOTORS — FOUR GE-731-D3
TRACTION MOTOR VENTILATION — FORCED
GEAR RATIO — 75/16 (4.69)
CONTROL VOLTAGE — 75V

MAXIMUM SPEED OF LOCOMOTIVE — ✫ 60 M.P.H.
CONTINUOUS RATING - TRACTIVE EFFORT — 34,000 LBS
SPEED — 8.0 M.P.H.

▲ APPLIES TO LOCOS. 8633 – 8667
■ " " " 8590 – 8632
✫ 75/16 GEAR RATIO SPEED. LOCOMOTIVE RESTRICTED TO 45 MPH.

CLASS DES-11K,11L

PRINTED 4-15-57

Class		No.	Re '66	Builder	Order Number	c/n	Date	Disposition
DES-11L	P&LE	* 8646	9746 mu	Alco	(S-3231)	80932	10/53	PC Rt 3/76 So
"	"	8647	(9747)mu	"	"	80933	"	So /66 (b)
"	"	*8648	9748 mu	"	"	80934	"	PC Rt 6/71 SC
"	"	8649	(9749)mu	"	"	80935	"	So 3/66 (a)
"	"	8650	(9750)mu	"	"	80936	"	So 3/66 (a)
"	"	*8651	9751 mu	"	"	80937	"	PC Rt 4/71 SS
"	"	*8652	9752 mu	"	"	80938	"	PC,CR Rt 10/78 So
"	"	*8653	9753 mu	"	"	80939	"	PC Rt 3/72 SS
"	"	8654	(9754)mu	"	"	80940	11/53	So 3/66 (a)
"	"	8655	(9755)mu	"	"	80941	"	So 2/66 (b)
"	"	*8656	9756 mu	"	"	80942	"	PC,CR Rt 4/77 EMD
"	"	*8657	9757 mu	"	"	80943	"	PC Rt 1/71 EMD
"	"	*8658	9758 mu	"	"	80944	"	PC Rt 3/76 SS
"	"	*8659	9759 mu	"	"	80945	"	PC Rt 12/70 SS
"	"	*8660	9760 mu	"	"	80946	"	PC Rt 7/68 Sc
"	"	*8661	9761 mu	"	"	80947	"	PC Rt 4/71 EMD
"	"	*8662	9762 mu	"	"	80948	"	PC So 6/68 (c)
"	"	*8663	9763 mu	"	"	80949	"	PC,CR Rt 10/77 SS
"	"	8664	(9764)mu	"	"	80950	"	So 3/66 (a)
"	"	*8665	9765 mu	"	"	80951	"	PC Rt 8/74 SS
"	"	*8666	9766 mu	"	"	80952	"	PC So 6/69
"	"	8667	(9767)mu	"	"	80953	"	So 3/66 (d)

Notes: * Acquired 3/66 by NYC. (a) 8654, 8649, 8650, 8664 to South Buffalo 108-111 (b) to Genesee & Wyoming 36. (c) to Precision Engrg. (d) to Armco Steel.

Class DES-12 Baldwin Westinghouse 1000HP Model DS-4-4-10

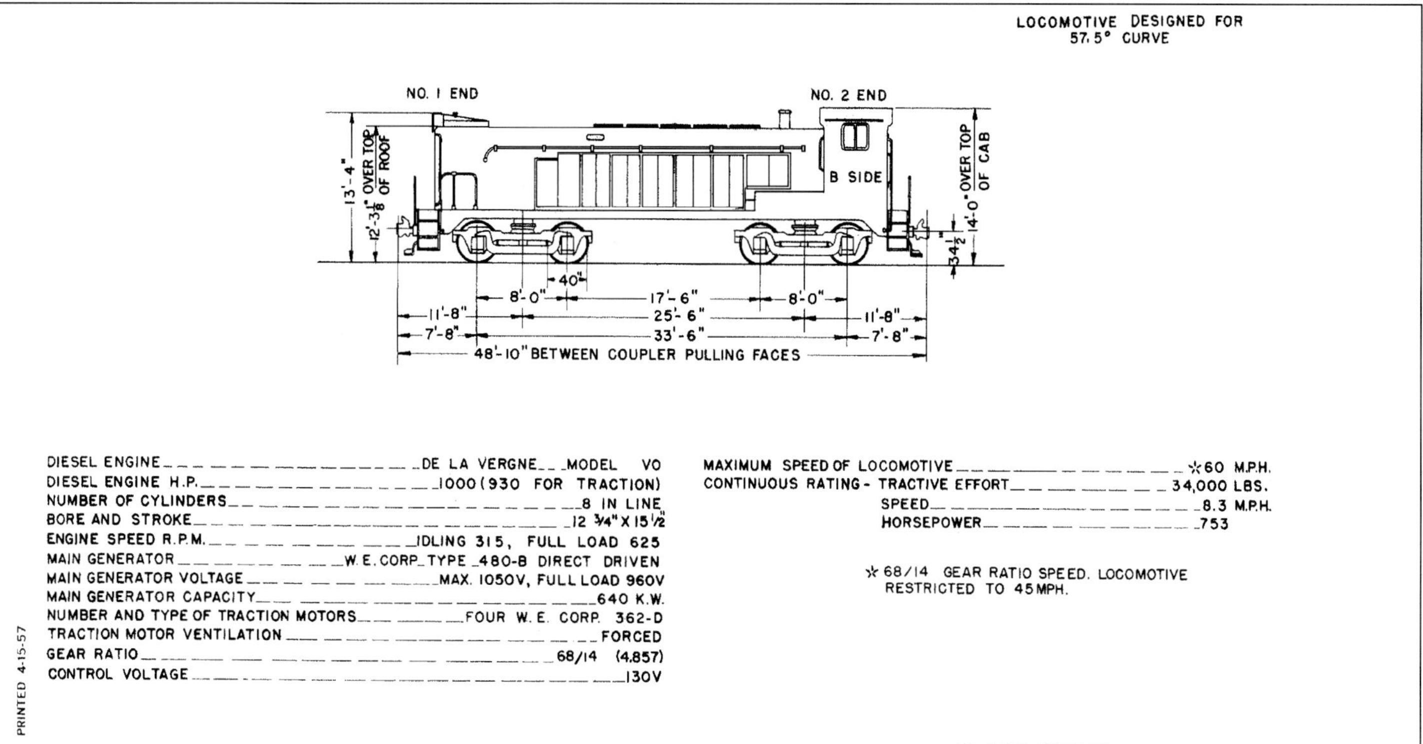

Class	Original No.	Re '52	Re '66	Builder	Order Number	c/n	Date	Disposition
DES-12A	8600	9300	(8047)	BLW	(43510-N)	71958	9/44	Rt 2/66, Sc
"	8601	9301	(8048)	"	"	71959	"	Rt 3/66
"	8602	9302		"	"	71960	"	Rt 2/65
"	8603	9303		"	(43512-C)	70300	10/44	Sc 3/64
"	8604	9304		"	"	70301	"	Rt 2/65, SS
DES-12B	8605	9305		"	(44504-B)	71730	2/45	Sc 3/64
"	8606	9306		"	"	71731	"	Sc 2/64
"	8607	9307		"	"	71732	"	Sc 3/64

NYCSHS Collection

No. 8606 Class DES-12B was a model DS-4-4-10 (VO-1000) switcher built by Baldwin in February 1945.

Class DES-13 (ES-10, m) Electro-Motive 1000HP Model NW2

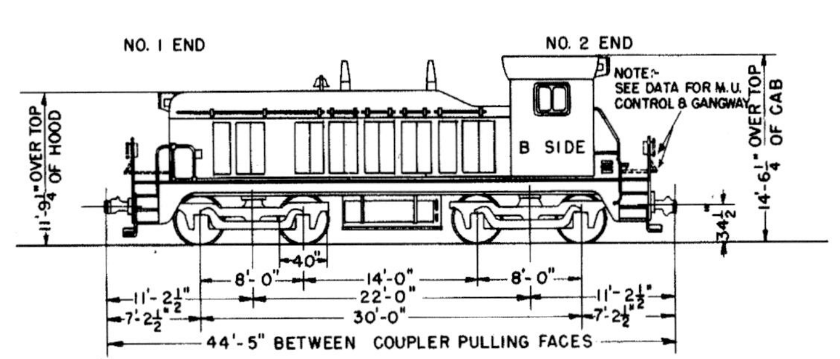

DIESEL ENGINE ---------- GM -- MODEL 567A
DIESEL ENGINE H.P. ---------- 1080 (1000 FOR TRACTION)
NUMBER OF CYLINDERS ---------- 12-V TYPE
BORE AND STROKE ---------- 8½" x 10"
ENGINE SPEED R.P.M. ---------- IDLING 275, FULL LOAD 800
MAIN GENERATOR ---------- EMD TYPE D-4-D DIRECT DRIVEN
MAIN GENERATOR VOLTAGE ---------- MAX. 1120 V., FULL LOAD 1070V.
MAIN GENERATOR CAPACITY ---------- 700 K.W.
NUMBER AND TYPE OF TRACTION MOTORS ---------- FOUR EMD D-7, D-17 OR D-27
TRACTION MOTOR VENTILATION ---------- FORCED
GEAR RATIO ---------- 62/15 (4.133)
CONTROL VOLTAGE ---------- 75 V.

MAXIMUM SPEED OF LOCOMOTIVE ---------- ☆65 M.P.H.
CONTINUOUS RATING - TRACTIVE EFFORT ---------- 31,200 LBS.
SPEED ---------- 10.0 M.P.H.
HORSEPOWER ---------- 832

☆ 62/15 GEAR RATIO SPEED. LOCOMOTIVE RESTRICTED TO 45 M.P.H.

4-15-57

Class	Road	No.	Builder	Order Number	c/n	Date	Disposition
DES-13A		8700	EMC	(E-696)	3606	7/48	PC,CR,RB to NW2u 9165
"		8701	"	"	3607	"	PC,CR re 9200
"		8702	"	"	3608	"	PC,CR,RB to NW2u 9167
"		8703	"	"	3609	"	PC,CR,RB to NW2u 9175
"		8704	"	"	3610	"	PC,CR re 9133
DES-13B	P&LE	8705	"	(E-888)	5249	12/47	P&LE So 2/71 PNC-Bab.& Wil.
"	"	8706	"	"	5250	"	P&LE So 2/71 PNC-C&NW 1001
"	"	8707	"	"	5251	"	P&LE So 2/71 PNC-USStl.30
"	"	8708	"	"	5252	"	P&LE So 11/71 CRI&P 4901
"	"	8709	"	"	5253	"	P&LE So 3/71 PNC-Bab.& Wil.
"	"	8710	"	"	5254	"	P&LE So 11/71 CRI&P 4902
"	"	8711	"	"	5255	"	P&LE So 3/71 PNC-YS&T 915
"	"	8712	"	"	5256	"	P&LE So 11/71 CRI&P 4900
"	"	8713	"	"	5257	"	P&LE So 11/71 CRI&P 4903
"	"	8714	"	"	5258	"	P&LE So 12/71 PNC-USStl.38
DES-13C	IHB	8715 mu	"	(E-1011)	6422	1/48	PC,CR as 2nd 8907 (re 4/66)
"	"	8716 mu	"	"	6423	"	IHB
"	"	8717 mu	"	"	6424	"	IHB RB 3/75 to DHT 478
"	"	8718 mu	"	"	6425	"	IHB
DES-13D	IHB	8719 mu	"	(E-985)	6219	5/48	IHB
"	"	8720 mu	"	"	6220	"	IHB
"	"	8721 mu	"	"	6221	"	IHB
"	"	8722 mu	"	"	6222	"	IHB
"	"	8723 mu	"	"	6223	"	IHB
"	"	8724 mu	"	"	6224	"	IHB
"	"	8725 mu	"	"	6225	"	IHB
"	"	8726 mu	"	"	6226	6/48	IHB
"	"	8727 mu	"	"	6227	"	IHB
"	"	8728 mu	"	"	6228	"	IHB RB by 76 to Slug PB-2
"	"	8729 mu	"	"	6376	"	IHB So 1/88 Pielet
"	"	8730 mu	"	"	6377	8/48	IHB
"	"	8731 mu	"	"	6378	"	IHB RB 8/87 to Booster BU50
"	"	8732 mu	"	"	6379	"	IHB
"	"	8733 mu	"	"	6380	9/48	IHB,PC,CR RB to NW2u 9158

Class	Road	No.	Builder	Order Number	c/n	Date	Disposition
DES-13D	IHB	8734 mu	EMD	(E-985)	6416	9/48	IHB
"	"	8735 mu	"	"	6417	"	IHB,PC,CR RB to NW2u 9159
"	"	8736 mu	"	"	6418	"	IHB,PC,CR RB to NW2u 9160
"	"	8737 mu	"	"	6419	10/48	IHB,PC,CR RB to NW2u 9161
"	"	8738 mu	"	"	6420	"	IHB
"	"	8739 mu	"	"	6421	"	IHB
DES-13E	P&LE	8740	"	(E-1056)	7418	3/49	P&LE So 11/71 CRI&P 4904
"	"	8741	"	"	7419	"	P&LE So 11/71 CRI&P 4905
"	"	8742	"	"	7420	"	P&LE So 11/71 CRI&P 4906
"	"	8743	"	"	7421	"	P&LE So 9/70 PE-Bab.& Wil.
"	"	8744	"	"	7422	"	P&LE So 4/71 PNC-Con&BL 126
"	"	8745	"	"	7423	"	P&LE So 9/70 PE-USStl.116
"	"	8746	"	"	7424	"	P&LE So 2/71 PNC-ECam&H.60
"	"	8747	"	"	7425	"	P&LE So 11/71 CRI&P 4907
"	"	8748	"	"	7426	"	P&LE So 11/71 CRI&P 4908
"	"	8749	"	"	7427	4/49	P&LE So 11/71 CRI&P 4909
DES-13F		8750	"	(E-984)	6195	10/48	PC,CR re 9201
"		8751	"	"	6196	"	PC,CR re 9202
"		8752	"	"	6197	11/48	PC,CR re 9203
"		8753	"	"	6198	"	PC,CR re 9204
"		8754	"	"	6199	12/48	PC
"		8755	"	"	6200	"	PC,CR re 9205
"		8756	"	"	6201	"	PC,CR re 9206
"		8757	"	"	6202	"	PC
"		8758	"	"	6203	"	PC
"		8759	"	"	6204	"	PC,CR re 9207
"		8760	"	"	6205	"	PC
"		8761	"	"	6206	"	PC,CR re 9208
"		8762	"	"	6207	"	PC,CR re 9276
"		8763	"	"	6208	"	PC
"		8764	"	"	6209	"	PC,CR RB to NW2u 9168
"		8765	"	"	6210	"	PC,CR re 9277
"		8766	"	"	6211	"	PC,CR re 9278
"		8767	"	"	6212	"	PC,CR re 9279
"		8768	"	"	6213	"	PC,CR re 9280
"		8769	"	"	6214	"	PC,CR re 9281
"		8770	"	"	6215	"	PC,CR re 9282
"		8771	"	"	6216	"	PC,CR re 9283
"		8772	"	"	6217	"	PC
"		8773	"	"	6218	"	PC,CR re 9284
DES-13G	IHB	8774 mu	"	(E-1043)	7185	7/49	IHB
"	"	8775 mu	"	"	7186	"	IHB So 1/88 Pielet
"	"	8776 mu	"	"	7187	"	IHB So 1/88 Pielet
"	"	8777 mu	"	"	7188	9/49	IHB RB 7/61 DHT 477
"	"	8778 mu	"	"	7189	"	IHB
"	"	8779 mu	"	"	7190	"	IHB
"	"	8780 mu	"	"	7191	"	IHB
"	"	8781 mu	"	"	7192	"	IHB,PC,CR RB NW2u 9162
"	"	8782 mu	"	"	7193	"	IHB
"	"	8783 mu	"	"	7194	"	IHB
"	"	8784 mu	"	"	7195	"	IHB
"	"	8785 mu	"	"	7196	"	IHB
"	"	8786 mu	"	"	7197	"	IHB
"	"	8787 mu	"	"	7198	"	IHB
"	"	8788 mu	"	"	7199	"	IHB
"	"	8789 mu	"	"	7200	"	IHB

Class	Road	No.	Builder	Order Number	c/n	Date	Disposition
DES-13H	IHB	8790 mu	EMD	(E-1230)	7201	9/49	IHB
"	"	8791 mu	"	"	7202	"	IHB
"	"	8792 mu	"	"	7203	"	IHB
"	"	8793 mu	"	"	7204	"	IHB,PC,CR RB NW2u 9163
"	"	* 8794	"	"	7205	"	PC
"	"	* 8795	"	"	7206	"	PC,CR re 9285
"	"	* 8796	"	"	7207	"	PC,CR re 9286
"	"	* 8797	"	"	7208	"	So 5/66 EMD
"	"	* 8798	"	"	7209	"	PC,CR re 9287
"	"	* 8799	"	"	7210	"	PC,CR re 9288
"	"	* 8800	"	"	7211	"	PC,CR re 9289
"	"	** 8801	"	"	7212	"	PC,CR re 9290
"	"	** 8802	"	"	7213	"	PC,CR re 9291
DES-13J		8803	"	(E-1042)	7177	11/49	PC,CR re 9292
"		8804	"	"	7178	"	PC,CR RB to NW2u 9166
"		8805	"	"	7179	"	PC,CR re 9293
"		8806 mu	"	"	7180	"	PC,CR re 9294
"		8807 mu	"	"	7181	"	PC,CR re 9295
"		8808 mu	"	"	7182	"	PC,CR re 9296
"		8809	"	"	7183	"	PC
"		8810	"	"	7184		PC,CR RB to NW2u 9170
DES-13K	IHB	8811 mu	"	(E-1267)	9456	10/49	IHB
"	"	8812 mu	"	"	9457	"	IHB
"	"	8813 mu	"	"	9458	"	IHB So 1/88 Pielet
"	"	8814 mu	"	"	9459	"	IHB
"	"	8815 mu	"	"	9461	12/49	IHB
"	"	8816 mu	"	"	9462	"	IHB
"	"	8817 mu	"	"	9463	"	IHB
"	"	8818 mu	"	"	9464	"	IHB
"	"	8819 mu	"	"	9465	"	IHB So 3/87 CarKni&Sh.
"	"	8820 mu	"	"	9466	"	IHB,PC,CR RB NW2u 9164
"	"	8821 mu	"	"	9467	"	IHB
"	"	8822 mu	"	"	9468	"	IHB So 1/88 Pielet
"	"	8823 mu	"	"	9469	"	IHB RB to Slug PB-3
"	"	8824 mu	"	"	9470	"	IHB
"	"	8825 mu	"	"	9471	"	IHB RB 4/88 Boos. BU54
"	"	8826 mu	"	"	9472	"	IHB
"	"	8827 mu	"	"	9473	"	IHB
"	"	8828 mu	"	"	9474	"	IHB
"	"	8829 mu	"	"	9475	"	IHB
"	"	8830 mu	"	"	9476	"	IHB
"	"	8831 mu	"	"	9477	"	IHB
"	"	8832 mu	"	"	9478	"	IHB Wreck 8/58, Rt 1/59
"	"	8833 mu	"	"	9479	"	IHB
"	"	8834 mu	"	"	9480	"	IHB

Notes: * Acquired 5/66 by NYC. ** Acquired 4/67 by NYC.
8700 had double-end train control and layover heating.
Units 8701, 8790-8792 had hump trailer control No. 1 end.
DES-13C, D, G, K had MU controls both ends.
8765, 8773 had layover heating.
DES-13F had 930 gallon fuel tank; all others 600 gallon.
Parts of 8777 used in DHT No. 477.

No. 8797 Class DES-13H was a model NW2 switcher rated at 1000 HP built by EMD in September 1949 for the Indiana Harbor Belt but transferred years later to the NYC.

Both: NYCSHS Collection

No. 8809 Class DES-13J was a model NW2 switcher built by EMD in November 1949. Note that even as late as 1949, NYC switchers were still being delivered without the "safety yellow" paint applied to the handrails and grab irons.

Class DES-13L (ES-10) Acquired 1957 from New York, Ontario & Western

Class	NYO&W	Re '57	Re '66	Builder	Order Number	c/n	Date	Disposition
DES-13L	114	9500	8683	EMC	(E-B24)	3167	3/48	PC,CR re 9263
"	116	9501	8684	"	"	3169	6/48	PC,CR re 9264
"	117	9502	8685	"	"	3170	"	PC,CR re 9265
"	118	9503	8686	"	"	3171	"	PC,CR RB to NW2u 9156
"	119	9504	8687	"	"	3172	"	PC,OR re 9266
"	120	9505	8688	"	"	3173	"	PC
"	121	9506	8689	"	"	3174	"	PC,CR re 9267
"	122	9507	8690	"	"	3175	"	PC,CR re 9268
"	123	9508	8691	"	"	3176	"	PC,CR re 9269
"	124	9509	8692	"	"	3177	7/48	PC,CR re 9270
"	125	9510	8693	"	"	3178	"	PC,CR re 9271
"	126	9511	8694	"	"	3179	"	PC,CR re 9272
"	127	9512	8695	"	"	3180	"	PC,CR RB to NW2u 9177
"	128	9513	8696	"	"	6160	"	PC,CR RB to NW2u 9101
"	129	9514	8697	"	"	6161	"	PC,CR re 9273
"	130	9515	8698	"	"	6162	"	PC,CR re 9274
"	131	9516	8699	"	"	6163	"	PC,CR re 9275

Collection of Louis A. Marre

No. 9511 Class DES-13L was far from its original road; the New York Ontario and Western when photographed at Toledo, Ohio on August 15, 1965. The 9511would be renumbered in 1966 to 8694 and once again by Conrail to 9272.

CLASS DES-14 FAIRBANKS-MORSE 1000 HP Model LCC

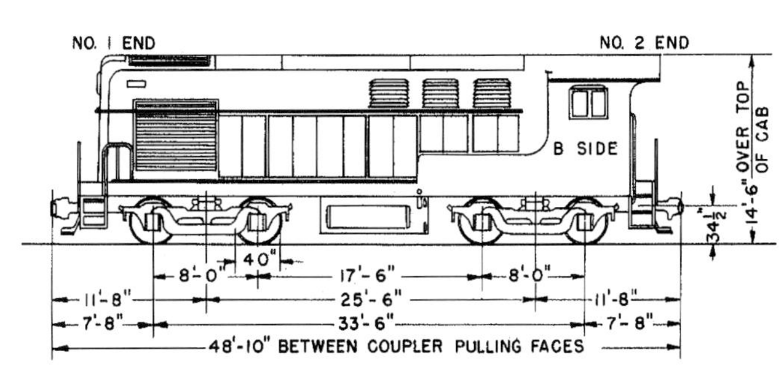

DIESEL ENGINE — F. M. MODEL 38 D 8 1/8
DIESEL ENGINE H. P. — 1108 (1000 FOR TRACTION)
NUMBER OF CYLINDERS — 6 IN LINE (O.P.)
BORE AND STROKE — 8 1/8 x 10"
ENGINE SPEED R.P.M. — IDLING 350, FULL LOAD 800
MAIN GENERATOR — W.E. CORP. TYPE 481-B DIRECT DRIVEN
MAIN GENERATOR VOLTAGE — MAX. 1040V, FULL LOAD 1000V
MAIN GENERATOR CAPACITY — 690KW
NUMBER AND TYPE OF TRACTION MOTORS — FOUR W. E. CORP. 362-D
TRACTION MOTOR VENTILATION — FORCED
GEAR RATIO — 68/14 (4.857)
CONTROL VOLTAGE — 130 V.

4-15-57

MAXIMUM SPEED OF LOCOMOTIVE — ☆ 60 M.P.H.
CONTINUOUS RATING – TRACTIVE EFFORT — 34,600 LBS.
SPEED — 8.3 M.P.H.
HORSEPOWER — 766

☆ 68/14 GEAR RATIO SPEED. LOCOMOTIVE RESTRICTED TO 45 MPH.

Class	Road	Original Number	Re '48	Re '49	Re '66	Builder	Order Number	c/n	Date	Disposition
DES-14A	P&LE	8800	8900	9100	(8200)	FM	(LD28)	L1023	12/46	P&LE So66 GE
"	"	8801	8901	9101	(8201)	"	"	L1024	"	P&LE So66 GE
DES-14B			8902	9102	(8202)	"	(LD33)	10L64	8/48	P&LE So66 GE
"			8903	9103	(8203)	"	"	10L65	"	P&LE So66 GE
DES-14C	IHB*		8904	9104	8204	"	(LD60)	10L146	6/49	dr by '67
"	IHB*		8905	9105	8205	"	"	10L147	"	dr by '67
DES-14D				9106	8206	"	(LD73)	10L170	12/49	PC Rt 4/68
"				9107	8207	"	"	10L171	"	PC Rt EMD
"				9108	8208	"	"	10L172	"	PC
"				9109	(8209)	"	"	10L173	2/50	Rt66 Sc
DES-14E				9110	8210	"	(LD77)	10L176	"	Rt /67

Note * Acquired 2/50 by NYC.

NYCSHS Collection

No. 9110 Class DES-14E was an H-10-44 model switcher. It was originally ordered for the Indiana Harbor, but delivered as shown.

Class DES-15A LIMA 1000 HP and DES-15b LIMA 1200 HP Switcher

LOCOMOTIVE DESIGNED FOR
57.5° CURVE

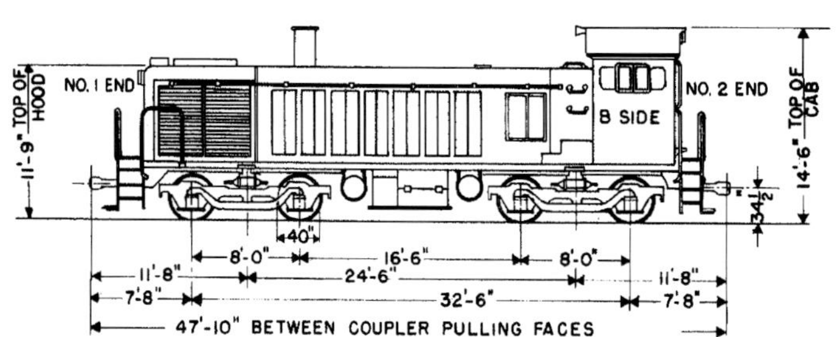

DIESEL ENGINE	LIMA MODEL T89 SA
DIESEL ENGINE H.P.	1000 FOR TRACTION
NUMBER OF CYLINDERS	8 IN LINE
BORE AND STROKE	9" X 12"
ENGINE SPEED R.P.M.	IDLING 425, FULL LOAD 950
MAIN GENERATOR	W. E. CORP. TYPE 499-A DIRECT DRIVEN
MAIN GENERATOR VOLTAGE	MAX. 1050V, FULL LOAD 1000V
MAIN GENERATOR CAPACITY	700 K.W.
NUMBER AND TYPE OF TRACTION MOTORS	FOUR W. E. CORP. 362-D
TRACTION MOTOR VENTILATION	FORCED
GEAR RATIO	68/14 (4.857)
CONTROL VOLTAGE	75V

MAXIMUM SPEED OF LOCOMOTIVE	✲60 M.P.H.
CONTINUOUS RATING - TRACTIVE EFFORT	34,000 LBS.
SPEED	8.9 M.P.H.

✲ 68/14 GEAR RATIO SPEED. LOCOMOTIVE RESTRICTED TO 45MPH.

PRINTED 4-15-57

CLASS DES-15A

Class	Road	Number	Builder	Order Number	c/n	Date	Disposition
DES-15A		8400	Lima	(1203)	9334	9/49	Rt 5/64 So 10/64 EMD
"		8401	"	"	9335	"	Rt 5/64 So 10/65 GE
"		8402	"	"	9336	"	Rt 5/64 So 10/64 EMD
"		8403	"	"	9337	"	Rt 5/64 So 10/65 GE
"		8404	"	"	9338	"	Rt 5/64
"		8405	"	"	9339	10/49	Rt 10/64 So10/65 GE
DES-15B	CR&I	8406	"	(1219)	9492	5/51	Rt 10/64 SS 1 /65
"	"	8407	"	"	9493	"	Rt 10/64 SS 1 /65
"	"	8408	"	"	9494	"	Rt 10/64 SS 1 /65
"	"	8409	"	"	9495	"	Rt 10/64 SS 1 /65
"	"	8410	"	"	9496	"	Rt 10/64 SS 1 /65
"	"	8411	"	"	9497	"	Rt 10/64 SS 1 /65

No. 8407 Class DES-15B was an LH-1200 switcher built for the Chicago River and Indiana RR. It lasted 13 years.

NYCSHS Collection

NYCSHS Collection

No 8407 Class DES-15B ready for delivery from Lima in 1951.

Louis A. Marre

No. 8408 Class DES-15B is almost at the end of its career at Chicago in October 1963.

Class DES-16A to H (ES-12, m) Electro-Motive 1200 HP Model SW7

LOCOMOTIVE DESIGNED FOR
57.5° CURVE

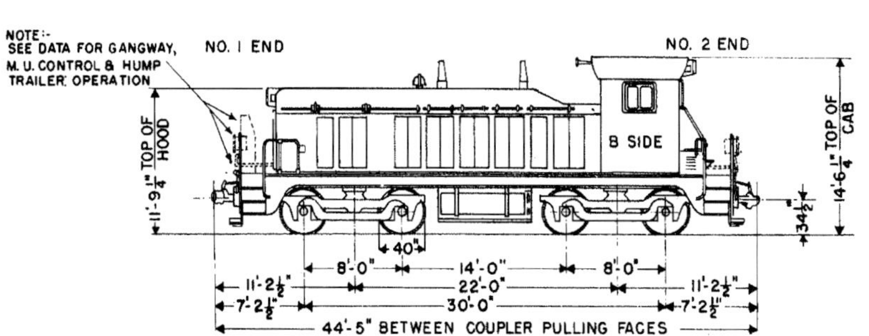

DIESEL ENGINE — GM MODEL 567B
DIESEL ENGINE H.P. — 1280 (1200 FOR TRACTION)
NUMBER OF CYLINDERS — 12-V TYPE
BORE AND STROKE — 8½"x10"
ENGINE SPEED R.P.M. — IDLING 275, FULL LOAD 800
MAIN GENERATOR — EMD TYPE D-15-A OR D-15-C DIRECT DRIVEN
MAIN GENERATOR VOLTAGE — MAX. 1025V, FULL LOAD 980V.
MAIN GENERATOR CAPACITY — 850 KW.
NUMBER AND TYPE OF TRACTION MOTORS — FOUR EMD D-27
TRACTION MOTOR VENTILATION — FORCED
GEAR RATIO — 62/15 (4.133)
CONTROL VOLTAGE — 75V.

MAXIMUM SPEED OF LOCOMOTIVE — ✫ 65 M.P.H.
CONTINUOUS RATING - TRACTIVE EFFORT — 31,200 LBS.
SPEED — 12.0 M.P.H.
HORSEPOWER — 1000

✫ 62/15 GEAR RATIO SPEED. LOCOMOTIVE RESTRICTED TO 45 MPH.

PRINTED 4-15-57

CLASS DES-16

Class	Road	Number	Builder	Order Number	c/n	Date	Disposition
DES 16A	IHB	8835 mu	EMC	(E 1267)	9460	10/49	IHB
DES-16B	"	8836 *		(E-1136)	8127	1/50	PC, CR
"	"	8837 *	"	"	8128	"	PC (re 4/72) 8866, CR
"	"	8838 *	"	"	8129	"	PC (re 4/72) 8867, CR
"	"	8839 *	"	"	8130	"	PC (re 4/72) 8867, CR
"	"	8840 *	"	"	8131	"	PC,CR
"	"	8841 *	"	"	8132	"	PC,CR
"	"	8842 @	"	"	8133	"	PC,CR
"	"	8843 @	"	"	8134	"	PC,CR
"	"	8844 @	"	"	8135	2/50	PC,CR
"	"	8845 @	"	"	8136	"	PC,CR
"	"	8846 @	"	"	9446	"	PC,CR
"	"	8847 @	"	"	9447	"	PC CR
"	"	8848 @	"	"	9448	"	PC,CR
"	"	8849 @	"	"	9449	"	PC,CR
"	"	8850 @	"	"	9450	"	PC,CR
DES-16C		8851	"	"	9451	"	PC,CR
"		8852 mu	"	"	9452	"	PC,CR
"		8853	"	"	9453	"	PC,CR
"		8854	"	"	9454	"	PC,CR
"		8855 mu	"	"	9455	"	PC,CR
DES-16D	IHB	8856 mu	EMD	(4000)	9121	2/50	IHB R8 5/76 to Slug PB-1
"	"	8857 mu	"	"	9122	"	IHB RB 2/88 to Boos. BU-53
"	"	8858 mu	"	"	9123	"	IHB
"	"	8859 mu	"	"	9124	"	IHB
"	"	8860 mu	"	"	9125	"	IHB
"	"	8861 mu	"	"	9126	"	IHB
"	"	8862 mu	"	"	9127	"	IHB
"	"	8863 mu	"	"	9128	"	IHB RB 4/75 to DHT 479
		8864			9129		IHB

* Acquired 1/65 by CR&I. @ acquired circa 1967 by NYC. 8841 equipped with air signal.

Class	Road	Number	Builder	Order Number	c/n	Date	Disposition
DES-16D	IHB	8865	EMD	(4000)	9130	3/50	IHB
"	"	8866	"	"	9131	"	IHB
"	"	8867 mu	"	"	9132	4/50	IHB
"	"	8868	"	"	9133	"	IHB
"	"	8869	"	"	9134	"	IHB
"	"	8870	"	"	9135	"	IHB
"	"	8871	"	"	9136	"	IHB
"	"	8872 **	"	"	9137	"	PC,CR
"	"	8873 **	"	"	9138	"	PC,CR
"	"	8874 **	"	"	9139	"	PC,CR
"	"	8875	"	"	9140	"	IHB
"	"	8876	"	"	9141	"	IHB
"	"	8877	"	"	9215	"	IHB
"	"	8878	"	"	9216	"	IHB
"	"	8879	"	"	9217	"	IHB RB 12/87 Boos. BU52

Notes: ** Acq.4/67 by NYC
8835, 8852, 8855-8863, 8867, 8901 and 8902 had MU controls both ends,
DES-13E, H had MU controls No. 2 end.
8886, 8887, 8898-8910 had layover heating.
8841 had air signal.

NYCSHS Collection

Indiana Harbor Belt No 8835 Class DES-16A. The first of the model SW7 fleet. Shown here at EMD with horn, bell and stacks covered for shipment.

Class	Road	Number	Builder	Order Number	c/n	Date	Disposition
DES-16E		8880 mu	EMD	(4040)	9221	5/50	PC,CR
"		8881 mu	"	"	9222	"	PC,CR
"		8882 mu	"	"	9223	"	PC,CR
"		8883 mu	"	"	9224	"	PC,CR
"		8884 mu	"	"	9418	"	PC,CR
"		8885 mu	"	"	9419	"	PC,CR
"		8886 mu	"	"	9420	"	PC,CR
"		8887 mu	"	"	9421	"	PC,CR
"		8888 mu	"	"	9422	"	PC,CR
"		8889 mu	"	"	9423	"	PC,CR
"		8890 mu	"	"	9424	"	PC,CR
"		8891 mu	"	"	9425	"	PC,CR
"		8892 mu	"	"	9426	"	PC,CR
"		8893 mu	"	"	9427	"	PC,CR
"		8894 mu	"	"	9428	"	PC,CR
"		8895 mu	"	"	9429	"	PC,CR
"		8896 mu	"	"	9430	6/50	PC,CR
"		8897 mu	"	"	9431	"	PC,CR
DES-16F	CR&I	* 8898	"	(4058)	11774	"	PC,CR
"	"	* 8899	"	"	11775	"	PC,CR
"	"	* 8900	"	"	11776	"	PC,CR
"	"	* 8901 mu	"	"	11777	"	PC,CR
"	"	* 8902 mu	"	"	11778	"	PC,CR
"	"	* 8903	"	"	11779	"	PC,CR
DES-16G	P&E	8904	"	(6174)	13012	12/50	PC,CR
"	"	8905	"	"	13013	"	PC,CR
"	"	8906	"	"	13014	"	PC,CR
"	"	8907	"	"	13015	"	So 5/66 EMD as 8715
"	"	8908	"	"	13016	"	PC,CR
"	"	8909	"	"	13017	"	PC,CR
"	"	8910	"	"	13018	"	PC,CR
DES-16H		8911 mu	"	(4012)	9950	1/51	PC,CR
"		8912 mu	"	"	9951	"	PC,CR
"		8913 mu	"	"	9952	"	PC,CR
"		8914 mu	"	"	9953	"	PC,CR
"		8915 mu	"	"	9954	"	PC,CR
"		8916 mu	"	"	9955	"	PC,CR
"		8917 mu	"	"	9956	"	PC,CR
"		8918 mu	"	"	9957	"	PC,CR
"		8919 mu	"	"	9958	"	PC,CR
"		8920 mu	"	"	9959	"	PC,CR

Note: * Acq. 5/51 by NYC. 8898-8910, 8886, 8887 have layover heating.

NYCSHS Collection

No. 8887 Class DES-16E, a model SW7 switcher.

CLASS DES-16J to R (ES-12,m) Electro-Motive 1200HP Model SW9

Class	Road	Number	Builder	Order Number	c/n	Date	Disposition
DES-16J		8921 mu	EMD	(4113)	9960	2/51	PC,CR
"		8922 mu	"	"	9961	"	PC,CR
"		8923 mu	"	"	9962	"	PC,CR
"		8924 mu	"	"	9963	"	PC,CR
"		8925 mu	"	"	9964	"	PC,CR
"		8926 mu	"	"	9965	"	PC
"		8927 mu	"	"	9966	"	PC,CR
"		8928 mu	"	"	9967	"	PC,CR

No 8923 Class DES-16J. An SW9 switcher built by EMD in May 1950.

NYCSHS Collection

Class	Road	Number	Builder	Order Number	c/n	Date	Disposition
DES-16k		8929 mu	EMD	(4110)	9968	2/51	PC,CR
"		8930 mu	"	"	9969	"	PC,CR
DES-16L	P&LE	8931 mu	EMD	(6242)	14099	3/51	P&LE 1253. So 8/72 BAR 33
"	"	8932 mu	"	"	14100	"	P&LE (1252) Re 9/72 PC&Y 3
"	"	8933 mu	"	"	14101	"	P&LE (1251) So 8/72 BAR 35
"	"	8934 mu	"	"	14102	"	P&LE (1250) So 8/72 BAR 31
"	"	8935 mu	"	"	14103	"	P&LE 1249 So 8/72 BAR 30
"	"	8936 mu	"	"	14104	"	P&LE (1248) So 8/72 BAR 32
"	"	8937 mu	"	"	14105	"	P&LE (1247) Re 9/72 PC&Y 4
"	"	8938 mu	"	"	14106	"	P&LE (1246)-So 8/72 BAR 34
"	"	8939 mu	"	"	14107	"	P&LE (1245) So 9/72 PC&Y 5
"	"	8940 mu	"	"	14108	"	P&LE (1244) So 8/72 BAR 36
DES-16M		8941	EMD	(4108)	15487	2/52	PC,CR
"		8942	"	"	15488	"	PC,CR
"		8943 mu	"	"	15489	"	PC,CR
"		8944 mu	"	"	15490	"	PC,CR
"		8945 mu	"	"	15491	"	PC,CR
"		8946	"	"	15492	"	PC,CR
"		8947	"	"	15493	"	PC,CR
"		8948	"	"	15494	"	PC,CR
"		8949	"	"	15495	"	PC,CR
"		8950	"	"	15496	"	PC,CR
"		8951	"	"	15497	"	PC,CR re 8940

Note: 8929 and 8930 equipped for hump trailer operation.

Class	Road	Number	Builder	Order Number	c/n	Date	Disposition
DES-16N	P&LE	8952 mu	EMD	(6368)	16330	9/52	P&LE 1243 So/76 Md.& Pa.84
"	"	8953 mu	"	"	16331	"	P&LE 1242 So/74 Ms.& SV D4
"	"	8954 mu	"	"	16332	"	P&LE 1241 So/74 Beth.Steel
"	"	8955 mu	"	"	16333	10/52	P&LE 1240 So/73 GrCity Stl
"	"	8956 mu	"	"	16334	"	P&LE 1239 So11/73 TO&E D17
"	"	8957 mu	"	"	16335	"	P&LE 1238 So/74 GrCity Stl
"	"	8958 mu	"	"	16336	"	P&LE 1237 So/74 Beth.Steel
"	"	8959 mu	"	"	16337	"	P&LE 1236 So/74 GrCity Stl
"	"	8960 mu	"	"	16338	"	P&LE 1235 So 3/74 TO&E D19
"	"	8961 mu	"	"	16339	"	P&LE 1234 So 3/74 TO&E D18
DES-16P		8962 mu	EMD	(4143)	16284	1/53	PC,CR
"		8963 mu	"	"	16285	"	PC,CR
"		8964 mu	"	"	16286	"	PC,CR
"		8965 mu	"	"	16287	"	PC,CR
"		8966 mu	"	"	16288	"	PC,CR
"		8967 mu	"	"	16289	"	PC,CR
"		8968 mu	"	"	16290	"	PC,CR
"		8969 mu	"	"	16291	"	PC,CR
"		8970 mu	"	"	16292	"	PC,CR
"		8971 mu	"	"	16293	"	PC,CR
"		8972 mu	"	"	16294	"	PC,CR
DES-16P		8973 mu	EMD	(4143)	16295	1/53	PC,CR
"		8974 mu	"	"	16296	"	PC,CR
"		8975 mu	"	"	16297	"	PC,CR
"		8976 mu	"	"	16298	"	PC,CR
"		8977 mu	"	"	16299	"	PC,CR
"		8978 mu	"	"	16300	"	PC,CR
"		8979 mu	"	"	16301	"	PC,CR
"		8980 mu	"	"	16302	"	PC,CR
"		8981 mu	"	"	16303	"	PC,CR
"		8982 mu	"	"	16304	"	PC,CR
"		8983 mu	"	"	16305	"	PC,CR
"		8984 mu	"	"	16306	"	PC,CR
"		8985 mu	"	"	16307	"	PC,CR
"		8986 mu	"	"	16308	"	PC,CR
"		8987 mu	EMD	(4143)	16309	1/53	PC,CR
"		8988 mu	"	"	16310	"	PC,CR
"		8989 mu	"	"	16311	"	PC,CR

Notes: DES-16J, K, P had MU controls No. 2 end.
DES-16R MU both ends and air signal.
9004 also had air signal.

Class	Road	Number	Builder	Order Number	c/n	Date	Disposition
DES-16Q		8990	EMD	(4192)	16312	2/53	PC,CR
"		8991	"	"	16313	"	PC,CR
"		8992	"	"	16314	"	PC,CR
"		8993	"	"	16315	"	PC,CR
"		8994	"	"	16316	"	PC,CR
"		8995	"	"	16317	"	PC,CR
"		8996	"	"	16318	"	PC,CR
"		8997	"	"	16319	"	PC,CR
"		8998	"	"	16320	"	PC,CR
"		8999 mu	"	"	16321	"	PC,CR
"		9000	"	"	16322	"	PC,CR
"		9001	"	"	16323	"	PC,CR
DES-16R	IHB	9002 mu	EMD	(4239)	18790	10/53	IHB
"	"	9003 mu	"	"	18791	"	IHB
"	"	9004 mu	"	"	18792	"	IHB
"	"	9005 mu	"	"	18793	"	IHB
"	"	9006 mu	"	"	18794	"	IHB
"	"	9007 mu	"	"	18795	"	IHB
"	"	9008 mu	"	"	18796	"	IHB

Note: 9004 equipped with air signal.

No. 8907 Class DES-16G, built for Peoria and Eastern is at work at Lafayette, Indiana on April 2, 1960.

Both: Louis A. Marre

No. 8851 Class DES-16C, a model SW7 switcher. First used on Ohio Central at Columbus.

Class DES-17 (FS-12, m) Fairbanks-Morse 1200 HP Model H12-44

LOCOMOTIVE DESIGNED FOR 57.5° CURVE

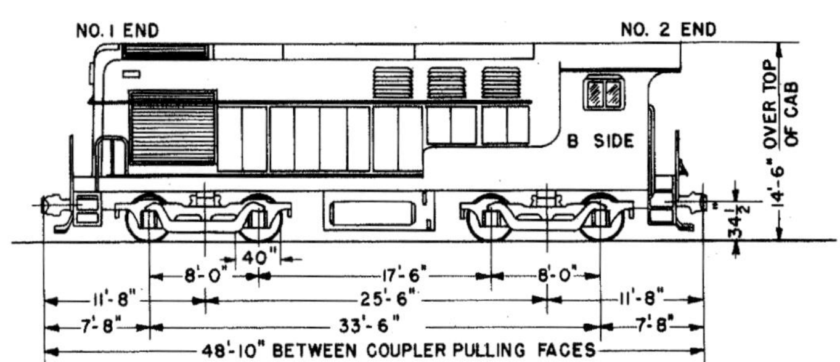

DIESEL ENGINE — F. M. MODEL 38 D 8 1/8
DIESEL ENGINE H.P. — 1347 (1200 FOR TRACTION)
NUMBER OF CYLINDERS — 6 IN LINE (O.P.)
BORE AND STROKE — 8⅛"x10"
ENGINE SPEED R.P.M. — IDLING 350, FULL LOAD 800
MAIN GENERATOR — W. E. CORP 481-G OR 481-GZ DIRECT DRIVEN
MAIN GENERATOR VOLTAGE — MAX. 1125V, FULL LOAD 1050V
MAIN GENERATOR CAPACITY — 820KW
NUMBER AND TYPE OF TRACTION MOTORS — FOUR W. E. CORP. 362-DF
TRACTION MOTOR VENTILATION — FORCED
GEAR RATIO — 68/14 (4.857)
CONTROL VOLTAGE — 75 V.

MAXIMUM SPEED OF LOCOMOTIVE — ☆60 M.P.H.
CONTINUOUS RATING - TRACTIVE EFFORT — 34,000 LBS.
SPEED — 11.3 M.P.H.
HORSEPOWER — 1025

☆ 68/14 GEAR RATIO SPEED. LOCOMOTIVE RESTRICTED TO 45 MPH.

PRINTED 4-15-57

Class	Number	Re '66	Builder	Order Number	c/n	Date	Disposition
DES-17A	9111	(8300) mu	F-M	(LD92)	12L378	12/50	RT 3/66 Sc
"	9112	8301 mu	"	"	12L379	"	Rt 5/67 GE
"	9113	8302 mu	"	"	12L380	"	Rt 5/67 GE
"	9114	8303 mu	"	"	12L381	"	PC Rt EMD
"	9115	8304 mu	"	"	12L382	"	Rt 5/67 GE
"	9116	8305 mu	"	"	12L383	"	PC
"	9117	8306 mu	"	"	12L384	1/51	Rt 8/67 SS 10/67
"	9118	8307 mu	"	"	12L385	"	PC
"	9119	8308 mu	"	"	12L386	"	Rt 5/67 GE
"	9120	8309 mu	"	"	12L387	"	PC
DES-17B	9121	8310 mu	"	(LD132)	12L613	5/52	PC Rt EMD
"	9122	8311 mu	"	"	12L614	"	PC Rt EMD
"	9123	8312 mu	"	"	12L615	"	PC
"	9124	8313 mu	"	"	12L616	"	PC
"	9125	8314	"	"	12L617	"	Rt 5/67 GE
"	9126	8315 mu	"	"	12L618	"	PC Rt EMD
"	9127	8316 mu	"	"	12L619	"	PC
"	9128	8317	"	"	12L620	"	Rt 8/67 SS 12/67
"	9129	8318 mu	"	"	12L621	6/52	PC
"	9130	8319	"	"	12L622	"	Rt 12/67 SS 2/68
"	9131	8320 mu	"	"	12L623	"	PC
"	9132	8321 mu	"	"	12L624	"	PC
"	9133	8322 mu	"	"	12L625	"	Rt 12/67 SS 2/68
"	9134	8323 mu	"	"	12L626	"	PC
"	9135	8324 mu	"	"	12L627	"	PC
"	9136	8325 mu	"	"	12L628	"	PC Rt 7/68
"	9137	8326	"	"	12L629	7/52	PC Rt EMD

Note: DES-17A equipped with double-end train control, speedometer, and MU on #2 end with gangway.

Both: NYCSHS Collection

No 9117 Class DES-17A a model H12-44 switcher built by Fairbanks-Morse in January 1951. The "lightning stripe" paint scheme was unusual for NYC yard switchers.

No 9117 and 9118 coupled in multiple at the F-M plant. All ten of the units in this class were assigned to the B&A at Beacon Park.

Class DES-18 (ES-8) Electro-Motive 800 HP Model SW8

LOCOMOTIVE DESIGNED FOR
57.5° CURVE

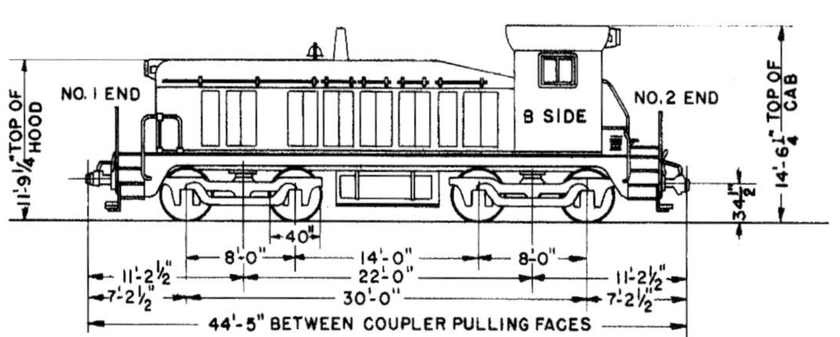

DIESEL ENGINE .... GM ... MODEL 567B
DIESEL ENGINE H.P. .... 865(800 FOR TRACTION)
NUMBER OF CYLINDERS .... 8-V TYPE
BORE AND STROKE .... 8 1/2" x 10"
ENGINE SPEED R.P.M. .... IDLING 275 FULL LOAD 800
MAIN GENERATOR .... EMD TYPE D-15-C DIRECT DRIVEN
MAIN GENERATOR VOLTAGE .... MAX. 1030V., FULL LOAD 1000V.
MAIN GENERATOR CAPACITY .... 567KW.
NUMBER AND TYPE OF TRACTION MOTORS .... FOUR EMD D-27
TRACTION MOTOR VENTILATION .... FORCED
GEAR RATIO 62/15 (4.133)
CONTROL VOLTAGE .... 75 V

MAXIMUM SPEED OF LOCOMOTIVE .... ☆ 65 M.P.H.
CONTINUOUS RATING - TRACTIVE EFFORT .... 31,200 LBS.
SPEED .... 7.0 M.P.H.
HORSEPOWER 581

☆ 75/16 GEAR RATIO SPEED. LOCOMOTIVE RESTRICTED TO 45 MPH.

PRINTED 4-15-57

CLASS DES-18

Class	Road	Number	Re '66	Builder	Order Number	c/n	Date	Disposition
DES-18A	CR&I	9600	*8600	EMD	(4059)	11780	10/50	PC,CR
"	CR&I	9601	*8601	EMD	"	11781	"	PC,CR
DES-18B		9602	8602	EMD	(4109)	15498	2/52	PC,CR
"		9603	8603	EMD	"	15499	"	PC,CR
"		9604	8604	EMD	"	15500	"	PC,CR
"		9605	8605	EMD	"	15501	"	Rt 1/67 Sc
"		9606	8606	EMD	"	15502	"	PC,CR
"		9607	8607	EMD	"	15503	"	PC,CR
DES-18C		9608	8608	EMD	(4144)	16183	2/53	PC,CR
"		9609	8609	EMD	"	16184	"	PC,CR
"		9610	8610	EMD	"	16185	"	PC,CR
"		9611	8611	EMD	"	16186	"	PC,CR
"		9612	8612	EMD	"	16187	"	PC,CR
"		9613	8613	EMD	"	16188	"	PC,CR
"		9614	8614	EMD	"	16189	"	PC,CR
"		9615	8615	EMD	"	16190	"	PC,CR
"		9616	8616	EMD	"	16191	"	PC,CR
"		9617	8617	EMD	"	16192	"	PC,CR
"		9618	8618	EMD	"	16193	"	PC,CR
"		9619	8619	EMD	"	16194	"	PC,CR
"		9620	8620	EMD	"	16195	"	PC,CR
"		9621	8621	EMD	"	16196	"	PC,CR
"		9622	8622	EMD	"	16324	"	PC,CR
"		9623	8623	EMD	"	16325	"	PC,AM 747
DES-18D		9624	8624	EMD	"	16326	"	PC,CR
"		9625	8625	EMD	"	16327	"	PC,AM 748
"		9626	8626	EMD	"	16328	"	PC,OR
"		9627	8627	EMD	"	16329	"	PC,CR

Note: * Acq.6/51 by NYC; Re 2/52 to L&JB 16,17; Re 5/55 9600, 9601 again.

Louis A. Marre

No. 9603 Class DES-18B is shown here at Moraine, Ohio on September 1, 1965. It would be renumbered to 8603 the following year.

NYCSHS Collection

No 9606 Class DES-18B was another SW8 switcher built by EMD in February 1952.

Collection of Louis A. Marre

No. 9620 Class DES-18C waits for a clear signal on a beautiful spring day at White Pigeon, Michigan on May 25, 1954.

Class DES-19 Lima 800 HP Switcher

LOCOMOTIVE DESIGNED FOR
57.5° CURVE

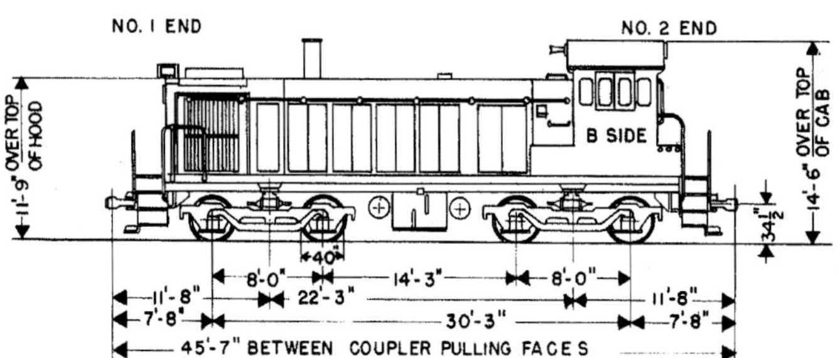

DIESEL ENGINE .... LIMA MODEL T69 SA
DIESEL ENGINE H.P. .... 800 FOR TRACTION
NUMBER OF CYLINDERS .... 6 IN LINE
BORE AND STROKE .... 9" x 12"
ENGINE SPEED R.P.M. .... IDLING 425, FULL LOAD 950
MAIN GENERATOR .... W.E. CORP. TYPE 499-A DIRECT DRIVEN
MAIN GENERATOR VOLTAGE .... MAX. 1020V., FULL LOAD 950V.
MAIN GENERATOR CAPACITY .... 541 KW.
NUMBER AND TYPE OF TRACTION MOTORS .... FOUR W. E. CORP. 362-D
TRACTION MOTOR VENTILATION .... FORCED
GEAR RATIO 68/14 (4.857)
CONTROL VOLTAGE .... 75V.

MAXIMUM SPEED OF LOCOMOTIVE .... 60 M.P.H.
CONTINUOUS RATING - TRACTIVE EFFORT .... 34,000 LBS.
SPEED .... 6.5 M.P.H.

PRINTED 4-15-57

CLASS DES-19

Class	Road	Number	Builder	Order Number	c/n	Date	Disposition
DES-19A	CR&I	9800	Lima	(1220)	9439	1/51	Rt SS
"	"	9801	"	"	9440	"	Rt SS
"	"	9802	"	"	9441	"	Rt SS
"	"	9803	"	"	9442	2/51	Rt SS
"	"	9804	"	"	9450	"	Rt 10/59
"	"	9805	"	"	9451	"	Rt SS
"	"	9806	"	"	9452	3/51	Rt SS
"	"	9807	"	"	9453	"	Rt SS
"	"	9808	"	"	9454	"	Rt 10/59
"	"	9809	"	"	9455	5/51	Rt 10/59
"	"	9810	"	"	9517	"	Rt SS
"	"	9811	"	"	9518	"	Rt SS
"	"	9812	"	"	9519	"	Rt SS
"	"	9813	"	"	9520	"	Rt SS
"	"	9814	"	"	9521	"	Rt SS
"	"	9815	"	"	9522	"	Rt SS
"	"	9816	"	"	9523	"	Rt SS
"	"	9817	"	"	9524	"	Rt SS
"	"	9818	"	"	9525	6/51	Rt 10/59
"	"	9819	"	"	9526	"	Rt 10/59
"	"	9820	"	"	9527	"	Rt 10/59

NYCSHS Collection

No. 9800 Class DES-19 first of the LH 800 switcher rated at 800 HP. Several in this class were retired when only eight years old.

H.L. Broadbelt Collection

No. 9310 Class DES-20A was a Baldwin model S-12, photographed at the Eddystone plant.

Class DES-20 (BS-12) Baldwin-Westinghouse Model S-12

LOCOMOTIVE DESIGNED FOR 44° CURVE

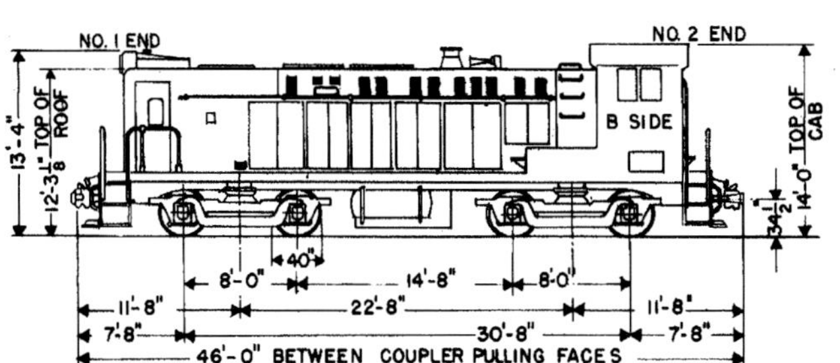

DIESEL ENGINE — BLH MODEL 606A
DIESEL ENGINE H.P. — 1257 (1200 FOR TRACTION)
NUMBER OF CYLINDERS — 6 IN LINE
BORE AND STROKE — 12 3/4" x 15 1/2"
ENGINE SPEED R.P.M. — IDLING 315, FULL LOAD 625
MAIN GENERATOR — W.E. CORP. TYPE 480-FZ DIRECT DRIVEN
MAIN GENERATOR VOLTAGE — MAX. 1065 V, FULL LOAD 1000 V.
MAIN GENERATOR CAPACITY — 865 K.W.
NUMBER AND TYPE OF TRACTION MOTORS — FOUR W.E. CORP. 362-DZ
TRACTION MOTOR VENTILATION — FORCED
GEAR RATIO — 68/14 (4.857)
CONTROL VOLTAGE — 75 V.

MAXIMUM SPEED OF LOCOMOTIVE — ✫60 M.P.H.
CONTINUOUS RATING - TRACTIVE EFFORT — 34,000 LBS.
SPEED — 10.8 M.P.H.
HORSEPOWER — 980

✫ 68/14 GEAR RATIO SPEED. LOCOMOTIVE RESTRICTED TO 45 MPH.

PRINTED 4-15-57

CLASS DES-20

Class	Original Number	Re '66	Builder	Order Number	c/n	Date	Disposition
DES-20A	9308	8092	BLH	(50545)	75275	10/51	PC
"	9309	8093	"	"	75276	"	PC
"	9310	8094	"	"	75277	"	PC re 8308
DES-20B	9311	8095	"	(51523)	75546	6/52	PC
"	9312	8096	"	"	75547	"	PC re 8309
	9313	8097	"	"	75548	"	Rt 5/67 GE
"	9314	8098	"	"	75549	"	PC re 8310
"	9315	8099	"	"	75550	"	PC re 8311
"	9316	8100	"	"	75551	"	PC re 8312
"	9317	8101	"	"	75552	"	
"	9318	8102	"	"	75553	"	Rt 5/67 GE
"	9319	8103	"	"	75554	7/52	Rt 5/67 GE
"	9320	8104	"	"	75555		Rt 5/67 GE
"	9321	8105	"	"	75556	"	Rt 5/67 GE
"	9322	8106	"	"	75557	"	PC re 8313
"	9323	8107	"	"	75558	"	PC re 8314
"	9324	8108	"	"	75559	"	PC
"	9325	8109	"		75560	"	Rt 5/67 GE
"	9326	8110	"	"	75561	"	PC re 8315
"	9327	8111	"	"	75562	"	PC re 8316
	9328	8112	"		75563	"	PC Rt 4/68

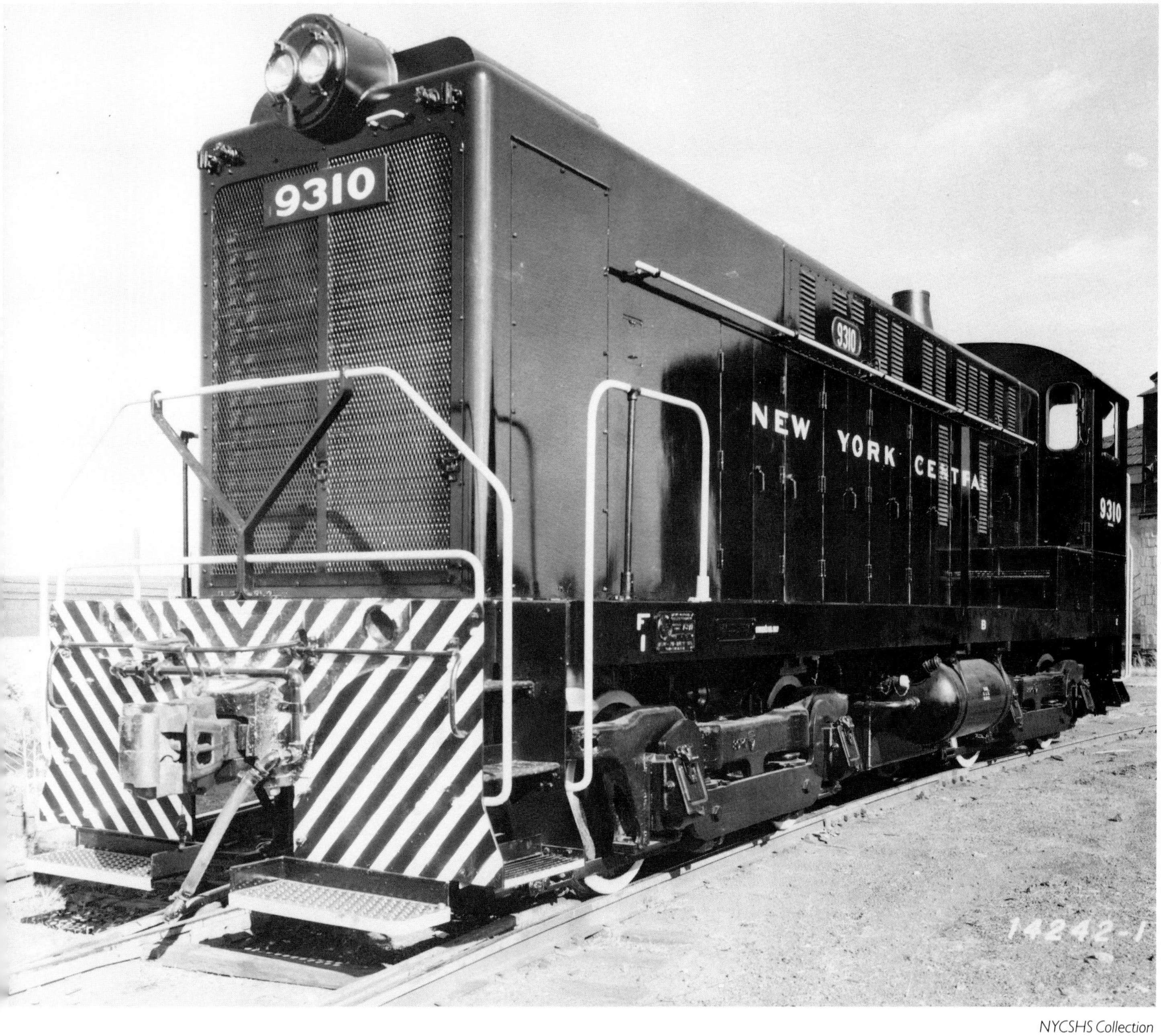

NYCSHS Collection

No 9310 Class DES-20A shown here new in October 1951 was renumbered 8094 in 1966 then to Penn Central and renumbered to 8308.

Class DES-21 (ES-9) Electro-Motive Model SW900

LOCOMOTIVE DESIGNED FOR
57.5° CURVE

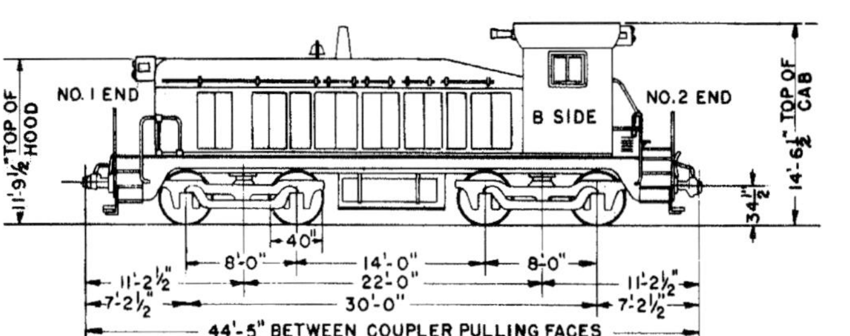

MODEL SW-900

DIESEL ENGINE — GM — MODEL 567C
DIESEL ENGINE H.P. — 900 FOR TRACTION
NUMBER OF CYLINDERS — 8-V TYPE
BORE AND STROKE — 8½" x 10"
ENGINE SPEED R.P.M. — IDLING 275 FULL LOAD 835
MAIN GENERATOR — EMD TYPE D-15-C DIRECT DRIVEN
MAIN GENERATOR VOLTAGE — MAX. 1020V., FULL LOAD 980 V.
MAIN GENERATOR CAPACITY — 638KW.
NUMBER AND TYPE OF TRACTION MOTORS — FOUR EMD D-37
TRACTION MOTOR VENTILATION — FORCED
GEAR RATIO — 62/15 (4.133)
CONTROL VOLTAGE — 75 V

MAXIMUM SPEED OF LOCOMOTIVE — 65 M.P.H.

PRINTED 4-15-57

CLASS DES-21

Class	Road	Number	Re '66	Builder	Order Number	c/n	Date	Disposition
DES-21A	CUT	9628*	8628	EMD	(4628)	19518	3/54	PC,CR
"	CUT	9629*	8629	"	"	19519	"	PC, CR
"	CUT	9630*	8630	"	"	19520	"	PC,CR
DES-21B		9631	8631	"	(4322)	20935	12/55	PC,CR re 9008
"		9632	8632	"	"	20936	"	PC, CR
"		9633	8633	"	"	20937	"	PC,CR
"		9634	8634	"	"	20938	"	PC,CR
"		9635	8635	"	"	20939	"	PC,CR
"		9636	8636	"	"	20940	"	PC,CR
"		9637	8637	"	"	20941	"	PC,CR
"		9638	8638	"	"	20942	"	PC,CR
"		9639	8639	"	"	20943	"	PC,CR
"		9640	8640	"	"	20944	"	PC,CR
"		9641	8641	"	"	20945	"	PC,CR
"		9642	8642	"	"	20946	"	PC,CR
"		9643	8643	"	(4324)	20947	"	PC,CR
"		9644	8644	"	"	20948	"	PC,CR
"		9645	8645	"	"	20949	"	PC,CR
"		9646	8646	"	"	20950	"	PC,CR

* equipped with double end train control

Cleveland Union Terminal No 9629 Class DES-21 was a model SW900 switcher. This locomotive was relettered for the NYC and renumbered 8629 in May 1966.

Louis A. Marre

he engineer side view of Cleveland Union Terminal No 9629 Class DES-21 at Collinwood on March 25, 1964. Note the large fuel tank nd double-end train control equipment.

DES-22 Planned but not assigned. New classification, ES-15 used.

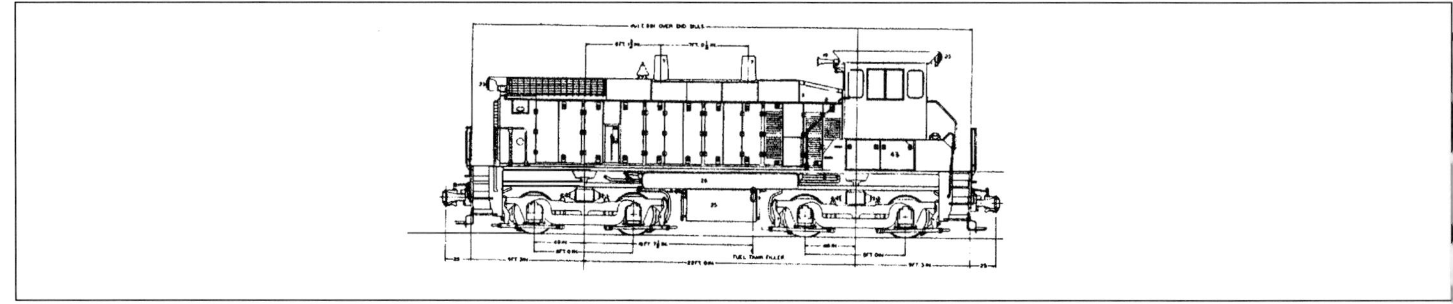

Class ES-15 B-B: EMD SW 1500 1500 HP 12-645E (V-12) 58000 - 247010 to 249650

Class	Road	Road Numbers	Builder	Order Number	c/n	Date	Disposition
ES-15M	IHB	9200-9207	EMD	7882	31719-31726	7,8/1966	
"	"	9208-9212	"	7982	33078-33082	3,4/1967	
"	"	9213-9215	"	7989	33083-33085	4/1967	
"	"	9216-9221	"	7111	34030-34035	6,7/1968	Note 1

Note: All Locomotives restricted to 45 MPH. All locomotives equipped with MU controls No. 1 and 2 ends.

9216-9221 ordered by NYC, delivered after merger into Penn Central. NYCS Classification DES-22 was to be assigned to these locomotives, but was never used due to the PC merger and the subsequent reclassification of all motive power

Louis A. Marr

No 9208 Class ES-15M at Riverside, Ohio on June 22, 1968. These units were the New York Central's last switchers.

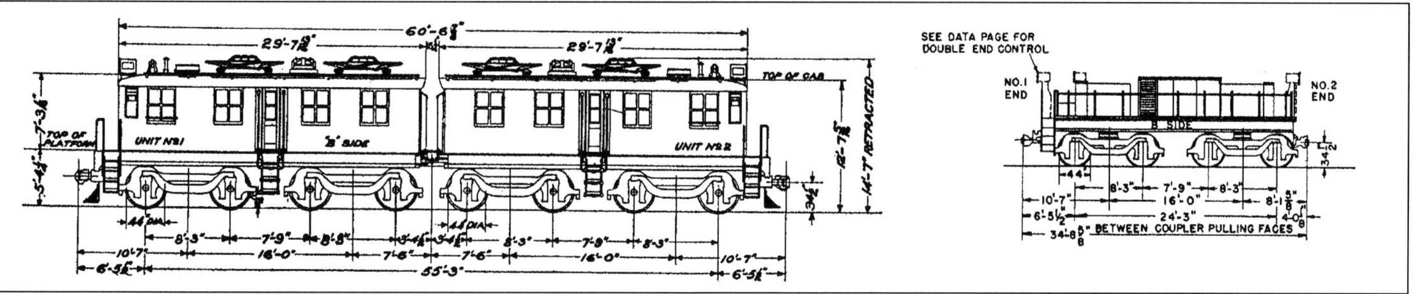

DHT-1

Class DHT-1A B-B: Built by NYC at Harmon Shop from retired class RA Electric Locos - 40MPH - 63425-253, 700

Class	Number	RA Loco #	Control	Operation	Rebuilt	Disposition
DHT-1A	450	300A	No	Single End	2/1945	Ret.12/63 Sc. l/64
"	451	300B	Yes	Double End	4/1945	Ret. after 8/66
"	452	301A	No	Single End	5/1945	Ret. 5/63Sc.10/63
"	453	301B	No	Single End	6/1945	Ret.10/63

quipped to operate with one DES-7, one or two DES-l 1's, one DES-13 or one DES-16 locomotive in Hump Yard Service.

NYC Photo, Collection of NYCSHS

No. 451 Hump Trailer Class DHT-1A rebuilt February, 1945 shown here MUed to Alco 8533, class DES-11C.

Diesel Hump Trailers

DHT-2A

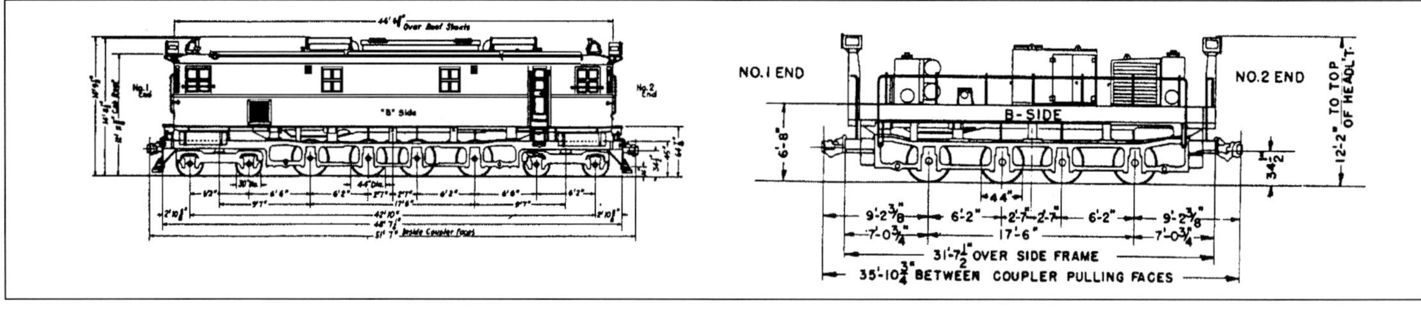

Class	Number	Re No. 7/51	Control	Operation	Rebuilt	Disposition
DHT-2A	454	469	Yes	Double End	12/1946	Sc. 11/1953

Equipped to operate with one or two DES-11"s, one DES-13 or one DES-16 Locomotive in Hump Yard Service.

DHT-2

Class DHT-2 B-B: Built by NYC from retired class DES-2 and DES-3 Locomotive

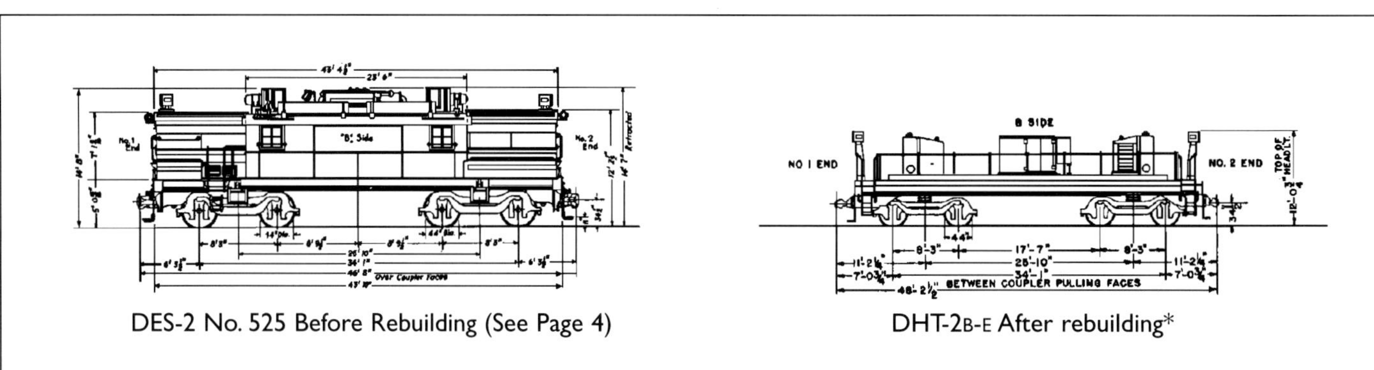

DES-2 No. 525 Before Rebuilding (See Page 4)

DHT-2B-E After rebuilding*

Class	Re Class 11/46	Number	Built From	Number	MU Control	Hump Trailer Operation	Built At	Date	Disposition
DHT-2A	DHT-2B	470	DES-2	525	Yes	Double end	H. E.Shop	12/45	Sc. 12/63
DHT-2B	DHT-2C	471	DES-3	562	"	"	"	8/46	Ret 9/63 SS12/63
DHT-2C	-	472	"	561	"	"	"	12/48	Ret 9/63 SS 12/63
DHT-2D	-	473 (IHB)	"	542	"	"	"	8/50	Reblt 5/52 as 477
DHT-2D		474 (IHB)	"	563	"	"	"	10/50	
DHT-2E		475	"	551	"	"	Collinwood	3/54	Ret 9/63 SS12/63
DHT-2E		476 (IHB)	"	535	"	"	"	5/54	

Equipped to operate with one or two DES-11"s, one DES-13 or one DES-16 Locomotive in Hump Yard Service.

*Some dimensions vary, depending on whether unit was rebuilt from DES-2 No. 525 or DES-3 units listed.

NYC Photo, Collection of NYCSHS

No. 469 Hump Trailer Class DHT-2A after rebuilding from DEF No. 500 at Harmon N.Y. Road No. 454 was originally assigned to this unit.

Collection of Louis A. Marre

No. 476 Hump Trailer Class DHT-2E after rebuilding from DES-3 No. 535 at Collinwood Shop in May 1954 for use at the hump yard at Gibson, Indiana. This view was made in July 1966 some time after retirement. The IHB equipped three DES-13H units 8790-8792 to work with DHT's.

Diesel Hump Trailer DHT-2F B-B: Built by IHB -40-61125 - 244500

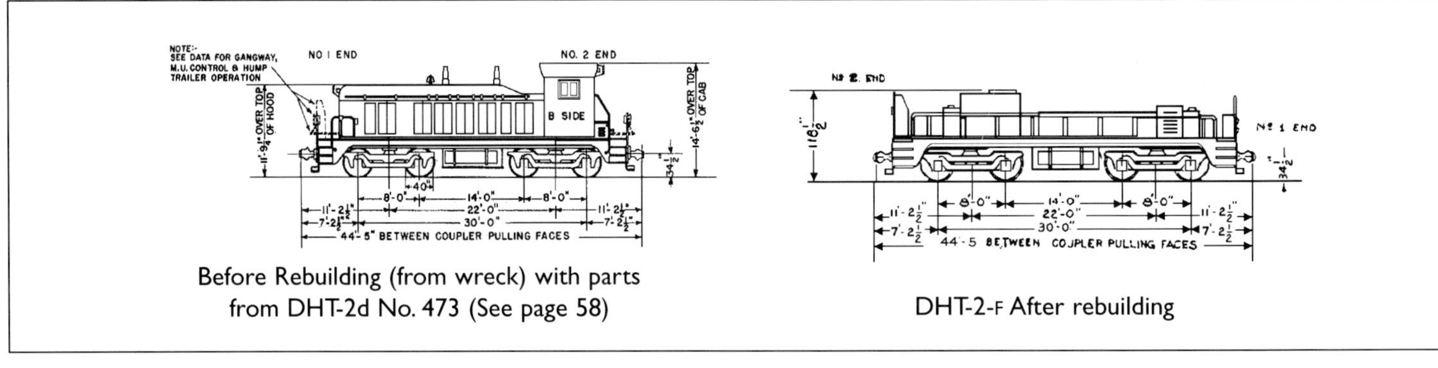

Before Rebuilding (from wreck) with parts from DHT-2d No. 473 (See page 58)

DHT-2-F After rebuilding

Class	Number	Built From	MU Control	Hump Trailer Operation	Built At	Date	Disposition
DHT-2F	477	DHT-473 and DES-13g No 8777	Yes	Single End	Gibson Indiana	8/62	

Equipped to operate with one DES-13 (ES-10) or one DES-16 (ES-12) Locomotive in hump yard service.

Road Freight Diesel Locomotives

CLASS DFA-IA and DFB-IA ELECTRO MOTIVE 1350HP Model FT

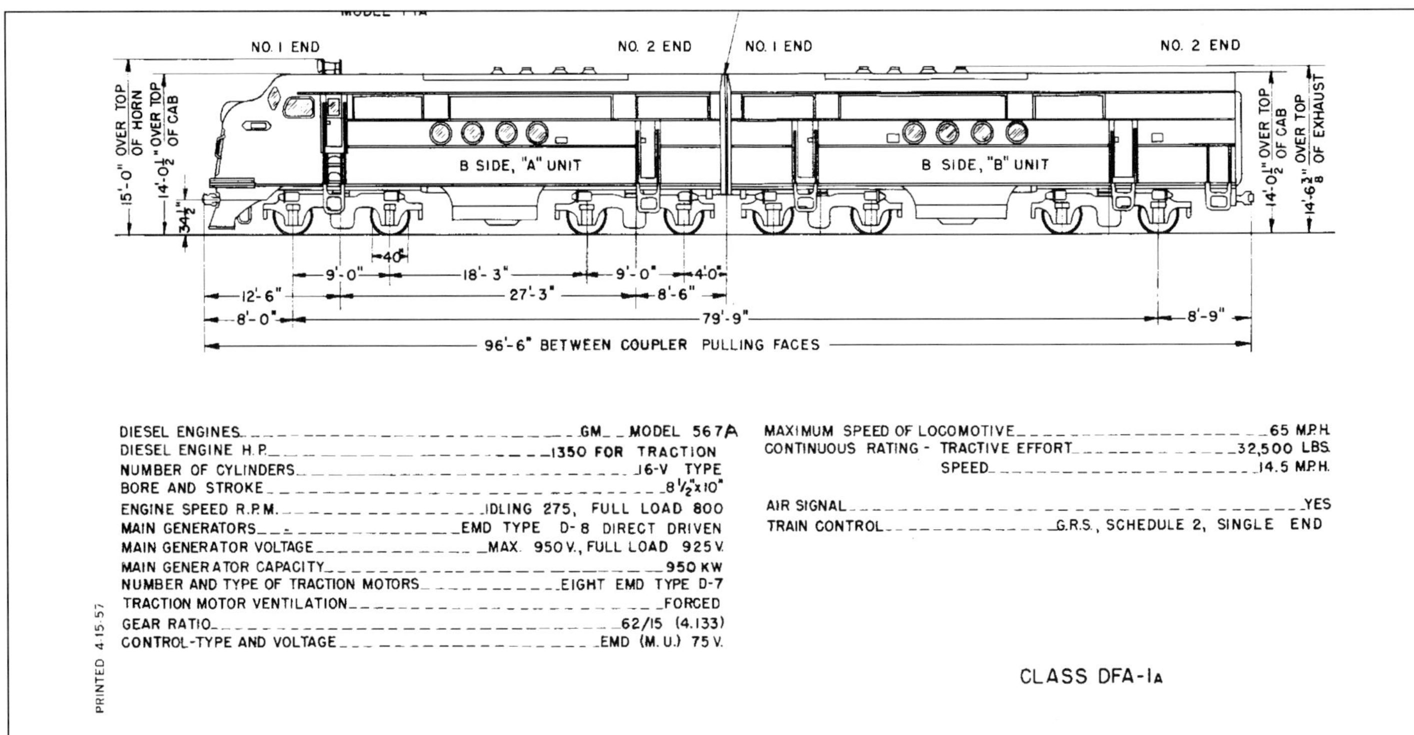

Class	Number	Builder	Order Number	c/n	Date	Disposition
DFA-IA	1600	EMC	(E-522)	1888	6/44	Rt, So10/64 EMD
	1601	"	"	1889	"	Rt, So 4/61 EMD
	1602	"	"	1890	"	Rt, So 4/61 EMD
	1603	"	"	1891	"	Rt, So 11/64 EMD
DFB-IA	2400	EMC	(E-523)	2183	6/44	Rt, So10/64 EMD
	2401	"	"	2184	"	Rt, So 4/61 EMD
	2402	"	"	2185	"	Rt, So 4/61 EMD
	2403	"	"	2186	"	Rt, So 11/64 EMD

William D. Edson

No. 1600 Class DFA-1A. NYC's first EMD FT diesel with DFB-1a No. 2400, photographed April 4, 1948 at Rotterdam Junction, New York with an eastbound freight.

Louis A. Marre

No. 1603 Class DFA-1A on its way to scrapping at EMD is seen here at Elkhart, Indiana on November 5, 1964.

CLASS DFA-1B EMD 1350HP Model F2

Class	Number	Builder	Order Number	c/n	Date	Disposition
DFA-1B	1604	EMC	(E-721)	3771	7/46	Rt 5/62 So EMD
"	1605	"	"	3772	"	Rt 9/65 So 12/65 EMD

CLASS DFA-2A, B and DFB-2A, B (EF-15) EMD 1500HP Model F3

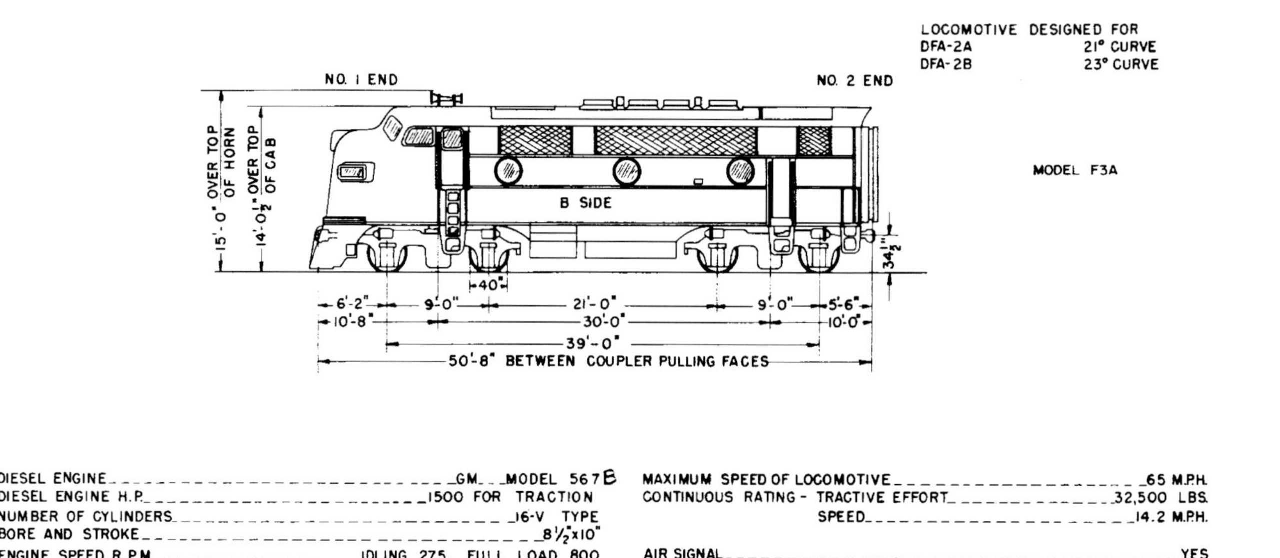

Class	Number	Builder	Order Number	c/n	Date	Disposition
DFA-2A	1606	EMC	(E-752)	4183	6/47	So 10/64 EMD
"	1607	"	"	4184	"	So 12/65 EMD
"	1608	"	"	4185	"	Rt 9/65 So 10/65 EMD
"	1609	"	"	4186	"	Rt 9/65 So 10/65 EMD
"	1610	"	"	4187	"	So 12/65 EMD
"	1611	"	"	4188	7/47	Rt 9/65 So 12/65 EMD
"	1612	"	"	4189	"	Rt 10/64 So 3/65 EMD
"	1613	"	"	4190	"	So 5/62 EMD
"	1614	"	"	4191	"	So 10/65 EMD
"	1615	"	"	4192	"	So 5/61 EMD
"	1616	"	"	4193	"	So 5/61 EMD
"	1617	"	"	4194	"	PC Rt 4/68
"	1618	"	"	4195	"	So 5/62 EMD
"	1619	"	"	4196	"	PC Rt 12/68
"	1620	"	"	4197	"	So 12/65 EMD
"	1621	"	"	4198	"	Rt 9/65 So 12/65 EMD
"	1622	"	"	4199	"	Rt 9/65 So 10/65 EMD
"	1623	"	"	4200	"	So 12/65 EMD

One of the pair of F2 units, No. 1605 Class DFA-1B as delivered by EMD in July 1946. Note small number boards and three carbody portholes.

Both: NYCSHS Collection

No. 1611 Class DFA-2B as delivered with an older version of the gray "lightning stripe" paint scheme. "B" units were painted solid black, a standard that was to appear again in later years.

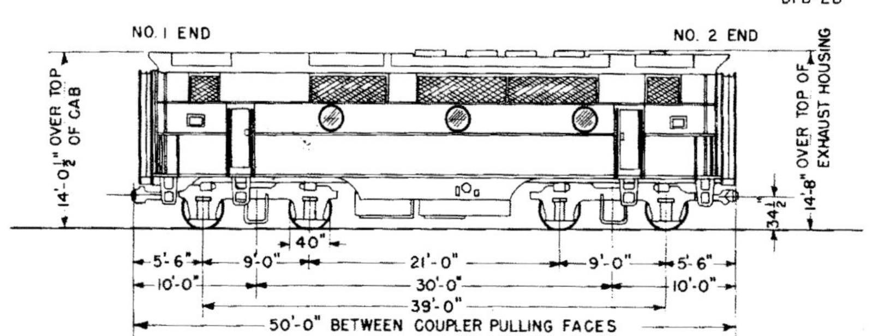

DIESEL ENGINE — GM — MODEL 567B
DIESEL ENGINE H.P. — 1620 (1500 FOR TRACTION)
NUMBER OF CYLINDERS — 16-V TYPE
BORE AND STROKE — 8½"x10"
ENGINE SPEED R.P.M. — IDLING 275, FULL LOAD 800
MAIN GENERATOR — EMD TYPE D-12 DIRECT DRIVEN
MAIN GENERATOR VOLTAGE — MAX. 1000V., FULL LOAD 950V.
MAIN GENERATOR CAPACITY — 1064 KW.
NUMBER AND TYPE OF TRACTION MOTORS — FOUR EMD D-17
TRACTION MOTOR VENTILATION — FORCED
GEAR RATIO — 62/15 (4.133)
CONTROL-TYPE AND VOLTAGE — EMD (M.U.) 75 V.

MAXIMUM SPEED OF LOCOMOTIVE — 65 M.P.H.
CONTINUOUS RATING - TRACTIVE EFFORT — 32,500 LBS.
SPEED — 14.2 M.P.H.
HORSEPOWER — 1231
AIR SIGNAL — YES
TRAIN CONTROL — NONE

PRINTED 5-1-53

CLASS DFB-2A, DFB-2B

Class	Number	Builder	Order Number	c/n	Date	Disposition
DFB-2A	2404	EMC	(E-752)	4201	6/47	Rt 9/65 So 12/65 EMD
"	2405	"	"	4202	"	Rt 5/62 So EMD
"	2406	"	"	4203	"	Rt 10/64 So 12/64 EMD
"	2407	"	"	4204	"	Rt 5/62 So EMD
"	2408	"	"	4205	"	So 5/61 EMD
"	2409	"	"	4206	7/47	Rt 5/62 So EMD
"	2410	"	"	4207	"	So 12/65 EMD
"	2411	"	"	4208	"	So 12/65 EMD
"	2412	"	"	4209	"	Rt 5/62 So EMD
"	2413	"	"	4210	"	Rt 9/65 So 10/65 EMD
DFA-2B	1624	EMC	(E-841)	4859	4/48	Rt 6/62 So 6/62 EMD?
"	1625	"	"	4860	"	So 5/61 EMD
"	1626	"	"	4861	"	So 4/61 EMD
"	1627	"	"	4862	"	So 4/61EMD
"	1628	"	"	4863	"	So 12/65 EMD
"	1629	"	"	4864	"	So 9/65 EMD
"	1630	"	"	4865	"	So 12/65 EMD
"	1631	"	"	4866	"	Rt 5/62 So EMD?
"	1632	"	"	4867	"	So 4/61 EMD
"	1633	"	"	4868	"	PC
"	1634	"	"	4869	"	So 4/61 EMD
"	1635	"	"	4870	"	PC Rt 4/68
DFB-2B	2414	EMC	(E-841)	4871	4/48	Rt 9/65 So 11/65 EMD
"	2415	"	"	4872	"	Rt 6/62 So EMD
"	2416	"	"	4873	"	So 12/65 EMD
"	2417	"	"	4874	"	So 12/65 EMD
"	2418	"	"	4875	"	So 9/65 EMD
"	2419	"	"	4876	"	So 12/65 EMD

NYCSHS Collection

No. 1626 and No. 1627 Class DFA-2B with DFB-2B No. 2415 sandwiched in between at EMD in April of 1948.

No. 1635 Class DFA-2B at South Bend, Indiana on October 14, 1959, shows a lot of road dirt and fading paint on the herald on the nose. The coupler shields are long since gone off of the pilot.

Louis A. Marre

Louis A. Marre

No. 1611 Class DFA-2A was built by EMD in July 1947. Shown here before being sold back to EMD in December 1965

CLASS DFA-2C to 2H and DFB-2C to 2G (EF-15) EMD 1500HP F7

Class	Original Number	Re '66	Builder	Order Number	c/n	Date	Disposition
DFA-2C	1636		EMC	(E-986)	6229	5/49	PC
"	1637		"	"	6230	"	PC
"	1638		"	"	6231	"	PC
"	1639		"	"	6232	"	PC,CR
"	1640		"	"	6233	"	So 12/64 EMD
"	1641		"	"	6234	"	PC
"	1642		"	"	6235	"	PC
"	1643		"	"	6236	"	So 1/67 GE re L&N 800
"	1644		"	"	6237	"	PC
"	1645		"	"	6238	"	So 12/64 EMD
"	1646		"	"	6239	"	PC
DFB-2C	2420		EMC	(E-986)	6240	5/49	So 12/65 EMD
"	2421		"	"	6381	"	So 12/65 EMD
DFA-2D	1647		EMC	(E-1041)	7153	7/49	So 12/64 EMD
"	1648		"	"	7154	"	PC,CR re 1792
"	1649		"	"	7155	"	PC
"	1650		"	"	7156	"	PC,CR re 1793
"	1651		"	"	7157	"	PC
"	1652		"	"	7158	"	So 12/64 EMD
"	1653		"	"	7159	"	So 6/65 EMD
"	1654		"	"	7160	"	PC Rt 7/68
"	1655		"	"	7161	"	PC
"	1656		"	"	7162	"	PC,CR
"	1657		"	"	7163	"	PC
"	1658		"	"	7164	"	PC
"	1659		"	"	7165	"	PC,CR
"	1660	1698	"	"	7166	"	PC (Re '65 2nd 1698)
"	1661		"	"	7167	"	PC
"	1662		"	"	7168	"	So 12/66 GE
DFB-2D	2422		EMC	(E-1041)	7169	7/49	So 12/65 EMD
"	2423	3423	"	"	7170	"	PC
"	2424		"	"	7171	"	So 12/65 EMD
"	2425	3425	"	"	7172	"	PC
"	2426		"	"	7173	"	So 12/64 EMD
"	2427		"	"	7174	"	So 9/65 EMD
"	2428		"	"	7175	"	So 12/65 EMD
"	2429	3429	"	"	7176	"	PC
DFA-2E	1663		EMC	(E-1137)	8137	11/49	PC
"	1664		"	"	8138	"	PC
"	1665		"	"	8139	"	PC
"	1666		"	"	8140	"	PC
"	1667		"	"	8141	"	PC
"	1668		"	"	8142	"	PC
"	1669		"	"	8143	"	PC
"	1670		"	"	8144	"	PC
"	1671		"	"	8145	"	PC
"	1672		"	"	8146	"	PC,CR
"	1673		"	"	8147	"	So 12/66 GE
"	1674		"	"	8148	"	PC
"	1675		"	"	8149	"	PC,CR
"	1676		"	"	8150	"	So 12/65 EMD

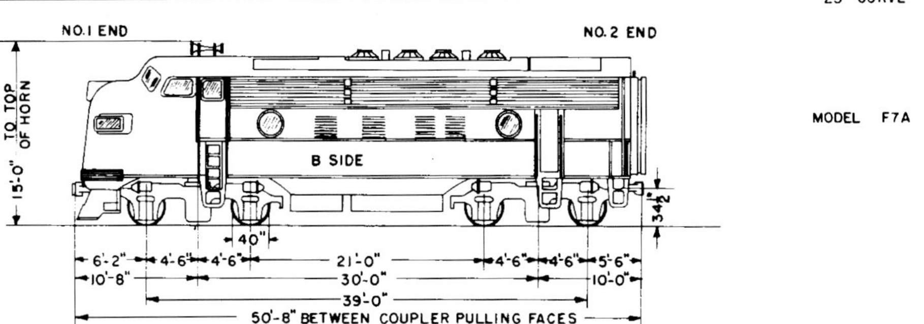

DIESEL ENGINE — GM — MODEL 567B
DIESEL ENGINE H.P. — 1500 FOR TRACTION
NUMBER OF CYLINDERS — 16-V TYPE
BORE AND STROKE — 8½"x10"
ENGINE SPEED R.P.M. — IDLING 275, FULL LOAD 800
MAIN GENERATOR — EMD TYPE D-12 OR D-12B DIRECT DRIVEN
MAIN GENERATOR VOLTAGE — MAX. 1000V, FULL LOAD 950V
MAIN GENERATOR CAPACITY — 1064KW
NUMBER AND TYPE OF TRACTION MOTORS — FOUR EMD D-27
TRACTION MOTOR VENTILATION — FORCED
GEAR RATIO — 62/15 (4.133)
CONTROL-TYPE AND VOLTAGE — EMD (M.U.) 75V.

MAXIMUM SPEED OF LOCOMOTIVE — 65 M.P.H.
CONTINUOUS RATING - TRACTIVE EFFORT — 40,000 LBS
SPEED — 11.5 M.P.H.
AIR SIGNAL — YES
TRAIN CONTROL — G.R.S., SCHEDULE 2, SINGLE END

PRINTED 4-15-57

CLASS DFA-2C, DFA-2D, DFA-2E, DFA-2F, DFA-2G, DFA-2H

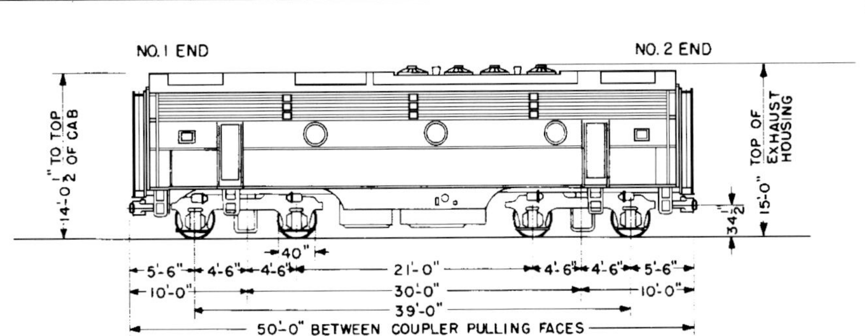

DIESEL ENGINE — GM MODEL 567B
DIESEL ENGINE H.P. — 1620 (1500 FOR TRACTION)
NUMBER OF CYLINDERS — 16-V TYPE
BORE AND STROKE — 8½"x10"
ENGINE SPEED R.P.M. — IDLING 275, FULL LOAD 800
MAIN GENERATOR — EMD TYPE D-12 OR D-12B DIRECT DRIVEN
MAIN GENERATOR VOLTAGE — MAX. 1000V., FULL LOAD 950V.
MAIN GENERATOR CAPACITY — 1064KW.
NUMBER AND TYPE OF TRACTION MOTORS — FOUR EMD D-27
TRACTION MOTOR VENTILATION — FORCED
GEAR RATIO — 62/15 (4.133)
CONTROL-TYPE AND VOLTAGE — EMD (M.U.) 75V.

MAXIMUM SPEED OF LOCOMOTIVE — 65 M.P.H.
CONTINUOUS RATING - TRACTIVE EFFORT — 40,000 LBS.
SPEED — 11.5 M.P.H.
HORSEPOWER — 1227
AIR SIGNAL — YES
TRAIN CONTROL — NONE

PRINTED 5-1-53

CLASS DFB-2C, DFB-2D, DFB-2E, DFB-2F, DFB-2G

Class	Original Number	Re '66	Builder	Order Number	c/n	Date	Disposition
DFB-2E	2430	3430	EMC	(E-1137)	8151	11/49	PC
"	2431	3431	“	“	9664	“	PC, Rt 7/68
	2432	3432	“	“	9665	“	PC
"	2433		"	"	9666	"	So 12/65 EMD
"	2434		"	"	9667	"	Rt 10/64 So 2/65 EMD
"	2435		"	"	9668	"	Rt 10/64 So 12/64 EMD
DFA-2F	1677		EMD	(3012)	9101	4/51	PC,CR re 1794
"	1678		“	“	9102	“	PC,CR re 1795
"	1679		“	“	9103	“	PC
"	1680		“	“	9104	“	Rt 5/67 EMD
"	1681		“	“	9105	“	PC,CR
"	1682		“	“	9106	“	PC
"	1683		“	“	9107	“	PC,CR re 1798
"	1684		“	“	9108	“	PC,CR
"	1685		“	“	9109	“	PC
"	1686		“	“	9110	“	PC,CR
"	1687		“	“	9111	“	PC,CR
"	1688		“	“	9112	“	PC
"	1689		“	“	9113	“	PC,CR
"	1690		“	“	9114	“	PC
"	1691		“	“	9115	“	PC
"	1692		“	“	9116	“	PC,CR re 1799
"	1693		“	“	9117	“	PC,CR
"	1694		“	“	9118	“	PC,CR
"	1695		“	“	9119	“	PC
"	1696		“	“	9120	“	PC,CR
"	1697		“	“	9995	“	PC,CR
"	1698		“	“	9996	“	So 6/65 EMD as 1660
"	1699		“	“	9997	“	PC
"	1700		“	“	9998	“	PC Rt 7/68
"	1701		“	“	9999	“	PC,CR
"	1702		“	“	10000	“	PC
"	1703		“	“	10001	“	PC,CR
"	1704		“	“	10002	“	PC
"	1705		“	“	10003	“	PC
"	1706		“	“	10004	“	PC
"	1707		“	“	10005	“	PC,CR
"	1708		“	“	10006	“	PC Rt 7/68
"	1709		“	“	10007	“	PC,CR
"	1710		“	“	10008	“	PC,CR

NYCSHS Collection

No. 1650 and 1649 Class DFA-2D and 2423 Class DFB-2D. These 1500 HP units were built by EMD in July 1949 for service on the Ohio Central between Thurston and Toledo.

Collection H.L.. Vail

No. 1684 and 1683 Class DFA-2F. Built by EMD in April 1951. These 1500 HP units would continue to serve with Penn Central and then Conrail. This was the last sub-class built with coupler doors.

NYCSHS Collection

No. 2438 Class DFB-2F. Built by EMD in November 1951. Note the later style stainless steel radiator grills.

Class	Original Number	Builder	Order Number	c/n	Date	Disposition
DFA-2G	1711	EMD	(3082)	15322	3/52	PC,CR
"	1712	"	"	15323	"	PC,CR
"	1713	"	"	15324	"	PC Rt 7/68
"	1714	"	"	15325	"	PC,CR
"	1715	"	"	15326	"	PC
"	1716	"	"	15327	"	PC,CR
"	1717	"	"	15328	"	PC
"	1718	"	"	15329	"	PC,CR
"	1719	"	"	15330	"	PC
"	1720	"	"	15331	"	PC Rt 7/68
"	1721	"	"	15332	"	PC
"	1722	"	"	15333	"	PC,CR
"	1723	"	"	15334	"	PC
"	1724	"	"	15335	"	PC
"	1725	"	"	15336	"	PC,CR
"	1726	"	"	15337	"	PC,CR
"	1727	"	"	15338	"	PC
"	1728	"	"	15339	"	PC
"	1729	"	"	15340	"	PC,CR
"	1730	"	"	15341	"	PC,CR
"	1731	"	"	15342	"	PC,CR
"	1732	"	"	15343	"	PC,CR

Loius A. Marre

Two generations of freight diesels, DFA-2G No. 1722 with 2523, a GE U-25B at Elkhart on October 1, 1964.

Class	Number	Builder	Order Number	c/n	Date	Disposition
DFA-2G	1733	EMD	(3082)	15344	3/52	PC,CR
"	1734	"	"	15345	"	PC,CR
"	1735	"	"	15346	"	PC
"	1736	"	"	15347	"	PC Rt 7/68
"	1737	"	"	15348	"	PC
"	1738	"	"	15349	"	PC Rt 7/68
"	1739	"	"	15350	"	PC
"	1740	"	"	15351	"	PC
"	1741	"	"	15352	"	PC
"	1742	"	"	15353	"	PC,CR
"	1743	"	"	15354	"	PC,CR
"	1744	"	"	15355	"	PC,CR
"	1745	"	"	15356	"	PC,CR
"	1746	"	"	15357	"	PC
"	1747	"	"	15358	"	PC,CR
"	1748	"	"	15359	"	PC,CR
"	1749	"	"	15360	"	PC,CR
"	1750	"	"	15361	"	PC,CR
"	1751	"	"	15362	"	PC
"	1752	"	"	15363	5/52	PC,CR
"	1753	"	"	15364	"	PC
"	1754	"	"	15365	"	PC
"	1755	"	"	15366	"	PC,CR
"	1756	"	"	15367	"	PC,CR
"	1757	"	"	15368	"	PC
"	1758	"	"	15369	"	PC,CR
"	1759	"	"	15370	"	PC
"	1760	"	"	15371	"	PC,CR
"	1761	"	"	15372	"	PC,CR
"	1762	"	"	15373	"	PC,CR
"	1763	"	"	15374	"	PC,CR
"	1764	"	"	15375	"	PC
"	1765	"	"	15376	"	PC
"	1766	"	"	15377	"	PC,CR
"	1767	"	"	15378	"	PC
"	1768	"	"	15379	"	PC
"	1769	"	"	15380	"	PC
"	1770	"	"	15381	"	PC
"	1771	"	"	15382	"	PC
"	1772	"	"	15383	"	PC,CR
"	1773	"	"	15384	"	PC,CR
"	1774	"	"	15385	"	PC,CR
"	1775	"	"	15386	"	PC,CR
"	1776	"	"	15387	6/52	PC
"	1777	"	"	15388	"	PC
"	1778	"	"	15389	"	PC
"	1779	"	"	15390	"	PC,CR
"	1780	"	"	15391	"	PC
"	1781	"	"	15392	"	PC
"	1782	"	(3098)	15393	11/51	PC,CR
"	1783	"	"	15394	"	PC,CR
"	1784	"	"	15395	"	PC,CR
"	1785	"	"	15396	"	PC,CR
"	1786	"	"	15397	12/51	PC
"	1787	"	"	15398	"	PC,CR
"	1788	"	"	15399	"	PC,CR

Class	Number	Builder	Order Number	c/n	Date	Disposition
DFA-2G	1789	EMD	(3098)	15400	12/51	PC
"	1790	"	"	15401	"	PC,CR
"	1791	"	"	15402	"	PC,CR
"	1792	"	"	15403	"	PC
"	1793	"	"	15404	"	PC
"	1794	"	"	15405	1/52	PC
"	1795	"	"	15406	"	PC
"	1796	"	"	15407	"	PC,CR
"	1797	"	"	15408	"	PC,CR
"	1798	"	"	15409	"	PC
"	1799	"	"	15410	"	PC
"	1800	"	"	15411	"	Rt 9/67 EMD
"	1801	"	"	15412	"	So 10/64 as 1875
"	1802	"	"	15413	"	PC
"	1803	"	"	15414	"	PC
"	1804	"	"	15415	"	PC
"	1805	"	"	15416	"	PC
"	1806	"	"	15417	"	PC
"	1807	"	"	15418	"	PC,CR
"	1808	"	"	15419	"	PC
"	1809	"	"	15420	"	PC Rt 7/68
"	1810	"	"	15421	"	PC
"	1811	"	"	15422	"	PC
"	1812	"	"	15423	"	PC
"	1813	"	"	15424	2/52	PC
"	1814	"	"	15425	"	PC
"	1815	"	"	15426	"	PC
"	1816	"	"	15427	"	PC
"	1817	"	"	15428	"	PC
"	1818	"	"	15429	"	PC Rt 7/68
"	1819	"	"	15430	"	PC
"	1820	"	"	15431	"	PC,CR
"	1821	"	"	15432	"	PC,CR
"	1822	"	"	15433	"	PC
"	1823	"	"	15434	"	PC
"	1824	"	"	15435	"	PC
"	1825	"	"	15436	2/52	PC,CR
"	1826	"	"	15437	"	PC,CR
"	1827	"	"	15438	"	PC
"	1828	"	"	15439	"	PC
"	1829	"	"	15440	"	PC,CR
"	1830	"	"	15441	"	PC
"	1831	"	"	15442	"	PC
"	1832	"	"	15443	"	PC,CR
"	1833	"	"	15114	"	PC,CR
"	1834	"	"	15445	"	PC
"	1835	"	"	15446	"	PC
"	1836	"	"	15447	3/52	So 12/66 GE
"	1837	"	"	15448	"	PC
"	1838	"	"	15449	"	PC
"	1839	"	"	15450	"	PC,CR
"	1840	"	"	15451	"	PC,CR
"	1841	"	"	15452	"	PC,CR

Class	Number	re '66	Builder	Order Number	c/n	Date	Disposition
DFB-2F	2436	3436	EMD	(3098)	15453	11/51	PC Rt 7/68
"	2437	3437	"	"	15454	"	PC,CR re 3874
"	2438	3438	"	"	15455	12/51	PC
"	2439	3439	"	"	15456	"	PC
"	2440	3440	"	"	15457	"	PC
"	2441	3441	"	"	15458	1/52	PC re Work 73600
"	2442	3442	"	"	15459	"	PC
DFA-2H	1842		EMD	(3124)	16220	9/52	PC
"	1843		"	"	16221	"	PC
"	1844		"	"	16222	"	PC,CR
"	1845		"	"	16223	"	PC
"	1846		"	"	16224	"	PC Rt 7/68
"	1847		"	"	16225	"	PC,CR
"	1848		"	"	16226	"	PC,CR
"	1849		"	"	16227	"	PC
"	1850		"	"	16228	"	PC,CR
"	1851		"	"	16229	"	PC,CR
"	1852		"	"	16230	"	PC
"	1853		"	"	16231	"	PC,CR
"	1854		"	"	16232	"	PC,CR
"	1855		"	"	16233	"	PC,CR
"	1856		"	"	16234	"	PC
"	1857		"	"	16235	10/52	PC
"	1858		"	"	16236	"	PC,CR
"	1859		"	"	16237	"	PC
"	1860		"	"	16238	"	PC,CR
"	1861		"	"	16239	"	PC
"	1862		"	"	16240	"	PC,CR
"	1863		"	"	16241	"	PC,CR
"	1864		"	"	16242	"	PC
"	1865		"	"	16243	"	PC,CR
"	1866		"	"	16244	"	PC,CR
"	1867		"	"	16245	"	PC Rt 4/68
"	1868		"	"	16246	"	PC
"	1869		"	"	16247	"	PC
"	1870		"	"	16248	"	PC
"	1871		"	"	16249	"	PC
"	1872		"	"	16250	"	PC
"	1873		"	"	16251	"	PC
DFB-2G	2443	3443	EMD	(3124)	16252	9/52	PC
"	2444	3444	"	"	16253	"	PC
"	2445	3445	"	"	16254	"	PC
"	2446	3446	"	"	16255	"	PC Rt 7/68
"	2447		"	"	16256	"	So 12/63 EMD
"	2448		"	"	16257	"	So 12/63 EMD
"	2449	3449	"	"	16258	"	PC
"	2450	3450	"	"	16259	"	PC
"	2451	3451	"	"	16260	"	PC
"	2452	3452	"	"	16261	"	PC
"	2453	3453	"	"	16262	"	PC,CR re 3866
"	2454	3454	"	"	16263	"	PC
"	2455	3455	"	"	16264	"	PC
"	2456	3456	"	"	16265	"	PC
"	2457	3457	"	"	16266	"	PC Rt 7/68

Class	Number	re '66	Builder	Order Number	c/n	Date	Disposition
DFA-2G	2458	3458	EMD	(3124)	16267	10/52	PC
"	2459	3459	"	"	16268	"	PC
"	2460	3460	"	"	16269	"	PC,CR re 3867
"	2461	3461	"	"	16270	"	PC
"	2462	3462	"	"	16271	"	PC
"	2463	3463	"	"	16272	"	PC
"	2464	3464	"	"	16273	"	PC, CR re 3868
"	2465	3465	"	"	16274	"	PC Rt 7/68
"	2466	3466	"	"	16275	"	PC,CR re 3869
"	2467	3467	"	"	16276	"	PC
"	2468	3468	"	"	16277	"	PC
"	2469	3469	"	"	16278	"	PC re 3870
"	2470	3470	"	"	16279	"	So 9/67 EMD
"	2471	3471	"	"	16280	"	PC re 3871
"	2472	3472	"	"	16281	"	PC Rt 7/68
"	2473	3473	"	"	16282	"	PC
"	2474	3474	"	"	16283	"	PC

No. 2464 Class DFB-2G. Built by EMD in October 1952.

Both: NYCSHS Collection

No. 1718 and 1717 Class DFA-2G. Built by EMD in March 1952.

CLASS DFA-2J and DFB-2H EMD F3 Converted from DCA-la, DCB-la

Class	Number	re '66		Date	Disposition
DFA-2J	1874		Conv. from 3500	1/59	So 5/61 EMD
"	1875	1801	" " 3501	12/58	PC Rt 4/68
"	1877		" " 3503	2/61	So 9/67 EMD
DFB-2H	2475		" " 3600	12/58	So 5/61 EMD
"	2476		" " 3601	8/59	So 12/65 EMD

Notes: Conversion included removal of steam generators and water tanks, addition of ballast and changing gearing. Dynamic braking not added. A units retained cast ovals on nose doors.

Collection of Louis A. Marre

No. 1875 Class DFA-2J. Originally Class DCA-1A No. 3501, converted to freight service in December 1958 was later renumbered to 1801 in 1966. This rare shot was made at LaPorte, Indiana on June 4, 1960.

CLASS DFA-3 and DFB-3 ALCO-GE 1500HP Model FA-1 and FB-1

LOCOMOTIVE DESIGNED FOR
21° CURVE

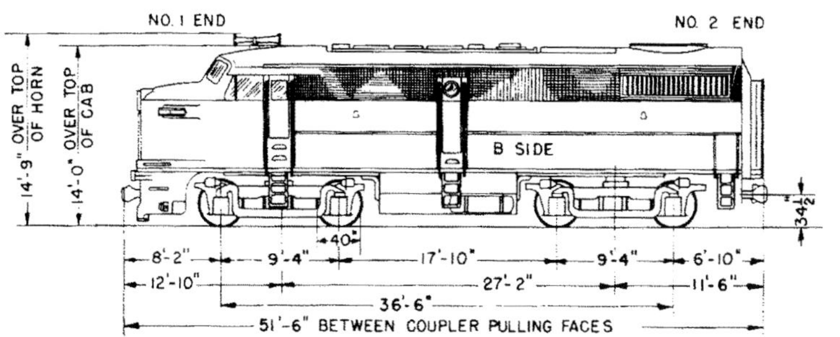

MODEL FA-1

DIESEL ENGINE .... ALCO ... MODEL 244
DIESEL ENGINE H.P. .... 1500 FOR TRACTION
NUMBER OF CYLINDERS .... 12-V TYPE
BORE AND STROKE .... 9"x10½"
ENGINE SPEED R.P.M. .... IDLING 350, FULL LOAD 1000
MAIN GENERATOR .... G.E. CO. TYPE GT-564-C1 DIRECT DRIVEN
MAIN GENERATOR VOLTAGE .... MAX. 900V., FULL LOAD 850V.
MAIN GENERATOR CAPACITY .... 1050 K.W.
NUMBER AND TYPE OF TRACTION MOTORS .... FOUR GE-752-A1 OR B1
TRACTION MOTOR VENTILATION .... FORCED
GEAR RATIO 74/18 (4.111)
CONTROL-TYPE AND VOLTAGE .... G.E. CO., P, (M.U.) 75 V.

MAXIMUM SPEED OF LOCOMOTIVE .... 65 M.P.H.
CONTINUOUS RATING - TRACTIVE EFFORT .... 42,500 LBS.
SPEED .... 11.0 M.P.H.

AIR SIGNAL .... YES
TRAIN CONTROL .... G.R.S., SCHEDULE 2, SINGLE END

LOCOMOTIVE DESIGNED FOR
21° CURVE

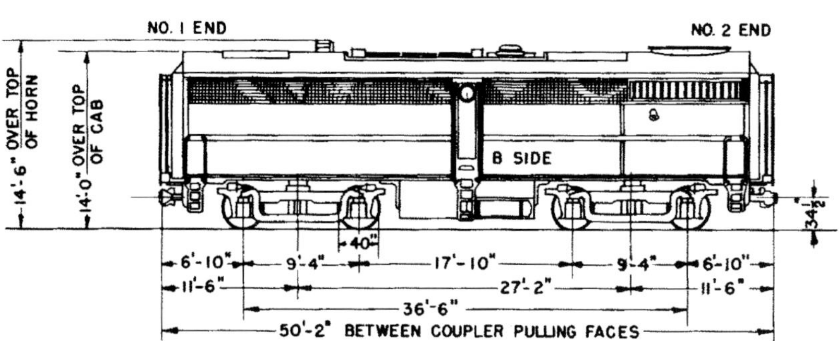

DIESEL ENGINE .... ALCO ... MODEL 244
DIESEL ENGINE H.P. .... 1630 (1500 FOR TRACTION)
NUMBER OF CYLINDERS .... 12-V TYPE
BORE AND STROKE .... 9"x10½"
ENGINE SPEED R.P.M. .... IDLING 350, FULL LOAD 1000
MAIN GENERATOR .... G.E. CO. TYPE GT-564-C1 DIRECT DRIVEN
MAIN GENERATOR VOLTAGE .... MAX. 900V., FULL LOAD 850V.
MAIN GENERATOR CAPACITY .... 1050 K.W.
NUMBER AND TYPE OF TRACTION MOTORS .... FOUR GE-752-A1 OR B1
TRACTION MOTOR VENTILATION .... FORCED
GEAR RATIO 74/18 (4.111)
CONTROL-TYPE AND VOLTAGE .... G.E. CO., P, (M.U.) 75 V.

MAXIMUM SPEED OF LOCOMOTIVE .... 65 M.P.H.
CONTINUOUS RATING - TRACTIVE EFFORT .... 42,500 LBS.
SPEED .... 11.0 M.P.H.
HORSEPOWER 1247
AIR SIGNAL .... YES
TRAIN CONTROL .... NONE

7-1-51

Class	Original Number	Re '65	Builder	Order Number	c/n	Date	Disposition
DFA-3a	1000	1119	Alco-GE	(S-1973)	73675	2/47	PC (1319)
"	1001		"	"	73676	"	So 6/64 GE
"	1002		"	"	73677	"	So 6/64 GE
"	1003		"	"	73678	3/47	So 1/64 GE

Class	Original Number	Re 4/51	Builder	Order Number	c/n	Date	Disposition
DFB-3a	2300	3300	Alco-GE	(S-1974)	73685	2/47	So 6/64 GE
"	2301	3301	"	"	73686	3/47	So 10/65 GE

No. 1000 Class DFA-3A. NYC's first Alco FA-1 unit. This 1500 HP locomotive was built in February 1947.

Both: NYCSHS Collection

No. 2300 Class DFB-3A. NYC's first Alco FB-1 unit was originally numbered 2300 when built in February 1947, but was renumbered 3300 in April 1951.

Class	Original Number	Re 4/51	Builder	Order Number	c/n	Date	Disposition
DFA-3b	1004		Alco-GE	(S-3054)	75709	2/48	So 9/65 GE
"	1005		“	“	75710	“	So 10/65 GE
"	1006		“	“	75711	3/48	Sc 4/61
"	1007		“	“	75712	“	So 4/65 GE
"	1008		“	“	75713	“	So 4/65 GE
"	1009		“	“	75714	“	PC Re 1300 Rt 7/68
"	1010		“	“	75715	“	So 2/64 GE
"	1011		“	“	75716	“	Sc 6/61
"	1012		“	“	75717	“	Sc 6/61
"	1013		“	“	75718	“	Sc 5/61
DFB-3b	2302	3302	Alco-GE	(S-3055)	75757	2/48	So 6/65 GE
"	2303	3303	“	“	75758	3/48	Sc 5/61
"	2304	3304	“	“	75759	“	So 6/64 GE
"	2305	3305	“	“	75760	“	Sc 5/61
"	2306	3306	“	“	75761	“	Sc 4/61
DFA-3c	1014		Alco-GE	(S-3076)	76275	11/48	So 6/64 GE
"	1015		“	“	76276	“	Sc 5/61
"	1016		“	“	76520	“	So 4/64 GE
"	1017		“	“	76521	“	So 4/65 GE
"	1018		“	“	76522	12/48	So 6/65 GE
"	1019		“	“	76523	“	Sc 5/61
"	1020		“	“	76524	“	So 3/64 GE
"	1021		“	“	76525	“	So 2/64 GE
"	1022		“	“	76526	“	Sc 5/61
"	1023		“	“	76527	“	So 5/64 GE
"	1024		“	“	76528	“	So 5/65 GE
"	1025		“	“	76529	“	So 3/64 GE
"	1026		“	“	76530	“	So 6/65 GE
"	1027		“	“	76531	“	So 5/64 GE
"	1028		“	“	76532	“	Sc 5/61
"	1029		“	“	76533	“	Sc 5/61
"	1030		“	“	76534	“	So 6/64 GE
"	1031	1056*	“	(S-3084)	76547	“	Rt 7/67 GE
"	1032		“	“	76548	“	Sc 6/61
DFB-3c	2307	3307	Alco-GE	(S-3078)	76297	11/48	So 5/64 GE
"	2308	3308	“	“	76298	“	So 5/64 GE
"	2309	3309	“	“	76299	“	So 5/64 GE
"	2310	3310	“	“	76300	“	So 5/64 GE
"	2311	3311	“	“	76301	“	So 6/65 GE
DFA-3d	1033	1110*	Alco-GE	(S-3099)	76844	5/49	PC re 1310 So GE
"	1034		“	“	76845	“	So 6/64 GE
"	1035		“	“	76846	“	So 6/64 GE
"	1036		“	“	76847	“	So 6/65 GE
"	1037		“	“	76848	“	So 5/65 GE
"	1038		“	“	76849	“	So 1/65 GE
"	1039		“	“	76850	“	So 6/64 GE
"	1040		“	‘	76851	“	So 5/65 GE

Note: * renumbered 1964 to second 1056 and 1110.

Class	Original Number	Re 4/51	Builder	Order Number	c/n	Date	Disposition
DFB-3d	2312	3312	Alco-GE	(S-3101)	76874	5/49	So 6/64 GE
"	2313	3313	"	"	76875	"	So 6/64 GE
"	2314	3314	"	"	76876	"	So 6/64 GE
"	2315	3315	"	"	76877	"	So 6/64 GE
DFA-3e	1041		Alco-GE	(S-3107)	77007	8/49	So 6/65 GE
"	1042		"	"	77008	"	So 1/65 GE
"	1043		"	"	77009	9/49	So 1/65 GE
DFB-3e	2316	3316	Alco-GE	(S-3101)	76882	8/49	So 5/64 GE
"	2317	3317	"	"	76883	"	So 6/64 GE
"	2318	3318	"	"	76884	"	So 1/65 GE
"	2319	3319	"	"	76885	"	So 1/65 GE
"	2320	3320	"	"	76886	"	Rt 5/67 GE
"	2321	3321	"	"	76887	9/49	So 3/65 GE
"	2322	3322	"	"	76888	"	So 10/64 GE

No. 1010 Class DFA-3B. Built by Alco in March 1948 was first assigned to the B&A.

Louis A. Marre

No. 2307 Class DFB-3C. Built by Alco in November 1948, renumbered 3307 in April 1951.

NYCSHS Collection

CLASS DFA-4 and DFB-4 BALDWIN WEST. 1500HP Model DR-4-4-15

LOCOMOTIVE DESIGNED FOR 21° CURVE

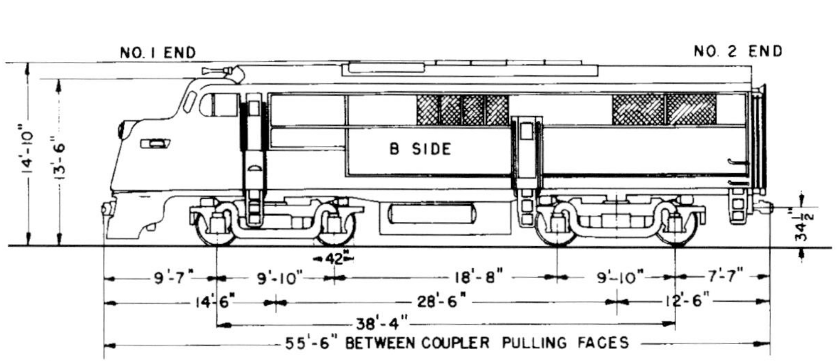

DIESEL ENGINE	BLW MODEL 608 SC
DIESEL ENGINE H.P.	1701 (1500 FOR TRACTION)
NUMBER OF CYLINDERS	8 IN LINE
BORE AND STROKE	12¾ x 15½
ENGINE SPEED R.P.M.	IDLING 315, FULL LOAD 625
MAIN GENERATOR	W.E. CORP. TYPE 471-A DIRECT DRIVEN
MAIN GENERATOR VOLTAGE	MAX. 910 V., FULL LOAD 880 V.
MAIN GENERATOR CAPACITY	1100 KW.
NUMBER AND TYPE OF TRACTION MOTORS	FOUR W.E. CORP. 370-G
TRACTION MOTOR VENTILATION	FORCED
GEAR RATIO	63/15 (4.20)
CONTROL-TYPE AND VOLTAGE	W.E. CORP., EP, (M. U.) 75 V.
MAXIMUM SPEED OF LOCOMOTIVE	65 M.P.H.
CONTINUOUS RATING - TRACTIVE EFFORT	42,500 LBS.
SPEED	10.5 M.P.H.
HORSEPOWER	1198
AIR SIGNAL	YES
TRAIN CONTROL	G.R.S., SCHEDULE 2, SINGLE END, WITH SAFETY CONTROL.

5-1-53

LOCOMOTIVE DESIGNED FOR 21° CURVE

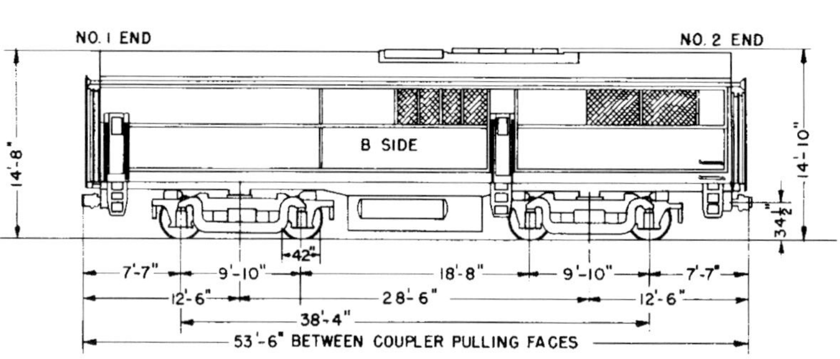

DIESEL ENGINE	BLW MODEL 608 SC
DIESEL ENGINE H.P.	1701 (1500 FOR TRACTION)
NUMBER OF CYLINDERS	8 IN LINE
BORE AND STROKE	12¾ x 15½
ENGINE SPEED R.P.M.	IDLING 315, FULL LOAD 625
MAIN GENERATOR	W.E. CORP. TYPE 471-A DIRECT DRIVEN
MAIN GENERATOR VOLTAGE	MAX. 910 V., FULL LOAD 880 V.
MAIN GENERATOR CAPACITY	1100 KW.
NUMBER AND TYPE OF TRACTION MOTORS	FOUR W.E. CORP. 370-G
TRACTION MOTOR VENTILATION	FORCED
GEAR RATIO	63/15 (4.20)
CONTROL-TYPE AND VOLTAGE	W.E. CORP., EP, (M. U.) 75 V.
MAXIMUM SPEED OF LOCOMOTIVE	65 M.P.H.
CONTINUOUS RATING - TRACTIVE EFFORT	42,500 LBS.
SPEED	10.5 M.P.H.
HORSEPOWER	1198
AIR SIGNAL	YES
TRAIN CONTROL	NONE

5-1-53

Class	Number	Renumbered 1951	Builder	Order Number	c/n	Date	Disposition
DFA-4a	3400	3800	BLW	(47510)	73676	10/48	Rt 12/60, Sc 7/62
"	3401	3801	"	"	73677	"	Rt 12/60, Sc 5/61
"	3402	3802	"	"	73678	"	Rt 12/60, Sc 7/62
"	3403	3803	"	"	73679	"	Rt 2/63, Sc 7/64 (Note)
DFB-4a	3700		"	"	73680	"	Rt 12/60, Sc 7/62
"	3701		"	"	73681	"	Rt 12/60, Sc 3/62

Note: 3800,3802,Scrapped 7/62, 3801 Scrapped 5/61; 3803 re-engined10/57at Collinwood Shop with EMD 567C V-16 Set at 1500HP (reduced speed) using original WE412 Generator and electrical equipment; Pneumatic throttle and MU replaced with EMD electric throttle and MU. Tractive Effort (Max) 62135, Weight 248540.

H. L. Vail Jr. Collection

No. 3400 Class DFA-4A. Built by Baldwin Locomotive Works in October 1948 and was renumbered 3800 in June 1951. This DR-4-4-15 unit was finally cut up for scrap in July 1962.

H. L. Vail Jr. Collection

Another view of No. 3400 Class DFA-4A. with B unit 3700 and matching A unit 3401. This view shows the stripe pattern used on a A-B-A freight set instead of the "full stripe" version.

No. 3803 Class DFA-4A. Shown here at South Gary, Indiana on April 10, 1958 shortly after re-powering with an EMD 567C at Collinwood Shop.

Louis A. Marre

Class DFA-5 and DFB-5 FM-GE "ERIE BUILT" 2000HP Freight

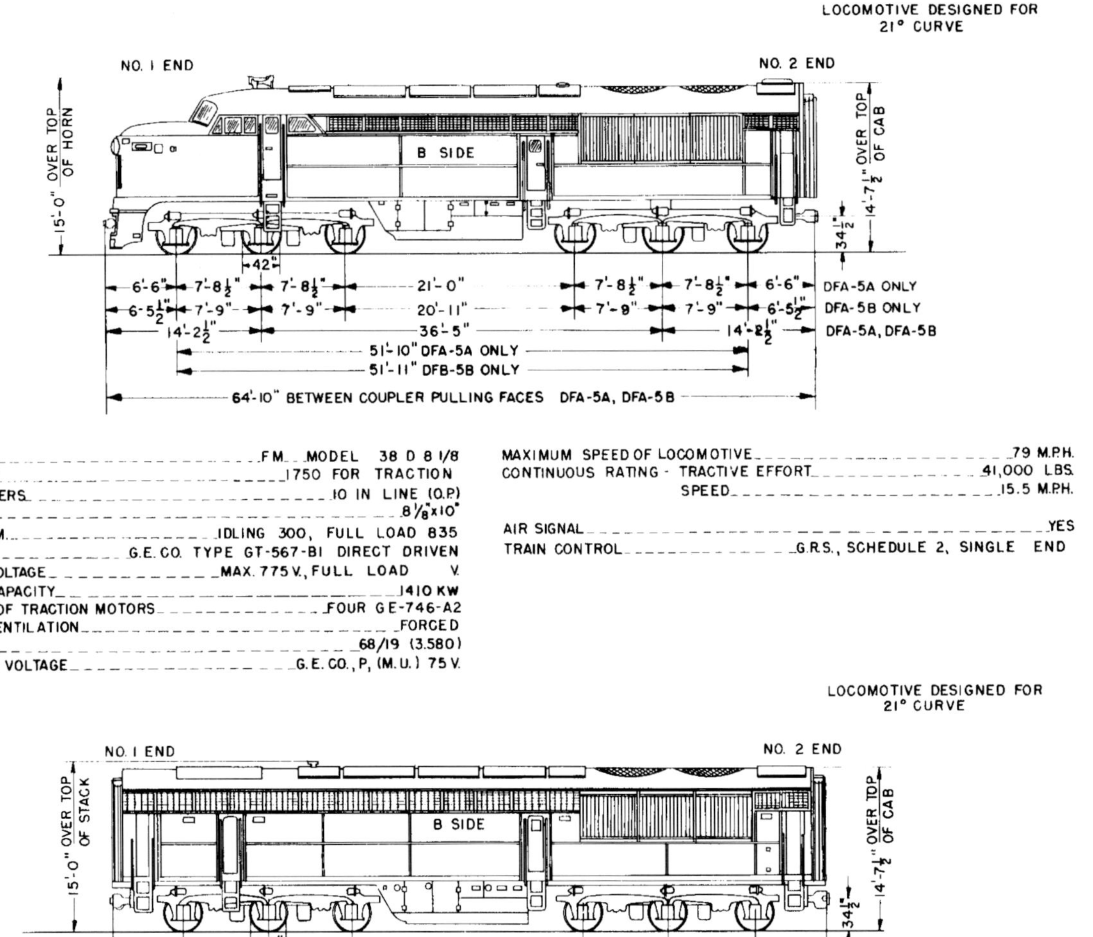

DIESEL ENGINE ... F.M. MODEL 38 D 8 1/8
DIESEL ENGINE H.P. ... 1750 FOR TRACTION)
NUMBER OF CYLINDERS ... 10 IN LINE (O.P.)
BORE AND STROKE ... 8⅛"x10"
ENGINE SPEED R.P.M. ... IDLING 300, FULL LOAD 835
MAIN GENERATOR ... G.E. CO. TYPE GT-567-B1 DIRECT DRIVEN
MAIN GENERATOR VOLTAGE ... MAX. 775 V., FULL LOAD V.
MAIN GENERATOR CAPACITY ... 1410KW
NUMBER AND TYPE OF TRACTION MOTORS ... FOUR GE-746-A2
TRACTION MOTOR VENTILATION ... FORCED
GEAR RATIO ... 68/19 (3.580)
CONTROL-TYPE AND VOLTAGE ... G.E. CO., P, (M.U.) 75 V.

MAXIMUM SPEED OF LOCOMOTIVE ... 79 M.P.H.
CONTINUOUS RATING - TRACTIVE EFFORT ... 41,000 LBS.
SPEED ... 15.5 M.P.H.
HORSEPOWER ... 1695
AIR SIGNAL ... YES
TRAIN CONTROL ... NONE

Class	Number	Builder	Order Number	c/n	Builder	c/n	Date	Re-Engine	Disposition
DFA-5a	5000	FM	(LD19)	L1105	GE	28631	10/47		Rt 12/60 Sc 1/62
"	5001	"	"	L1107	"	28632	"	9/57	Rt 4/63 Sc 10/63
DFA-5b	5002	"	(LD46)	L1170	"	29430	12/48	11/57	Rt 4/63 Sc 9/63
"	5003	"	"	L1174	"	30123	1/49	7/57	Rt 4/63 So 9/63
"	5004	"	"	L1175	"	30124	2/49		Rt 12/60 Sc 1/62
"	5005	"	"	L1176	"	30125	"		Rt 12/60 Sc 1/62
DFB-5a	5100	"	"	L1159	"	29443	12/48		Rt 12/60 Sc 2/62
"	5101	"	"	L1160	"	29444	1/49	5/57	Rt 4/63 SS 8/63

Notes: New 16-567C EMD engines installed at Collinwood on dates listed. Derated to 1750HP, using original GE electrical equipment. Dynamic brake removed. Units 5002-5005 and 5100-5101 equipped with cast steel drop equalizer trucks. Units 5000 and 5001 built with fabricated straight-equalizer trucks as shown on diagram.

H. L. Vail Jr. Collection

No. 5002 Class DFA-5B. FM "Erie Built" as pictured at Erie in December 1948. It was re-powered with an EMD 567CV-16 engine rated at 1750 HP in November 1957 at Collinwood. Note the cast steel drop equalizer trucks.

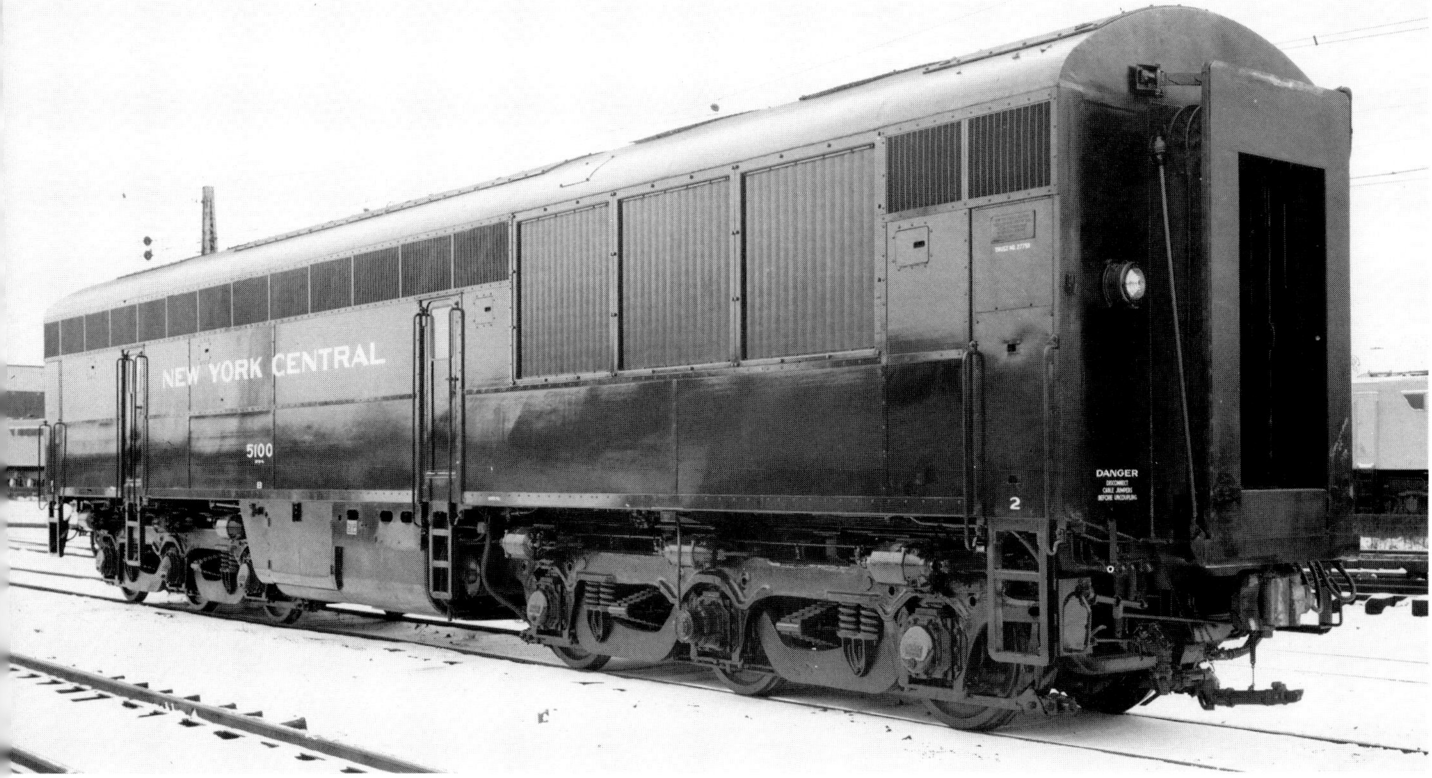

H. L. Vail Jr. Collection

No. 5100 Class DFB-5A. Also an FM "Erie Built" rated at 2000 HP. It kept it's original FM opposed piston engine until retirement in December 1960. It was scrapped in February 1962.

Class DFA-6 and DFB-6 FM 2000HP Model CFA & CFB-20-4

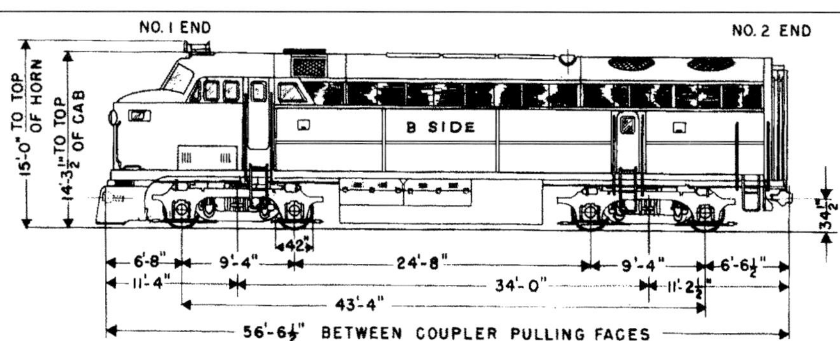

DIESEL ENGINE .... F.M. MODEL 38 D 8 1/8
DIESEL ENGINE H.P. .... 2214 (2000 FOR TRACTION)
NUMBER OF CYLINDERS .... 10 IN LINE (O.P.)
BORE AND STROKE .... 8⅛"x10"
ENGINE SPEED R.P.M. .... IDLING 300, FULL LOAD 850
MAIN GENERATOR .... W. E. CORP. 498-A DIRECT DRIVEN
MAIN GENERATOR VOLTAGE .... MAX. 1160V, FULL LOAD 1100V
MAIN GENERATOR CAPACITY 1370KW
NUMBER AND TYPE OF TRACTION MOTORS .... FOUR W. E. CORP. 370-DL OR G
TRACTION MOTOR VENTILATION .... FORCED
GEAR RATIO 63/15 (4.20)
CONTROL-TYPE AND VOLTAGE .... W. E. CORP. (M.U.) 75 V.

MAXIMUM SPEED OF LOCOMOTIVE .... 65 M.P.H.
CONTINUOUS RATING - TRACTIVE EFFORT .... 42,800 LBS.
SPEED .... 14.7 M.P.H.
HORSEPOWER 1678
AIR SIGNAL .... YES
TRAIN CONTROL .... G.R.S., SCHEDULE 2, SINGLE END, WITH SAFETY CONTROL

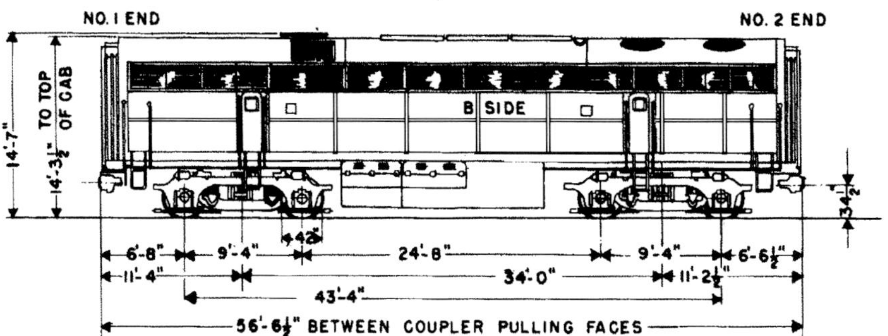

DIESEL ENGINE .... F.M. MODEL 38 D 8 1/8
DIESEL ENGINE H.P. .... 2214 (2000 FOR TRACTION)
NUMBER OF CYLINDERS .... 10 IN LINE (O.P.)
BORE AND STROKE .... 8⅛"x10"
ENGINE SPEED R.P.M. .... IDLING 300, FULL LOAD 850
MAIN GENERATOR .... W. E. CORP. 498-A DIRECT DRIVEN
MAIN GENERATOR VOLTAGE .... MAX. 1160V, FULL LOAD 1100V
MAIN GENERATOR CAPACITY 1370KW
NUMBER AND TYPE OF TRACTION MOTORS .... FOUR W. E. CORP. 370-DL OR G
TRACTION MOTOR VENTILATION .... FORCED
GEAR RATIO 63/15 (4.20)
CONTROL-TYPE AND VOLTAGE .... W. E. CORP. (M.U.) 75 V.

MAXIMUM SPEED OF LOCOMOTIVE .... 65 M.P.H.
CONTINUOUS RATING - TRACTIVE EFFORT .... 42,800 LBS.
SPEED .... 14.7 M.P.H.
HORSEPOWER 1678
AIR SIGNAL .... YES
TRAIN CONTROL .... NONE

Class	Number	Builder	Order Number	c/n	Date	Re-Engine	Disposition
DFA-6a	5006	FM	(LD62)	21L288	4/50	8/55	Rt 2/65 So
"	5007	"	"	21L289	"	10/56	So 8/64 GE
"	5008	"	"	21L290	"	8/56	Rt 7/64 Sc 9/64
"	5009	"	"	21L291	"	9/56	Rt 2/65 So
"	5010	"	"	21L292	"	3/55	So 8/64 GE
"	5011	"	"	21L293	"	11/56	Rt 2/65 So 9/65 GE
"	5012	"	"	21L294	"	6/56	So 9/65 GE
"	5013	"	"	21L295	"	7/55	So 9/65 GE

Class	Number	Builder	Order Number	c/n	Date	Re-Engine	Disposition
DFA-6B	5014	FM	(LD72)	21L296	6/50	9/55	Rt 2/65 PE
"	5015	"	"	21L297	"	5/56	Rt 2/65 PE
"	5016	"	"	21L298	"	11/56	Rt 2/65 PE
"	5017	"	"	21L299	7/50	2/56	Rt 2/65 SS
DFB-6A	5102	FM	"	21L270	6/50	1/57	Rt 1/65 So
"	5103	"	"	21L271	6/50	12/56	Rt 2/65 SS 3/66
"	5104	FM	"	21L272	7/50	1/57	Rt 11/64 So PE

Note: All units re-engined at Collinwood Shop with EMD engines: 5006, 5010, 5013, 5014 with 567A (V-16) 1500 HP and 5007-5009, 5011, 5012, 5015-5017, 5102-5104 with 567C (V-16) 1750 HP. All using original WE electrical equipment. Dynamic brake retained.

No. 5008 Class DFA-6A. FM CFA-20-4 2000 HP unit built in April 1950 was re-engined with an EMD engine in August of 1956.. It is shown here in April of 1960 at Elkhart, Indiana.

Both: Louis A. Marre

No. 5008 Class DFA-6A. This view shows the engineer's side of the same unit at South Bend, Indiana on April 18, 1960.

CLASS DFA-7 and DFB-7 (AF-16) ALCO-GE 1600HP FA-2 and FB-2.

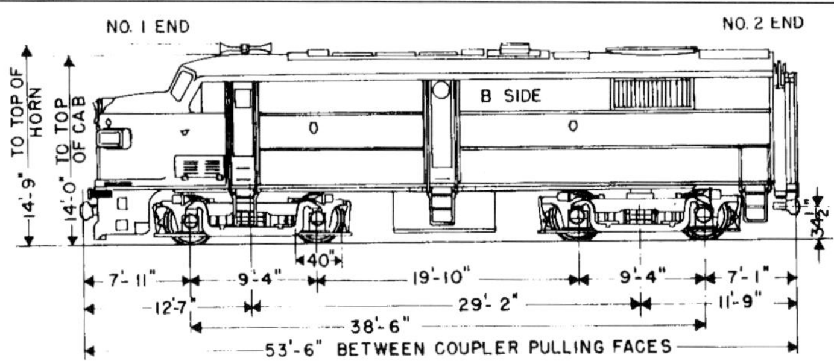

DIESEL ENGINE .... ALCO MODEL 244
DIESEL ENGINE H.P. .... 1600 FOR TRACTION
NUMBER OF CYLINDERS .... 12-V TYPE
BORE AND STROKE .... 9"x10½"
ENGINE SPEED R.P.M. .... IDLING 350, FULL LOAD 1000
MAIN GENERATOR .... G.E.CO. TYPE GT-581-A1 DIRECT DRIVEN
MAIN GENERATOR VOLTAGE .... MAX. 865 V., FULL LOAD 845 V.
MAIN GENERATOR CAPACITY .... 1100 K.W.
NUMBER AND TYPE OF TRACTION MOTORS .... FOUR GE-752-C1
TRACTION MOTOR VENTILATION .... FORCED
GEAR RATIO 74/18 (4.111)
CONTROL-TYPE AND VOLTAGE .... G.E. CO.,P, (M.U.) 75 V.

MAXIMUM SPEED OF LOCOMOTIVE .... 65 M.P.H.
CONTINUOUS RATING - TRACTIVE EFFORT .... 52,500 LBS.
SPEED .... 9.4 M.P.H.

AIR SIGNAL .... ☆ YES
TRAIN CONTROL .... G.R.S., SCHEDULE 2, SINGLE END

☆ APPLIES TO DFA-7A & DFA-7B ONLY

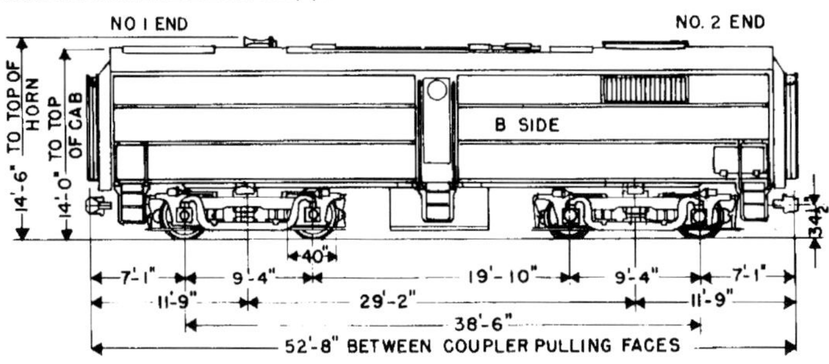

DIESEL ENGINE .... ALCO MODEL 244
DIESEL ENGINE H.P. .... 1760 (1600 FOR TRACTION)
NUMBER OF CYLINDERS .... 12-V TYPE
BORE AND STROKE .... 9"x10½"
ENGINE SPEED R.P.M. .... IDLING 350, FULL LOAD 1000
MAIN GENERATOR .... G.E. CO. TYPE GE-581-A1 DIRECT DRIVEN
MAIN GENERATOR VOLTAGE .... MAX. 865 V., FULL LOAD 845 V.
MAIN GENERATOR CAPACITY .... 1100 K.W.
NUMBER AND TYPE OF TRACTION MOTORS .... FOUR GE-752-C1
TRACTION MOTOR VENTILATION .... FORCED
GEAR RATIO 74/18 (4.111)
CONTROL-TYPE AND VOLTAGE .... G.E. CO.,P, (M.U.) 75 V.

MAXIMUM SPEED OF LOCOMOTIVE .... 65 M.P.H.
CONTINUOUS RATING - TRACTIVE EFFORT .... 52,500 LBS.
SPEED .... 9.4 M.P.H.
HORSEPOWER 1315
AIR SIGNAL .... ✱YES
TRAIN CONTROL .... NONE

✱ APPLIES TO DFB-7A & DFB-7B ONLY

Class	Number	Builder	Order Number	c/n	Date	Disposition
DFA-7A	1044	Alco-GE	(S-3161)	78652	6/51	Rt 9/67 GE
DFA-7A	1045	"	"	78653	"	PC re 1345 Rt GE
DFB-7A	3323	Alco-GE	(S-3162)	78670	5/51	PC Rt 7/68 GE
"	3324	"	"	78671	"	PC Rt 7/68 GE
"	3325	"	"	78672	"	PC
"	3326	"	"	78673	"	Rt 9/67 GE
"	3327	"	"	78674	"	PC Rt 6/68
"	3328	"	"	78675	"	PC
"	3329	"	"	78676	"	Rt 5/67 GE
"	3330	"	"	78677	6/51	PC Rt 68
"	3331	"	"	78678	"	PC Rt /68 GE
"	3332	"	"	78679	"	Rt 10/67

No. 1046 Class DFA-7B, was one of 80 FA-2 models built by Alco in 1951 and 1952.

Both: NYCSHS Collection

No. 3330 Class DFB-7B, was a FB-2 model, built by Alco in June 1951.

Class	Number	Builder	Order Number	c/n	Date	Disposition
DFA-7B	1046	Alco-GE	(S-3161)	78654	6/51	Rt 5/67 GE
"	1047	"	"	78655	"	Rt 1/67 GE
"	1048	"	(S-3170)	78961	6/51	Rt 7/67 GE
"	1049	"	"	78962	"	PC Re 1349 Rt GE
"	1050	"	"	78963	"	PC Rt 7/68 GE
"	1051	"	"	78964	"	PC Re 1351 Rt
"	1052	"	"	78965	"	PC Rt 6/68 GE
"	1053	"	"	78966	"	PC Rt 4/68 GE
"	1054	"	"	78967	6/51	PC re 1354
"	1055	"	"	78968	"	PC re 1355
"	1056	"	"	78969	"	So 5/64 GE as 1031
"	1057	"	"	78970	"	Rt 5/67 GE
"	1058	"	"	78971	"	Rt 7/67 GE
"	1059	"	"	78972	"	Rt 5/67 GE
"	1060	"	"	78973	"	PC Rt 4/68 GE
"	1061	"	"	78974	"	PC re 1361 Rt 7/68 GE
"	1062	"	"	78975	"	Rt 1167 Alco
"	1063	"	"	78976	7/51	PC Rt 7/68 GE
"	1064	"	"	78977	"	Rt 6/67 (Wrecked)
"	1065	"	"	78978	"	Rt 5/67 GE
"	1066	"	"	78979	"	Rt 11/67 Alco
"	1067	"	"	78980	"	PC Rt 4/68 GE
"	1068	"	"	78981	"	PC Rt 7/68 GE
"	1069	"	"	78982	"	PC re 1369
"	1070	"	"	78983	"	PC Rt 4/68 GE
"	1071	"	"	79001	8/51	PC re 1371
"	1072	"	"	79002	"	Rt 9/67 GE
"	1073	"	"	79003	9/51	PC re 1373
"	1074	"	"	79004	"	Rt 1/67 GE
"	1075	"	"	79005	"	PC re 1375
"	1076	"	"	79006	"	PC re 1376
"	1077	"	"	79007	"	Rt 5/67 GE
"	1078	"	"	79008	"	Rt 9/67 GE
"	1079	"	"	79009	"	Rt 5/67 GE
"	1080	"	"	79010	"	PC re 1380 Rt GE
"	1081	"	(S-3179)	79276	"	PC re 1381
"	1082	"	"	79277	"	PC re 1382
"	1083	"	"	79278	"	PC re 1383
"	1084	"	"	79279	"	PC re 1384 Rt GE
"	1085	"	"	79280	"	Rt 7/67 GE
"	1086	"	"	79281	"	PC re 1386 Rt 6/68 GE
"	1087	"	"	79282	"	PC.Rt 4/68 GE

Class	Number	Builder	Order Number	c/n	Date	Disposition
DFB-7B	3333	Alco-GE	(S-3162)	78680	6/51	Rt 6/67 (Wrecked)
"	3334	"	(S-3171)	79011	"	Rt 9/67 GE
"	3335	"	"	79012	"	Rt 11/67 Alco
"	3336	"	"	79013	"	Rt 9/67 GE
"	3337	"	"	79014	"	PC
"	3338	"	"	79015	"	PC
"	3339	"	"	79016	"	Rt 9/67 GE
"	3340	"	"	79017	"	Rt 11/67 Alco
"	3341	"	"	79018	"	PC Rt /68 GE
"	3342	"	"	79019	"	PC Rt 4/68 GE
"	3343	"	"	79020	"	Rt 9/67 GE
"	3344	"	"	79021	"	Rt 7/67 GE
"	3345	"	"	79022	"	PC Rt /68 GE
"	3346	"	(S-3180)	79318	8/51	PC Rt 4/68 GE
"	3347	"	"	79319	9/51	Rt 7/67 GE
"	3348	"	"	79320	"	PC
"	3349	"	"	79321	"	Rt 11/67 Alco
"	3350	"	"	79322	"	PC Rt /69
"	3351	"	"	79323	"	
"	3352	"	"	79324	"	Rt 9/67 GE
"	3353	"	"	79325	"	Rt 5/67 GE
"	3354	"	"	79326	"	Rt 11/67 Alco
DFA-7C	1088	Alco-GE	(S-3179)	79287	10/51	Rt 7/67 GE
"	1089	"	"	79288	"	PC re 1389
"	1090	"	"	79289	"	Rt 5/67 GE
"	1091	"	"	79290	"	PC re 1391
"	1092	"	"	79291	"	Rt 5/67 GE
"	1093	"	"	79292	"	Rt 2/67 GE
"	1094	"	"	79293	"	Rt 8/67 GE
"	1095	"	"	79294	"	Rt 5/67 GE
"	1096	"	"	79295	"	Rt 7/67 GE
"	1097	"	"	79296	"	Rt 7/67 GE
"	1098	"	"	79297	"	PC re 1398
"	1099	"	"	79298	"	PC re 1399
"	1100	"	"	79299	"	Rt 7/67 GE
"	1101	"	"	79300	"	Rt 8/67 GE
"	1102	"	"	79301	"	PC re 1302 Rt 6/71 LIRR 600
"	1103	"	"	79302	"	PC Rt 4/68 GE
"	1104	"	"	79303	"	PC re 1304
"	1105	"	"	79304	"	Rt 8/67 GE
"	1106	"	"	79305	"	Rt 7/67 GE
"	1107	"	"	79306	"	Rt 5/67 GE
DFB-7C	3355	Alco-GE	(S-3185)	79472	10/51	PC Rt 7/68 GE
"	3356	"	"	79473	"	PC Rt /68 GE
"	3357	"	"	79474	"	PC Rt /68 GE
"	3358	"	"	79475	"	PC Rt /68
"	3359	"	"	79476	"	Rt 6/67 (Wrecked)
"	3360	"	"	79477	"	Rt 5/67 GE
"	3361	"	"	79478	"	Rt 5/67 GE
"	3362	"	"	79479	"	PC Rt 7/68 GE
"	3363	"	"	79480	"	Rt 7/67 GE
"	3364	"	"	79481	"	PC Rt /68 GE

Class	Number	Builder	Order Number	c/n	Date	Disposition
DFA-7D	1108	Alco-GE	(S-3199)	79960	5/52	PC re 1308 Rt GE
"	1109	"	"	79961	"	PC Rt 6/68 GE
"	1110	"	"	79962	"	So 5/64 GE as 1033
"	1111	"	"	79963	6/52	PC re 1311
"	1112	"	"	79964	"	PC Rt 6/68 GE
"	1113	"	"	79965	"	PC Re 1313
"	1114	"	"	79966	"	Rt 8/67 GE
"	1115	"	"	79967	"	Rt 5/67 GE
"	1116	"	"	79968	7/52	Rt 5/67 GE
"	1117	"	"	79969	"	Rt 7/67 GE
"	1118	"	"	79972	8/52	Rt 11/67 Al co
"	1119	"	"	79973	"	So 4/65 GE as 1000
"	1120	"	"	79974	"	
"	1121	"	"	79975	9/52	Rt 7/67 GE
"	1122	"	"	79976	10/52	PC Rt 4/68 GE
"	1123	"	"	79977	"	Rt 7/67 GE
DFB-7D	3365	Alco GE	(S-3200)	80015	5/52	PC Rt 4/68 GE
"	3366	"	"	80016	6/52	Rt 5/67 GE
"	3367	"	"	80017	"	PC
"	3368	"	"	80018	"	PC Rt /69
"	3369	"	"	80019	7/52	So 10/65 GE as 3320
"	3370	"	"	80020	8/52	PC Rt /69
"	3371	"	"	80021	9/52	Rt 11/67 Alco
"	3372	"	"	80022	10/52	PC Rt /68 GE

Louis A. Marre

No. 1103 Class DFA-7C wears fading paint at Elkhart, Indiana on November 3, 1964.

NYCSHS Collection

No. 1101 Class DFA-7D was built by Alco in May 1952. This 1600 HP FA-2 model features a "full-length lightning stripe"

Collection of Louis A. Marre

No. 1073 Class DFA-7B shown here at Sharonville, Ohio with the large lettering placed low on the carbody.

CLASS DFA-8 and DFB-8 (BF-16) Baldwin 1600HP Model RF-16

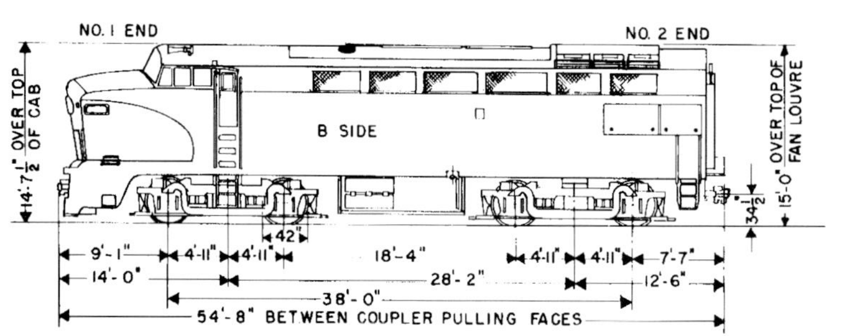

DIESEL ENGINE — BLH — MODEL 608 A
DIESEL ENGINE H.P. — 1723(1600 FOR TRACTION)
NUMBER OF CYLINDERS — 8 IN LINE
BORE AND STROKE — 12¾"X15½"
ENGINE SPEED R.P.M. — IDLING 315, FULL LOAD 625
MAIN GENERATOR — W.E. CORP. TYPE 471-BZ DIRECT DRIVEN
MAIN GENERATOR VOLTAGE — MAX. 905V., FULL LOAD 875V
MAIN GENERATOR CAPACITY — 1125 K.W.
NUMBER AND TYPE OF TRACTION MOTORS — FOUR W.E. CORP. 370-DEZ
TRACTION MOTOR VENTILATION — FORCED
GEAR RATIO — 63/15 (4.20)
CONTROL-TYPE AND VOLTAGE — W.E. CORP, P, (M.U.) 75V.

MAXIMUM SPEED OF LOCOMOTIVE — 70 M.P.H.
CONTINUOUS RATING - TRACTIVE EFFORT — 48,600 LBS.
SPEED — 9.9 M.P.H.
HORSEPOWER — 1283
AIR SIGNAL — NONE
TRAIN CONTROL — G.R.S., SCHEDULE 2, SINGLE END, WITH SAFETY CONTROL

CLASS DFA-8

Class	Number	Re '66	Builder	Order Number	c/n	Date	Disposition
DFA-8A	3804	1204	B-L-H	(50548)	75360	12/51	Rt 5/67 GE SS 10/67
"	3805	1205	"	"	75361	"	Rt 5/67 GE So 12/67 Mga RR
"	3806	1206	"	"	75362	"	Rt 5/67 GE
"	3807	1207	"	"	75363	"	Rt 5/67 GE So 12/67 Mga RR
"	3808	(1208)	"	"	75364	"	Rt 9/66
"	3809	1209	"	"	75365	1/52	Rt 5/67 GE So 12/67 Mga RR
"	3810	1210	"	"	75366	"	Rt 5/67 GE So 12/67 Mga RR
"	3811	1211	"	"	75367	"	Rt 5/67 GE So 12/67 Mga RR
"	3812	1212	"	"	75368	"	Rt 5/67 GE SS 10/67
"	3813	1213	"	"	75369	"	Rt 5/67 GE So 12/67 Mga RR
"	3814	1214	"	"	75370	"	Rt 5/67 GE
"	3815	1215	"	"	75371	"	Rt 5/67 GE SS 10/67
"	3816	1216	"	"	75372	"	Rt 5/67 GE So 12/67 Mga RR
"	3817	1217	"	"	75373	"	Rt 5/67 GE SS 10/67
"	3818	1218	"	"	75374	2/52	Rt 5/67 GE SS 10/67
"	3819	1219	"	"	75375	"	Rt 5/67 GE
"	3820	1220	"	"	75376	"	Rt 5/67 GE SS 10/67
"	3821	1221	"	"	75377	"	Rt 9/66, Sc
DFB-8A	3702		B-L-H	(50549)	75401	12/51	Rt 9/66
"	3703		"	"	75402	"	Rt 9/66
"	3704		"	"	75403	"	Rt 9/66
"	3705		"	"	75404	1/52	Rt 5/67 GE SS 10/67
"	3706		"	"	75405	"	Rt 9/66
"	3707		"	"	75406	"	Rt 9/66
"	3708		"	"	75407	"	Rt 5/67 GE So 12/67 Mga RR
"	3709		"	"	75408	2/52	Rt 5/67 GE So 12/67 Mga RR

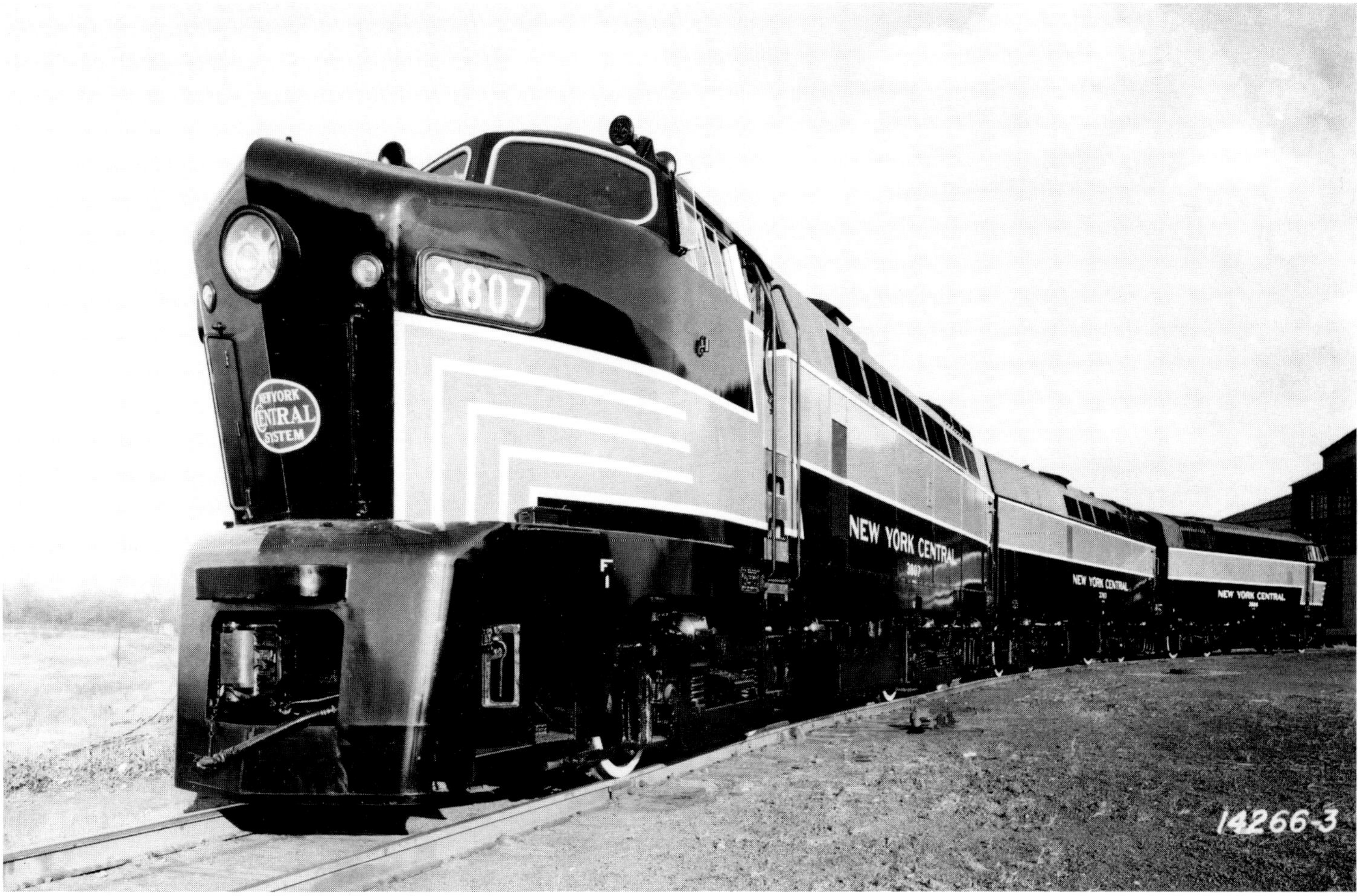

14266-3

NYCSHS Collection

No. 3807 Class DFA-8A was a 1600 HP RF-16 "Sharknose" built by Baldwin Locomotive Works in December 1951. These locomotives spent most of their service life on the Big Four.

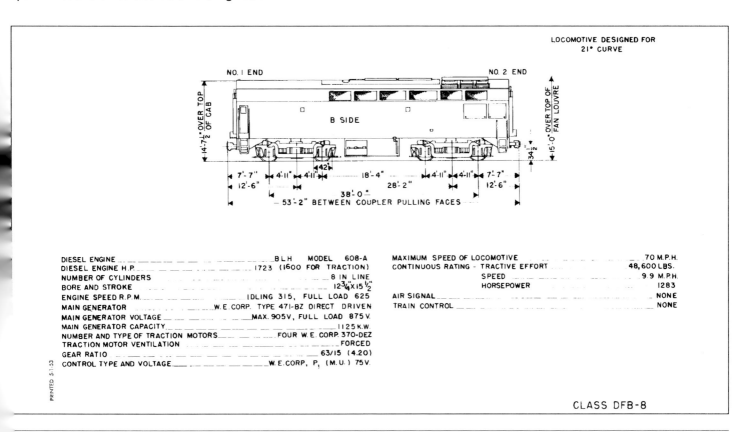

LOCOMOTIVE DESIGNED FOR
21° CURVE

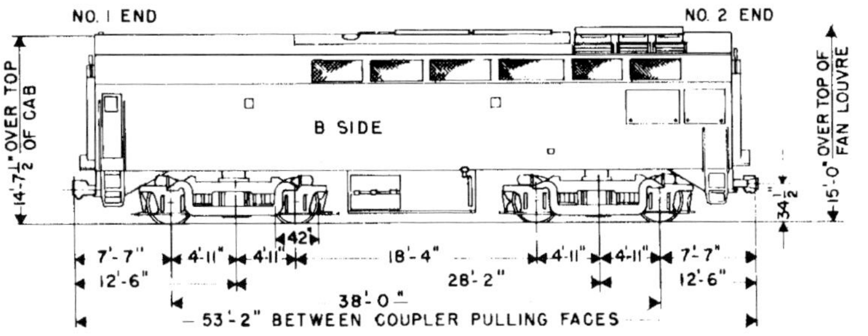

NO. 1 END

NO. 2 END

B SIDE

14'-7½" OVER TOP OF CAB

15'-0" OVER TOP OF FAN LOUVRE

34½"

42"

7'-7" 4'-11" 4'-11" 18'-4" 4'-11" 4'-11" 7'-7"

12'-6" 28'-2" 12'-6"

38'-0"

53'-2" BETWEEN COUPLER PULLING FACES

DIESEL ENGINE	BLH MODEL 608-A
DIESEL ENGINE H.P.	1723 (1600 FOR TRACTION)
NUMBER OF CYLINDERS	8 IN LINE
BORE AND STROKE	12¾"X15½"
ENGINE SPEED R.P.M.	IDLING 315, FULL LOAD 625
MAIN GENERATOR	W.E. CORP. TYPE 471-BZ DIRECT DRIVEN
MAIN GENERATOR VOLTAGE	MAX. 905V, FULL LOAD 875V.
MAIN GENERATOR CAPACITY	1125 K.W.
NUMBER AND TYPE OF TRACTION MOTORS	FOUR W.E. CORP. 370-DEZ
TRACTION MOTOR VENTILATION	FORCED
GEAR RATIO	63/15 (4.20)
CONTROL TYPE AND VOLTAGE	W.E. CORP, P_1 (M.U.) 75V.

MAXIMUM SPEED OF LOCOMOTIVE		70 M.P.H.
CONTINUOUS RATING -	TRACTIVE EFFORT	48,600 LBS.
	SPEED	9.9 M.P.H.
	HORSEPOWER	1283
AIR SIGNAL		NONE
TRAIN CONTROL		NONE

PRINTED 5-1-53

CLASS DFB-8

CLASS DFA-9 and DFB-9 FM 1600HP Model CFA & CFB-16-4.

LOCOMOTIVE DESIGNED FOR 21° CURVE

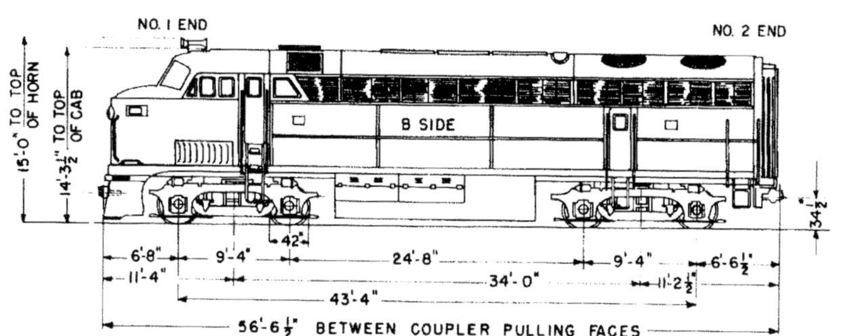

DIESEL ENGINE	FM MODEL 38 D 8 1/8
DIESEL ENGINE H.P.	(1600 FOR TRACTION)
NUMBER OF CYLINDERS	8 IN LINE (O.P.)
BORE AND STROKE	8⅛"x10"
ENGINE SPEED R.P.M.	IDLING 300, FULL LOAD 850
MAIN GENERATOR	W.E. CORP. TYPE 497-BZ DIRECT DRIVEN
MAIN GENERATOR VOLTAGE	MAX. 985V, FULL LOAD 950V
MAIN GENERATOR CAPACITY	
NUMBER AND TYPE OF TRACTION MOTORS	FOUR W.E. CORP. 370-DEZ
TRACTION MOTOR VENTILATION	FORCED
GEAR RATIO	63/15 (4.20)
CONTROL-TYPE AND VOLTAGE	W.E. CORP (M.U.) 75 V.
MAXIMUM SPEED OF LOCOMOTIVE	70 M.P.H.
CONTINUOUS RATING - TRACTIVE EFFORT	48,600 LBS.
SPEED	9.9 M.P.H.
HORSEPOWER	1283
AIR SIGNAL	NONE
TRAIN CONTROL	G.R.S. SCHEDULE 2, SINGLE END WITH SAFETY CONTROL

LOCOMOTIVE DESIGNED FOR 21° CURVE

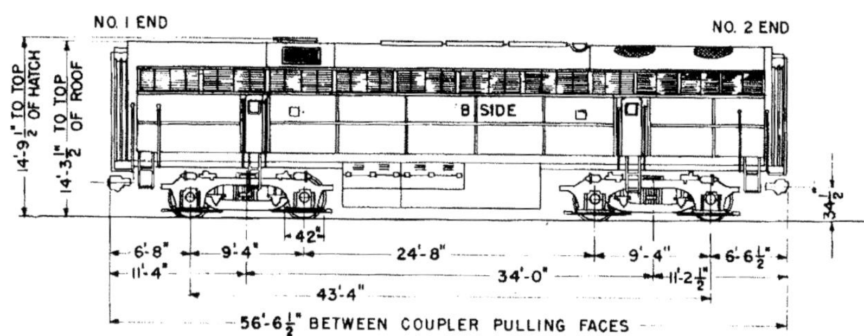

DIESEL ENGINE	FM MODEL 38 D 8 1/8
DIESEL ENGINE H.P.	(1600 FOR TRACTION)
NUMBER OF CYLINDERS	8 IN LINE (O.P.)
BORE AND STROKE	8⅛"x10"
ENGINE SPEED R.P.M.	IDLING 300, FULL LOAD 850
MAIN GENERATOR	W.E. CORP. TYPE 497-B OR 497BZ DIRECT DRIVEN
MAIN GENERATOR VOLTAGE	MAX. 985V., FULL LOAD 950V.
MAIN GENERATOR CAPACITY	
NUMBER AND TYPE OF TRACTION MOTORS	FOUR W.E. CORP. 370-DEZ
TRACTION MOTOR VENTILATION	FORCED
GEAR RATIO	63/15 (4.20)
CONTROL-TYPE AND VOLTAGE	W.E. CORP. (M.U.) 75V.
MAXIMUM SPEED OF LOCOMOTIVE	70 M.P.H.
CONTINUOUS RATING - TRACTIVE EFFORT	48,600 LBS
SPEED	9.9 M.P.H.
HORSEPOWER	1283
AIR SIGNAL	NONE
TRAIN CONTROL	NONE

Class	Number	Builder	Order Number	c/n	Date	Disposition
DFA-9A	6600	FM	(LD126)	16L541	2/52	Rt 9/66
"	6601	"	"	16L542	"	Rt 9/66
"	6602	"	"	16L543	"	Rt 9/66
"	6603	"	"	16L544	"	Rt 9/66
"	6604	"	"	16L545	"	Rt 9/66
"	6605	"	"	16L546	"	Rt 9/66
"	6606	"	"	16L547	3/52	Rt 9/66
"	6607	"	"	16L548	"	Rt 9/66
DFB-9A	6900	FM	(LD126)	16L549	2/52	Rt 9/66
"	6901	"	"	16L550	"	Rt 9/66
"	6902	"	"	16L551	"	Rt 9/66
"	6903	"	"	16L560	3/52	Rt 9/66

H. L. Vail Jr. Collection

No. 6607, 6903, and 6606. Fairbanks-Morse "C-Liners" 1600 HP units at F-M in February 1952. The silver painted trucks as shown in this photo were not "standard" for NYC freight power.

J. David Ingles, Louis A. Marre Collection

No. 6604 Class DFA-9A is at Greensburg, Indiana with two geeps on June 3, 1964.

CLASS DCA-1 and DCB-1 ELECTRO-MOTIVE 1500HP Model F3

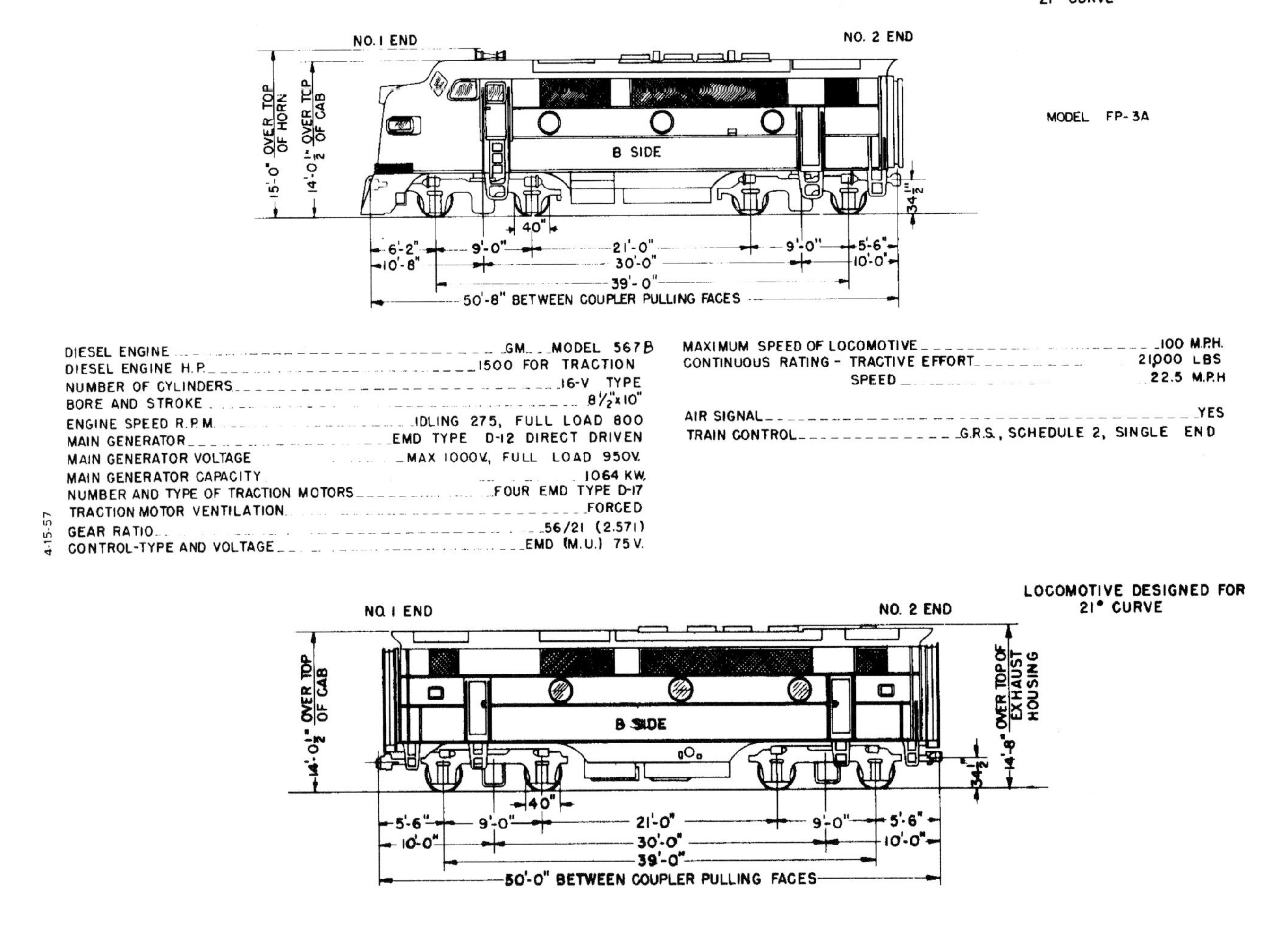

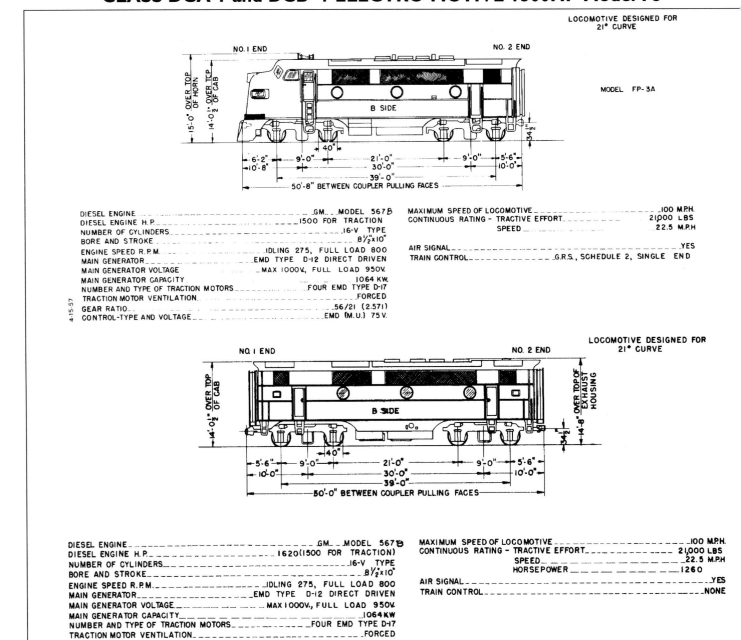

DIESEL ENGINE .... GM. MODEL 567B
DIESEL ENGINE H.P. .... 1620 (1500 FOR TRACTION)
NUMBER OF CYLINDERS .... 16-V TYPE
BORE AND STROKE .... 8½"x10"
ENGINE SPEED R.P.M. .... IDLING 275, FULL LOAD 800
MAIN GENERATOR .... EMD TYPE D-12 DIRECT DRIVEN
MAIN GENERATOR VOLTAGE .... MAX 1000V., FULL LOAD 950V.
MAIN GENERATOR CAPACITY .... 1064 KW
NUMBER AND TYPE OF TRACTION MOTORS .... FOUR EMD TYPE D-17
TRACTION MOTOR VENTILATION .... FORCED
GEAR RATIO 56/21 (2.571)
CONTROL-TYPE AND VOLTAGE .... EMD (M.U.) 75 V.

MAXIMUM SPEED OF LOCOMOTIVE .... 100 M.P.H.
CONTINUOUS RATING - TRACTIVE EFFORT .... 21,000 LBS
SPEED .... 22.5 M.P.H
HORSEPOWER 1260
AIR SIGNAL .... YES
TRAIN CONTROL .... NONE

Class	Original Number	Builder	Order Number	c/n	Date	Disposition	Converted Date	New Class	New Number
DCA-1A	3500	EMC	E-772	4211	7/47	Converted to freight	1/59	DFA-2J	1874
"	3501	"	"	4212	"	Converted to freight	12/58	DFA-2J	1875 (1)
"	3502	"	"	4213	"	Sold 5/61 EMD			
	3503	"	"	4214	"	Converted to freight	2/61	DFA-2J	1877
DCB-1A	3600	EMC	E-772	4215	7/47	Converted to freight	12/58	DFB-2H	2475
	3601	"	"	4216	"	"	8/59	DFB-2H	2476

Note: Converted at Collinwood Shop by removing steam generator and associated equipment, adding counterweight, and changing gear ratio to freight. See DFA-2, DFB-2 for specifications and disposition.

General: Delivered as 3 unit locomotives 3500-3600-3501 and 3502-3601-3503: Bodies painted Passenger 2 tone gray on "A" units, "B" units were originally dark gray. These locomotives not equipped with dynamic brakes - Overhead boiler water tanks installed instead of brake grids and blowers.

W.D. Edson

No. 3502, with "B" unit number 3601 and DCA-1A No. 3503 on train No. 415 at Lafayette, Indiana on September 22, 1953

No. 3503, and 3502 lead train No. 257 through South Bend, Indiana on April 24, 1960. Just over a year later the 3502 would be sold to EMD and the 3503 would be converted to freight service and renumbered 1877.

Louis A. Marre

CLASS DCA-2 and DCB- 2 Baldwin 1500HP Model DR-6-4-15

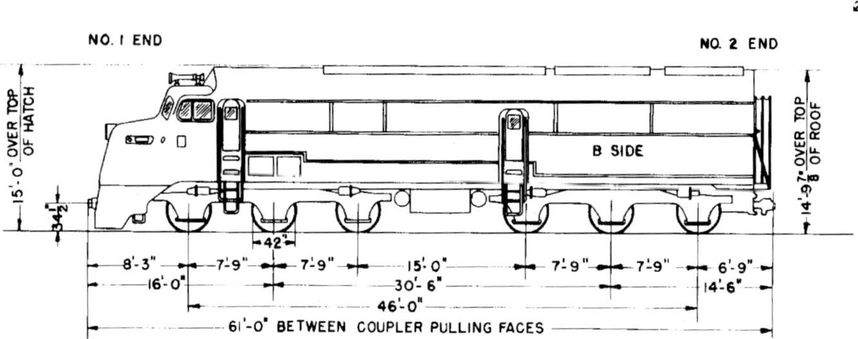

DIESEL ENGINE — BLW. MODEL 608 SC
DIESEL ENGINE H.P. — 1701 (1500 FOR TRACTION)
NUMBER OF CYLINDERS — 8 IN LINE
BORE AND STROKE — 12¾"x 15½"
ENGINE SPEED R.P.M. — IDLING 315, FULL LOAD 625
MAIN GENERATOR — W. E. CORP. TYPE 471-A DIRECT DRIVEN
MAIN GENERATOR VOLTAGE — MAX. 910 V., FULL LOAD 880 V.
MAIN GENERATOR CAPACITY — 1100 KW.
NUMBER AND TYPE OF TRACTION MOTORS — FOUR W. E. CORP. 370-F
TRACTION MOTOR VENTILATION — FORCED
GEAR RATIO — 57/22 (2.591)
CONTROL-TYPE AND VOLTAGE — W. E. CORP., EP, (M.U.) 75 V.

MAXIMUM SPEED OF LOCOMOTIVE — 100 M.P.H.
CONTINUOUS RATING - TRACTIVE EFFORT — 25,400 LBS.
SPEED — 18.1 M.P.H.
HORSEPOWER — 1226
AIR SIGNAL — YES
TRAIN CONTROL — G.R.S., SCHEDULE 2, SINGLE END, WITH SAFETY CONTROL

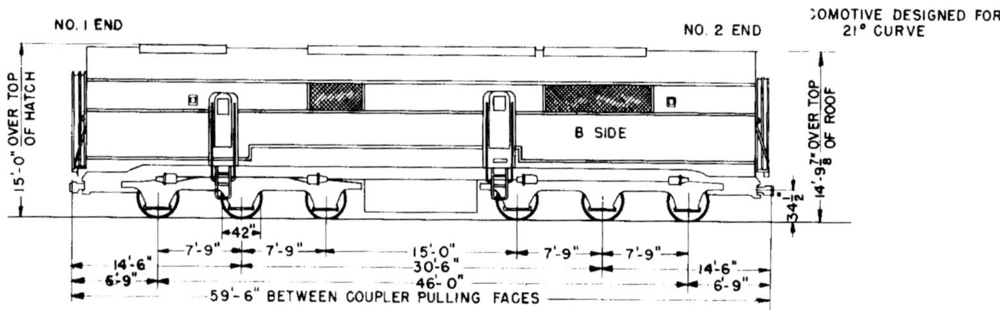

DIESEL ENGINE — BLW. MODEL 608 SC
DIESEL ENGINE H.P. — 1701 (1500 FOR TRACTION)
NUMBER OF CYLINDERS — 8 IN LINE
BORE AND STROKE — 12¾"x 15½"
ENGINE SPEED R.P.M. — IDLING 315, FULL LOAD 625
MAIN GENERATOR — W. E. CORP. TYPE 471-A DIRECT DRIVEN
MAIN GENERATOR VOLTAGE — MAX. 910 V., FULL LOAD 880 V.
MAIN GENERATOR CAPACITY — 1100 KW.
NUMBER AND TYPE OF TRACTION MOTORS — FOUR W. E. CORP. 370-F
TRACTION MOTOR VENTILATION — FORCED
GEAR RATIO — 57/22 (2.591)
5-1-53 CONTROL-TYPE AND VOLTAGE — W. E. CORP., EP, (M.U.) 75 V.

MAXIMUM SPEED OF LOCOMOTIVE — 100 M.P.H.
CONTINUOUS RATING - TRACTIVE EFFORT — 25,400 LBS.
SPEED — 18.1 M.P.H.
HORSEPOWER — 1226
AIR SIGNAL — YES
TRAIN CONTROL — NONE

Class	Original Number	Builder	Order Number	c/n	Date	Re-engined Date	New Class	Re 5/55	Disposition
DCA-2A	3200	Baldwin	46502	73132	10/47	3/55	DCA-3A	3504	Rt 12/60 Sc 2/62
"	3201	"	"	73133	"	3/55	"	3505	Rt 12/60 Sc 3/62
"	3202	"	"	73134	4/48	5/55	"	3506	Rt 12/60 Sc 3/62
"	3203	"	"	73135	"	3/55	"	3507	Rt 12/60 Sc 2/62

Class	Original Number	Builder	Order Number	c/n	Date	Re '51	Re-engined Date	New Class	Re 5/55	Disposition
DCB-2A	3300	Baldwin	46502	73136	10/47	3210	5/55	DCB-3A	3602	Rt 12/60 Sc 2/62
"	3301	"	"	73137	4/48	3211	3/55	"	3603	Rt 12/60 Sc 1/62

Note: (1) Originally built with 13'-3" WB straight equalized trucks. Trucks changed to drop equalized type with 15'-6" WB. Delivered as 3 unit Locomotive 3200-3300-3201 and 3202-3301-3203, painted passenger two tone gray.
(2) When re-engined, original WE 412 Generator and electrical equipment retained; pneumatic throttle and MU control replaced with EMD electric throttle and MU.

NYCSHS Collection

No. 3200 (later 3504) 3300 (later 3210 then 3602) and 3201 (later 3505) are shown new at Baldwin Locomotive Works in October 1947. The enclosed drop coupler is shown in the "up" or service position. The two sets of these 3-unit locomotives were intended to operate Boston-Chicago on the *Paul Revere*, but they failed miserably in this service.

Collection of Louis A. Marre

No. 3201 Class DCA-2A shown at La Grange, Illinois after re-engining by EMD in March 1955. Only two months later it would be renumbered 3505.

CLASS DPA-1 and DPB-1 (EP-20) EMD 2000HP Model E7

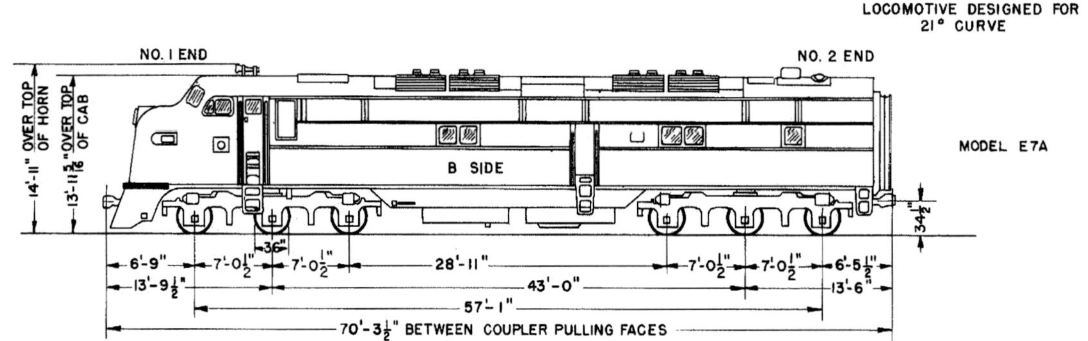

DIESEL ENGINES — TWO GM MODEL 567A
DIESEL ENGINE H.P. (TWO ENGINES) — 2000 FOR TRACTION
NUMBER OF CYLINDERS (EACH ENGINE) — 12-V TYPE
BORE AND STROKE — 8 1/2"x10"
ENGINE SPEED R.P.M. — IDLING 275, FULL LOAD 800
MAIN GENERATORS — TWO EMD TYPE D-4-D DIRECT DRIVEN
MAIN GENERATOR VOLTAGE — MAX. 1125V., FULL LOAD 1070 V.
MAIN GENERATOR CAPACITY (TWO GENERATORS) — 1425 KW.
NUMBER AND TYPE OF TRACTION MOTORS — FOUR EMD D-7, D-17 OR D-27
TRACTION MOTOR VENTILATION — FORCED
GEAR RATIO — 55/22 (2.5)
CONTROL-TYPE AND VOLTAGE — EMD (M. U.) 75 V.

PRINTED 4-15-57

MAXIMUM SPEED OF LOCOMOTIVE — 98 M.P.H.
CONTINUOUS RATING - TRACTIVE EFFORT — 18,400 LBS.
SPEED — 35.0 M.P.H.
AIR SIGNAL — YES
TRAIN CONTROL — G.R.S., SCHEDULE 2, SINGLE END

CLASS DPA-1

Class	Number	Builder	Order Number	c/n	Date	Disposition
DPA-1A	4000	EMC	(E-639)	2865	3/45	PC Rt 4/68
"	4001	"	"	2866	"	PC
"	4002	"	"	2867	"	PC
"	4003	"	"	2868	"	* PC
"	4004	"	"	2869	10/45	PC Rt 4/68
"	4005	"	"	2870	"	PC
"	4006	"	"	2871	"	PC
"	4007	"	"	2872	"	PC
DPB-1A	4100	EMC	(E-639)	2873	10/45	PC Rt 4/68
"	4101	"	"	2874	"	PC Rt 4/68
"	4102	"	"	2875	"	PC Rt 4/68
"	4103	"	"	2876	"	PC Rt 4/68
DPA-1B	4008	EMC	(E-751)	4163	4/47	PC
"	4009	"	"	4164	"	PC Rt 4/68
"	4010	"	"	4165	"	PC
"	4011	"	"	4166	"	PC
"	4012	"	'	4167		PC Rt /69
"	4013	"	"	4168	"	PC Rt 4/68
"	4014	"	"	4169	"	PC
"	4015	"	"	4170	"	PC
"	4016	"	"	4171	"	PC Rt 4/68
"	4017	"	"	4172	"	PC Rt 4/68
"	4018	"	"	4173	"	PC
"	4019	"	"	4174	"	PC
"	4020	"	"	4175	"	* PC re AM 255
"	4021	"	"	4176	"	PC
"	4022	"	"	4177	"	PC
"	4023	"	"	4178	"	PC

* Note: 4003 and 4020 converted to model E8 carbody.

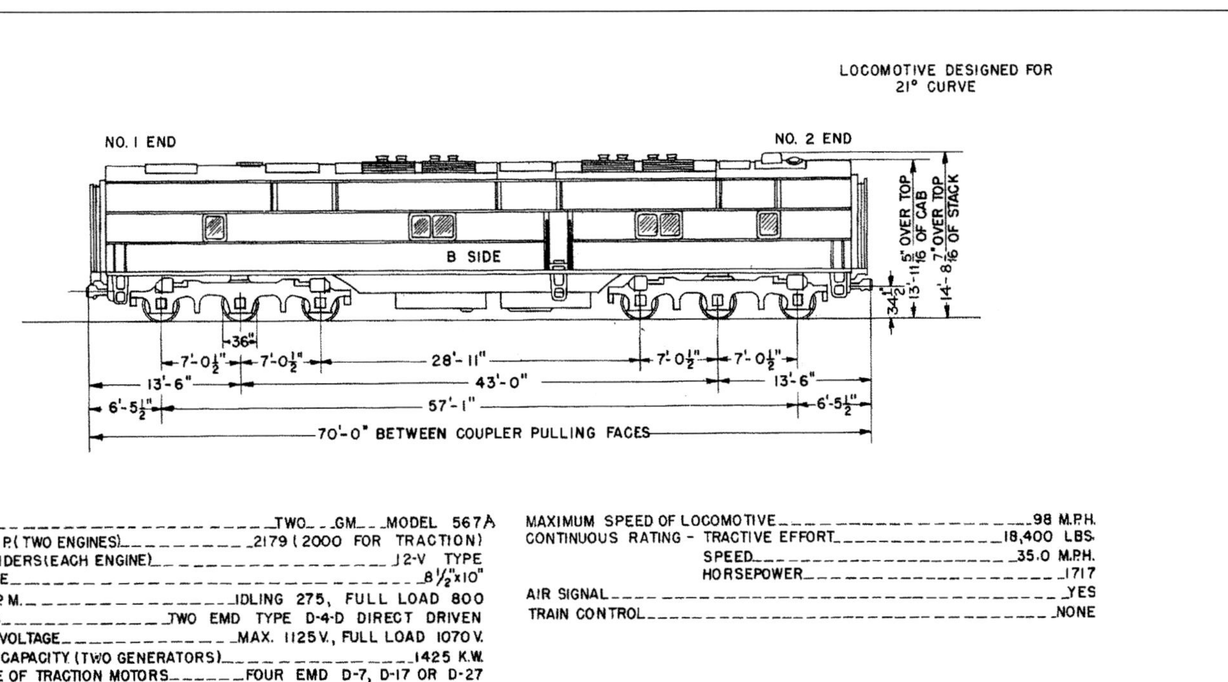

Class	Number	Builder	Order Number	c/n	Date	Disposition
DPB-1B	4104	EMC	(E-751)	4179	4/47	PC Rt 10/73
"	4105	"	"	4180	"	PC Rt 4/68
"	4106	"	"	4181	"	PC Rt 4/68
"	4107	"	"	4182	"	PC Rt 10/73
DPA-1C	4024	EMC	(E-840)	4847	2/48	PC
"	4025	"	"	4848	"	PC
"	4026	"	"	4849	"	PC
"	4027	"	"	4850	"	PC
"	4028	"	"	4851	"	PC
"	4029	"	"	4852	"	PC
DPB-1C	4108	EMC	(E-840)	4853	2/48	PC Rt /69
"	4109	"	"	4854	"	PC
"	4110	"	"	4855	"	PC Rt 4/68
"	4111	"	"	4856	"	PC
"	4112-	"	"	4857	"	PC Rt 4/68
"	4113	"	"	4858	"	PC Rt 4/68
DPA-1D	4030	EMC	(E-987)	6241	2/49	PC
"	4031	"	"	6242	"	PC
"	4032	"	"	6243	"	PC
"	4033	"	"	6244	"	PC
"	4034	"	"	6245	"	PC
"	4035	"	"	6246	"	PC

Notes: Units 4001, 4003 originally painted solid black with aluminumlettering and striping. All other DPA-1A and DPB-1A painted light grey with dark grey lightning stripes and imitation aluminum trim and a black roof. and running gear. E7 units that followed were painted painted dark grey with light grey lighting stripes.

Collection of H. L. Vail Jr.

No. 4009 Class DPA-1B and 4105 DPB-1b new at Harmon, New York in April 1947.

Louis A. Marr

No. 4003 Class DPA-1B leads train No. 357 at Dearborn, Michigan on September 6, 1963. No. 4003 was rebuilt with an E-8 carbody afte being wrecked ten years earlier at Conneaut, Ohio.

No. 4004 Class DPA-1A new at EMD in October 1945. Note the early striping scheme.

Both: Collection of H. L. Vail Jr.

No. 4028 Class DPA-1C and No. 4112 DPB-1C new at EMD in February 1948.

CLASS DPA-2 and DPB-2 ALCO-GE 2000HP Model PA-1, PB-1

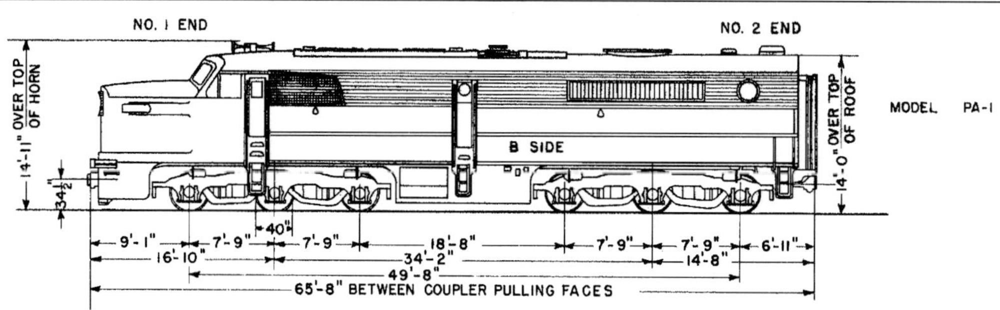

DIESEL ENGINE .... ALCO ... MODEL 244
DIESEL ENGINE H.P. .... 2000 FOR TRACTION
NUMBER OF CYLINDERS .... 16-V TYPE
BORE AND STROKE .... 9"x10½"
ENGINE SPEED R.P.M. .... IDLING 350, FULL LOAD 1000
MAIN GENERATOR .... G.E.CO. TYPE GT-566-C1 DIRECT DRIVEN
MAIN GENERATOR VOLTAGE .... MAX. 790V., FULL LOAD 735V.
MAIN GENERATOR CAPACITY .... 1400 K.W.
NUMBER AND TYPE OF TRACTION MOTORS .... FOUR GE-752-A1 OR B1
TRACTION MOTOR VENTILATION .... FORCED
GEAR RATIO 60/23 (2.609)
CONTROL-TYPE AND VOLTAGE .... G.E. CO., P, (M.U.) 75 V.

MAXIMUM SPEED OF LOCOMOTIVE .... 100 M.P.H.
CONTINUOUS RATING - TRACTIVE EFFORT .... 27,000 LBS.
SPEED .... 23.0 M.P.H.
AIR SIGNAL .... YES
TRAIN CONTROL .... G.R.S., SCHEDULE 2, SINGLE END

4-15-57

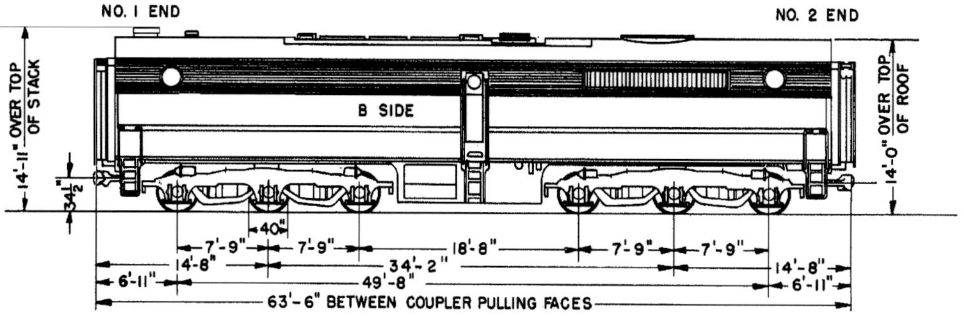

DIESEL ENGINE .... ALCO ... MODEL 244
DIESEL ENGINE H.P. .... 2150 (2000 FOR TRACTION)
NUMBER OF CYLINDERS .... 16-V TYPE
BORE AND STROKE .... 9"x10½"
ENGINE SPEED R.P.M. .... IDLING 350, FULL LOAD 1000
MAIN GENERATOR .... G.E.CO. TYPE GT-566-C1 DIRECT DRIVEN
MAIN GENERATOR VOLTAGE .... MAX. 790V., FULL LOAD 735V.
MAIN GENERATOR CAPACITY .... 1400 K.W.
NUMBER AND TYPE OF TRACTION MOTORS .... FOUR GE-752-A1 OR B1
TRACTION MOTOR VENTILATION .... FORCED
GEAR RATIO 60/23 (2.609)
CONTROL-TYPE AND VOLTAGE .... G.E. CO., P, (M.U.) 75 V.

MAXIMUM SPEED OF LOCOMOTIVE .... 100 M.P.H.
CONTINUOUS RATING - TRACTIVE EFFORT .... 27,000 LBS.
SPEED .... 23.0 M.P.H.
HORSEPOWER 1656
AIR SIGNAL .... YES
TRAIN CONTROL .... NONE

7-1-51

Class	Number	Builder	Order Number	c/n	Date	Disposition
DPA-2A	4200	Alco GE	(S-3040)	75328	1/48	Rt 4/62, Sc 7/62
"	4201	"	"	75329	"	Rt 4/62, Sc 6/62
DPB-2A	4300	Alco GE	(S-3049)	75605	1/48	Rt 4/62, Sc 5/62
"	4301	"	"	75606	"	Rt 4/62, Sc 6/62
DPA-2B	4202	Alco GE	(S-3067)	76086	12/48	Rt 4/62, Sc 5/62
"	4203	"	(S-3079)	76307	"	Rt 4/62, Sc 6/62

Class	Road	Number	Builder	Order Number	c/n	Date	Disposition
DPB-2B		4302	Alco-GE	(S-3049)	75610	12/48	*Rt 4/62, Sc 6/62
"		4303	"	"	75611	"	Rt 4/62, Sc 7/62
DPA-2C	P&LE	4204	Alco GE	(S-3103)	76913	4/49	Rt 12/60, SS 2/61
"	"	4205	"	"	76914	"	Rt 12/60, SS 2/61
"	"	4206	"	"	76915	"	Rt 12/60, SS 1/61
"	"	4207	"	"	76916	"	Rt 12/60, SS 2/61

* Note: Re-engined 11/55 at Collinwood Loco Shop with EMD 567 C V-16, 1750 HP using original GE 566-C1 generator, modified coupling, modified Woodward Governor and partial EMD transition, balance original equipment. Tractive effort (max) 50450, weight 299,300.

No. 4202 Class DPA-2B a 2250 HP model PA-2 locomotive built by Alco in December 1948 was retired in April 1962.

Both: NYCSHS Collection

NYCSHS Collection

No. 4302 Class DPB-2B built by Alco in December 1948 operated with the 4202 shown above. An EMD engine was substituted in 1955, but keeping the original GE equipment.

CLASS DPA-3 FM-GE "Erie Built" 2000HP Passenger

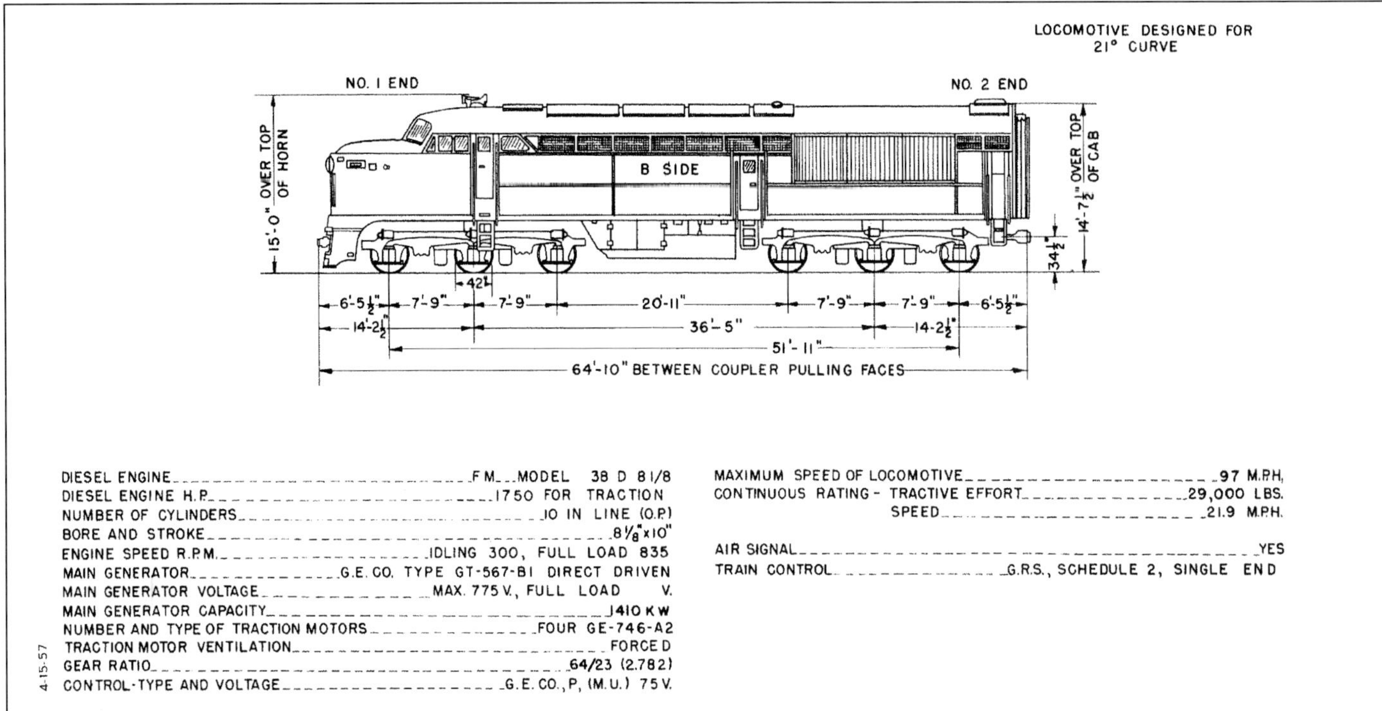

Class	Number	Builder	Order Number	c/n	Builder	c/n	Date	Disposition
DPA-3A	4400	FM	(LD47)	L1177	GE	30126	3/49	Rt 1/64, SS 2/64
"	4401	"	"	L1178	"	30127	"	Rt 1/64, SS 2/64
"	4402	"	"	L1179	"	30128	"	Rt 1/64, SS 2/64
"	4403	"	"	L1180	"	30129	"	Rt 1/64, SS 3/64
"	4404	"	"	L1181	"	30130	4/49	Rt 1/64, SS 1/64
"	4405	"	"	L1182	"	30131	"	Rt 1/64, SS 1/64

Note: All units built with 63/24 gear ratio. By 1957 all units de-rated to 1750HP, with 64/23 gear ratio, 97 mph; all units built with cast steel drop equalizer trucks (not "fabricated" shown in diagram) with indicated wheel base.

NYCSHS Collecti

No. 4403 Class DPA-3A was 2000 HP, 10 cylinder opposed-piston powered locomotive built for Fairbanks-Morse by GE at GE's Eri Pennsylvania works in April 1949.

No. 4405 Class DPA-3A. An F-M "Erie Built" in service at Waterford, Ontario in 1952.

Both: R. F. McMichael Photo, Collection of Louis A. Marre

The opposite or fireman's side of No. 4405 Class DPA-3A. One of six GE-FM "Erie Builts" at Harmon, New York on September 8, 1951.

CLASS DPA-4 and DPB-4 Alco-GE 2250HP Model PA-2, PB-2

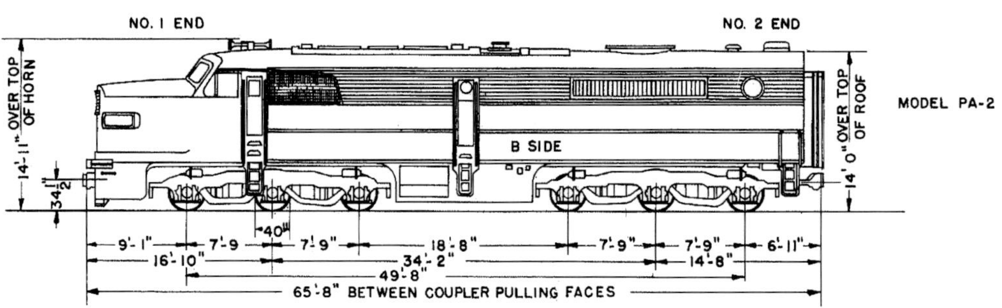

DIESEL ENGINE	ALCO MODEL 244
DIESEL ENGINE H.P.	2250 FOR TRACTION
NUMBER OF CYLINDERS	16-V TYPE
BORE AND STROKE	9"X10½
ENGINE SPEED R.P.M.	IDLING 350, FULL LOAD 1000
MAIN GENERATOR	G.E. CO. TYPE GT-566-C1 DIRECT DRIVEN
MAIN GENERATOR VOLTAGE	MAX 780V, FULL LOAD 755 V.
MAIN GENERATOR CAPACITY	1550 K.W.
NUMBER AND TYPE OF TRACTION MOTORS	FOUR GE-752-A1
TRACTION MOTOR VENTILATION	FORCED
GEAR RATIO	60/23 (2.609)
CONTROL-TYPE AND VOLTAGE	G.E. CO. P, (M.U.) 75 V.

4-15-57

MAXIMUM SPEED OF LOCOMOTIVE	100 M.P.H.
CONTINUOUS RATING - TRACTIVE EFFORT	33,000 LBS.
SPEED	21.8 M.P.H.
AIR SIGNAL	YES
TRAIN CONTROL	● G.R.S, SCHEDULE 2, SINGLE END ▲ US & S, SCHEDULE 896, SINGLE END.

● APPLIES TO DPA-4A, DPA-4B.
▲ APPLIES TO DPA-4C.

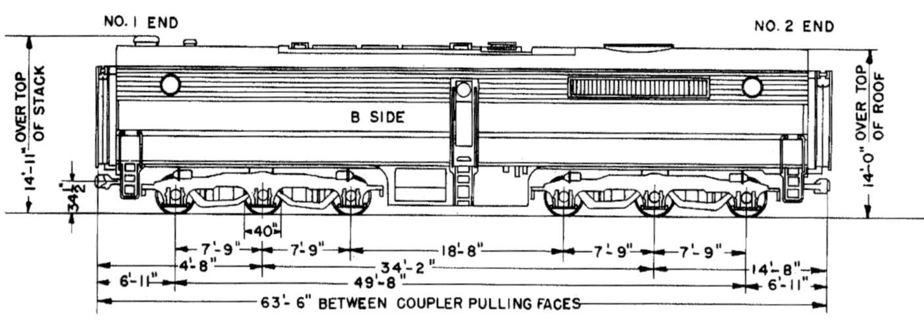

DIESEL ENGINE	ALCO MODEL 244
DIESEL ENGINE H.P.	2410(2250 FOR TRACTION)
NUMBER OF CYLINDERS	16-V TYPE
BORE AND STROKE	9"X10½"
ENGINE SPEED R.P.M.	IDLING 350, FULL LOAD 1000
GAIN GENERATOR	G. E. CO. TYPE GT-566-C1 DIRECT DRIVEN
MAIN GENERATOR VOLTAGE	MAX. 780V, FULL LOAD 755V
MAIN GENERATOR CAPACITY	1550KW
NUMBER AND TYPE OF TRACTION MOTORS	FOUR GE-752-A1
TRACTION MOTOR VENTILATION	FORCED
GEAR RATIO	60/23 (2.609)
CONTROL-TYPE AND VOLTAGE	G. E. CO. P, (M.U.) 75 V.

5-1-53

GEAR RATIO 60/23 (2.609)
CONTROL-TYPE AND VOLTAGE G. E. CO. P, (M.U.) 75 V.
5-1-53

MAXIMUM SPEED OF LOCOMOTIVE	100 M.P.H.
CONTINUOUS RATING - TRACTIVE EFFORT	33,000 LBS.
SPEED	21.8 M.P.H.
HORSEPOWER	1918
AIR SIGNAL	YES
TRAIN CONTROL	NONE

Class		Number	Builder	Order Number	c/n	Date	Disposition
DPA-4A		4208	Alco-GE	(S-3142)	78204	6/50	So 5/65 GE
"		4209	"	"	78205	"	So 5/65 GE
"		4210	"	"	78206	"	So 5/65 GE
"		4211	"	"	78207	"	So 5/65 GE
DPA-4B	Note	4212	Alco-GE	(S-3116)	75790	4/50	Rt 4/62, Sc 6/62
DPB-4A	"	4304	Alco-GE	(S-3057)	75789	"	Rt 4/62, Sc 7/62
DPA-4C	P&LE	4213	Alco-GE	(S-3172)	79040	5/52	Rt 12/60, SS 1/61
"	"	4214	"	"	79041	"	Rt 12/60, SS 1/61

Note: Acquired 8/51 from GE; ex-8375a and 8375b for GE's "More Power to America" special train.

No. 4208 Class DPA-4A a 2250 HP model PA-2 locomotive built by Alco in June 1950 and was sold to GE in May 1965. The enclosed coupler pilot doors shown here fully opened were removed at a later date. The four units in this class were first assigned to the *New England States*, but maintained at Collinwood.

Both: NYCSHS Collection

No. 4213 Class DPA-4C built for service on the P&LE between Pittsburgh and Buffalo, New York. Retired in December 1960 after only eight years.

CLASS DPA-5 (EP-22) ELECTRO-MOTIVE 2250HP Model E8

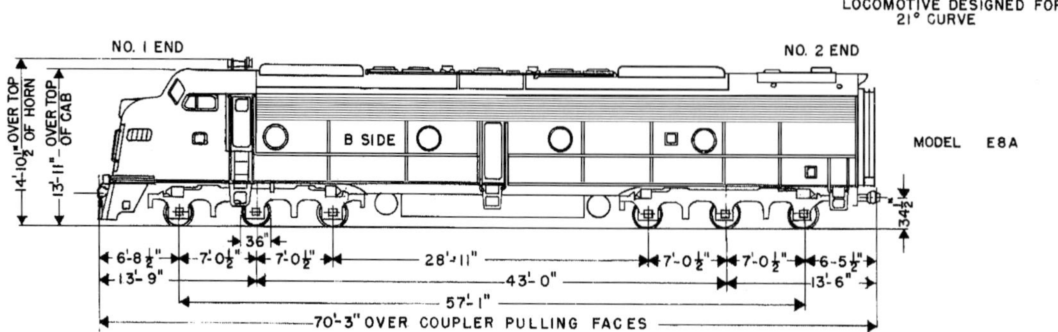

DIESEL ENGINE	GM. MODEL 567B
DIESEL ENGINE H.P. (TWO ENGINES)	2250 FOR TRACTION
NUMBER OF CYLINDERS (EACH ENGINE)	12-V TYPE
BORE AND STROKE	8½" x 10"
ENGINE SPEED R.P.M.	IDLING 275, FULL LOAD 800
MAIN GENERATOR	TWO EMD TYPE D-15B DIRECT DRIVEN
MAIN GENERATOR VOLTAGE	MAX. 995, FULL LOAD 930 V.
MAIN GENERATOR CAPACITY (TWO GENERATORS)	1600 KW.
NUMBER AND TYPE OF TRACTION MOTORS	FOUR EMD D-27
TRACTION MOTOR VENTILATION	FORCED
GEAR RATIO	55/22 (2.5)
CONTROL-TYPE AND VOLTAGE	EMD (M.U.) 75 V.

MAXIMUM SPEED OF LOCOMOTIVE	98 M.P.H.
CONTINUOUS RATING - TRACTIVE EFFORT	23,500 LBS.
SPEED	29.5 M.P.H.
AIR SIGNAL	YES
TRAIN CONTROL	G.R.S., SCHEDULE 2, SINGLE END

PRINTED 4-15-57

CLASS DPA-5

Class	Number	Builder	Order Number	c/n	Date	Disposition
DPA-5A	4036	EMD	(2016)	14425	6/51	PC, AM 256
"	4037	"	"	14426	"	PC
"	4038	"	"	14427	"	PC, AM 257
"	4039	"	"	14428	"	PC, CR
DPA-5B	4040	"	(6291)	14583	9/51	PC, AM 258
"	4041	"	"	14584	"	PC, AM 259
"	4042	"	"	14585	"	PC, CR
"	4043	"	"	14586	"	PC, AM 260
"	4044	"	"	14587	"	PC, AM 261
"	4045	"	"	15304	11/51	PC, AM 262
"	4046	"	"	15305	"	PC
"	4047	"	"	15306	"	PC, AM 263
"	4048	"	"	15307	1/52	PC, AM 264
"	4049	"	"	15308	"	PC, AM 265
"	4050	"	"	15309	"	PC
"	4051	"	"	15310	"	PC,AM 266
"	4052	"	"	15311	3/52	PC,AM 267
"	4053	"	"	15312	"	PC,AM 268
DPA-5C	4054	"	(6358)	15313	4/52	PC,AM 269
"	4055	"	"	15314	"	PC,AM 270
"	4056	"	"	15315	"	PC,AM 271
"	4057	"	"	15316	"	PC,AM 272
"	4058	"	"	15317	"	PC,AM 273
"	4059	"	"	15318	"	PC,AM 274
"	4060	"	"	15319	"	PC,AM 275
"	4061	"	"	15320	"	PC,AM 276
DPA-5D	4062	"	(6515)	18345	6/53	PC,CR
"	4063	"	"	18346	"	PC,CR

Class	Number	Builder	Order Number	c/n	Date	Disposition
DPA-5E	4064	EMD	(2055)	18522	6/53	PC
"	4065	"	"	18523	"	PC
"	4066	"	"	18524	"	PC
"	4067	"	"	18525	"	PC
"	4068	"	"	18526	"	PC re 10/73 4320 NJT
"	4069	"	"	18527	"	PC
"	4070	"	"	18528	"	PC re 10/73 4321 NJT
"	4071	"	"	18529	"	PC re 10/73 4322 NJT
"	4072	"	"	18530	"	PC
"	4073	"	"	18531	"	PC
"	4074	"	"	18532	"	PC
"	4075	"	"	18533	"	PC
"	4076	"	"	18534	8/53	PC re 10/73 4323 NJT
"	4077	"	"	18535	"	PC Wrecked 12/65, Sc 3/66
"	4078	"	"	18536	"	PC
"	4079	"	"	18537	"	PC re 10/73 4324 NJT
"	4080	"	"	18538	"	PC re 10/73 4325 NJT
"	4081	"	"	18539	"	PC
"	4082	"	"	18540	"	PC
"	4083	"	"	18541	"	PC re 10/73 4326 NJT
"	4084	"	"	18542	"	PC re 10/73 4327 NJT
"	4085	"	"	18543	"	PC re 10/73 4328 NJT
"	4086	"	"	18544	"	PC Rt 7/68, Sc
"	4087	"	"	18545	"	PC
"	4088	"	"	18546	"	PC
"	4089	"	"	18547	9/53	PC
"	4090	"	"	18548	"	PC
"	4091	"	"	18549	"	PC
"	4092	"	"	18550	"	PC
"	4093	"	"	18551	"	PC
"	4094	"	"	18552	"	PC
"	4095	"	"	18553	"	PC

NYCSHS Collection

There were sixty EMD model E8s on the NYC, including No. 4038 Class DPA-5A.

NYCSHS Collection

No. 4048 Class DPA-5B built by EMD January 1952 went on to Penn Central and then Amtrak as No. 264.

Collection of Louis A. Marre

No. 4074 Class DPA-5E while perfectly framed by the signal bridge, heads up train No. 27 the *New England States* as it leaves Boston on July 3, 1965.

NYCSHS Collection

CLASS DPA-6 Fairbanks-Morse 2400HP Model CPA-24-4

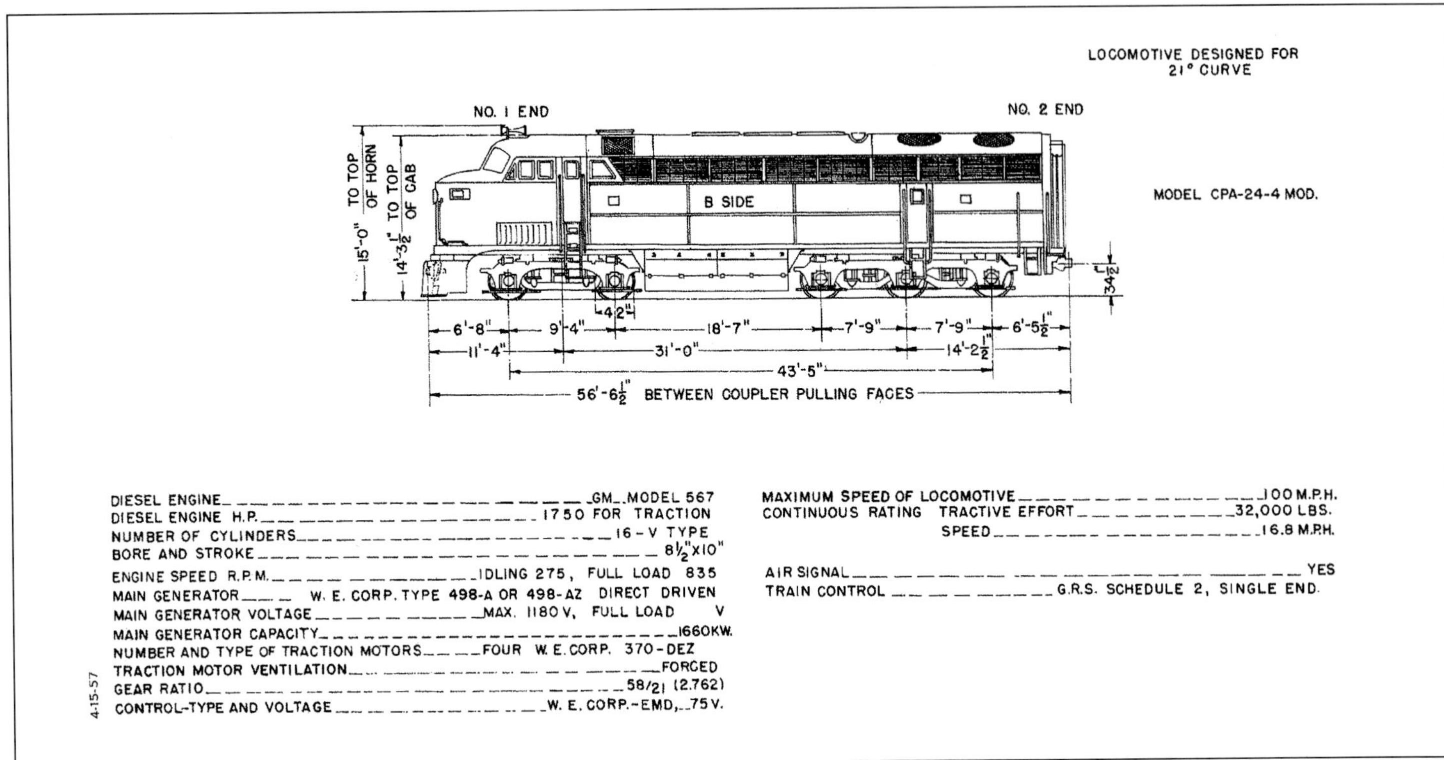

Class	Number	Builder	Order Number	c/n	Date	Re-Engined	Disposition
DPA-6A	4500	FM	(LD125)	24L552	3/52	10/55	Rt 10/66, SS 1/67
"	4501	"	"	24L553	"	12/55	Rt 10/66, SS 1/67
"	4502	"	"	24L554	"	11/55	Rt 10/66, SS 1/67
"	4503	"	"	24L555	"	4/56	Rt 10/66, SS 1/67
"	4504	"	"	24L556	"	3/56	Rt 10/66, SS 1/67
"	4505	"	"	24L557	"	10/55	Rt 10/66, SS 1/67
"	4506	"	"	24L558	4/52	2/56	Rt 10/66, SS 1/67
"	4507	"	"	24L559	"	3/56	Rt 10/66, SS 1/67

* Re-engined Collinwood Diesel Loco. Shop with EMD 567C (V-16) 1750 HP, using original Westinghouse electrical equipment. Tractive Effort (max) 62475, weight 306000.

NYCSHS Collection

No. 4503 Class DPA-6A a Fairbanks-Morse 2400 HP "C-Line" unit shown new at F-M in 1952. In three or four years all were equipped with EMD engines. All eight of the class was retired in October 1966.

CLASS DH-1 Baldwin 1000HP Model RP-210H Diesel Hydraulic

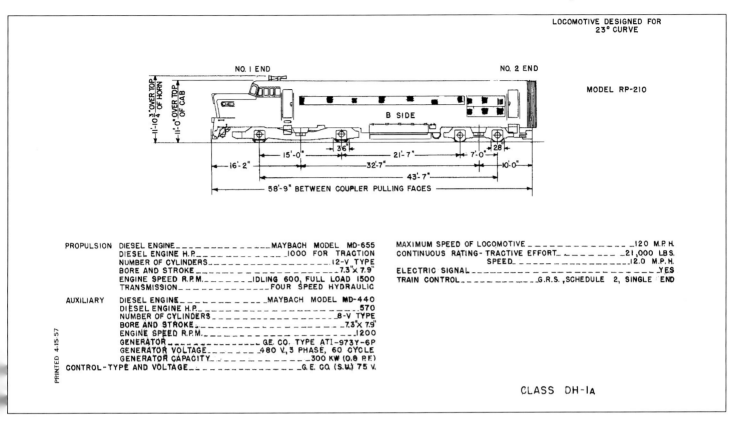

LOCOMOTIVE DESIGNED FOR 23° CURVE

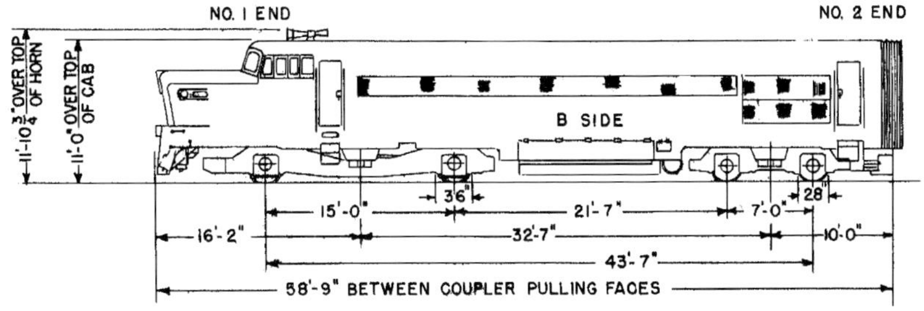

NO. 1 END — NO. 2 END — MODEL RP-210

B SIDE

11'-10¾" OVER TOP OF HORN — 11'-0" OVER TOP OF CAB

15'-0" — 3'6" — 21'-7" — 7'-0" — 28" — 16'-2" — 32'-7" — 10'-0" — 43'-7"

58'-9" BETWEEN COUPLER PULLING FACES

PROPULSION
- DIESEL ENGINE — MAYBACH MODEL MD-655
- DIESEL ENGINE H.P. — 1000 FOR TRACTION
- NUMBER OF CYLINDERS — 12-V TYPE
- BORE AND STROKE — 7.3"x 7.9"
- ENGINE SPEED R.P.M. — IDLING 600, FULL LOAD 1500
- TRANSMISSION — FOUR SPEED HYDRAULIC

AUXILIARY
- DIESEL ENGINE — MAYBACH MODEL MD-440
- DIESEL ENGINE H.P. — 570
- NUMBER OF CYLINDERS — 8-V TYPE
- BORE AND STROKE — 7.3"x 7.9"
- ENGINE SPEED R.P.M. — 1200
- GENERATOR — G.E. CO. TYPE ATI-973Y-6P
- GENERATOR VOLTAGE — 480 V., 3 PHASE, 60 CYCLE
- GENERATOR CAPACITY — 300 KW (0.8 P.F.)

CONTROL-TYPE AND VOLTAGE — G.E. CO. (S.U.) 75 V.

- MAXIMUM SPEED OF LOCOMOTIVE — 120 M.P.H.
- CONTINUOUS RATING-TRACTIVE EFFORT — 21,000 LBS.
- SPEED — 12.0 M.P.H.
- ELECTRIC SIGNAL — YES
- TRAIN CONTROL — G.R.S., SCHEDULE 2, SINGLE END

PRINTED 4-15-57

CLASS DH-1A

Class	Number	Builder	Order Number	c/n	Date	Disposition
DH-1A	20	Baldwin	120-1020	76108	5/56	Ret 12/60

Note: Equipped with Maybach Mech-Hydro 4 speed hydraulic transmission and Cardan drive to gears on driving axles.

Collection of Louis A. Marre

No. 20, Class DH-1A was built by Baldwin-Lima-Hamilton in May, 1956 for the lightweight "Explorer" train. This blue and yellow locomotive spent much of its service life in storage or the repair shops where it acquired the nickname "Mickey Mouse." After retirement in December 1960, the "X-Plorer" was sold to the Pickens Railroad.

Diesel Freight Transfer Locomotives

CLASS DFT-1 FAIRBANKS MORSE 2000HP Model H20-44

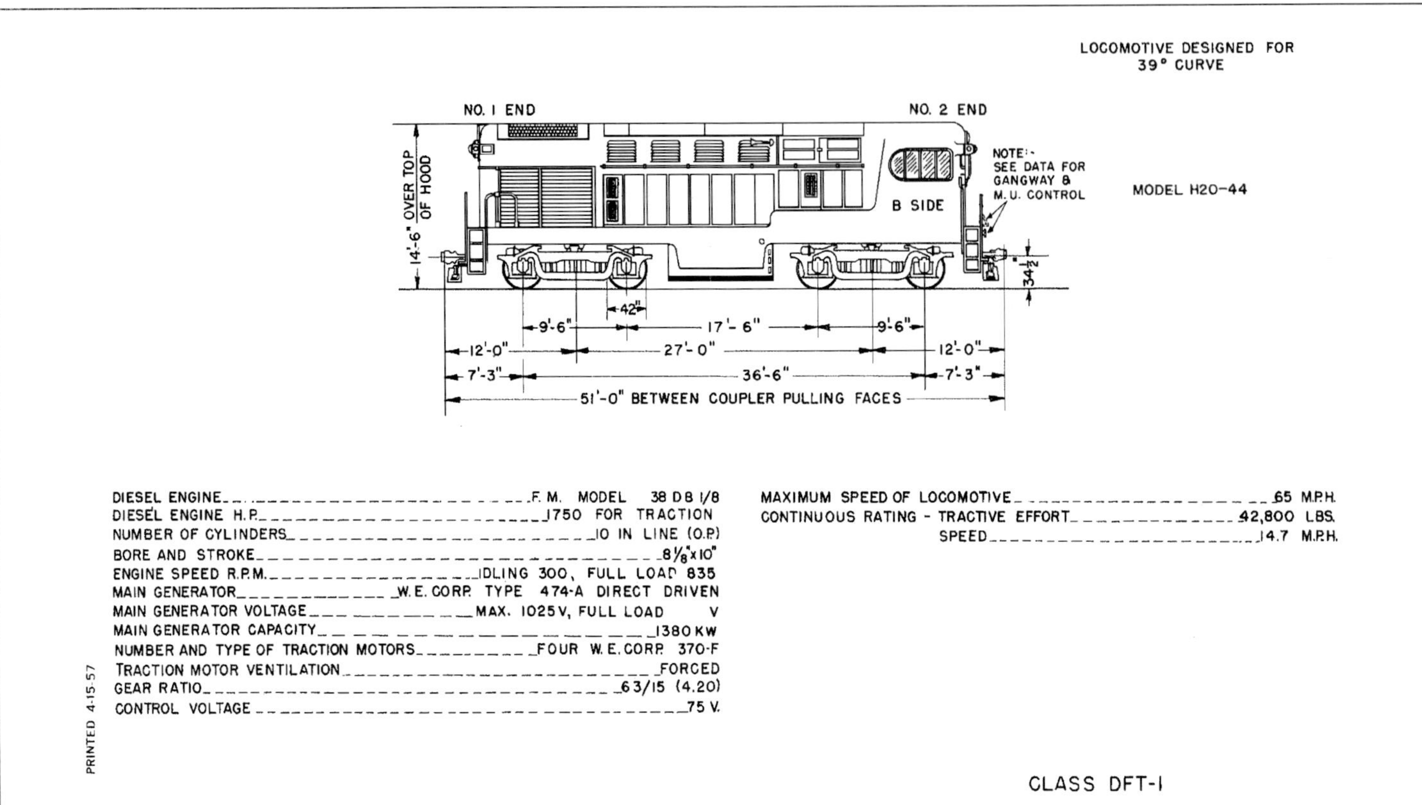

Class	Road	Number	Builder	Order Number	c/n	Date	Disposition
DFT-1A		7100	FM	(LD44)	20L23	7/48	So 6/64 GE
"		7101	"	"	20L24	"	So 11/64 GE
"		7102	"	"	20L25	8/48	Rt 7/65 GE
"		7103	"	"	20L26	"	Rt 8/65 GE
"		7104	"	"	20L27	"	Rt 8/65 GE
"		7105	"	"	20L28	9/48	Rt 8/65 GE
DFT-1D		7106	"	"	20L29	10/48	So 6/64 GE
"		7107	"	"	20L30	"	So 12/64 GE
"		7108	"	"	20L31	"	So 1/65 GE
"		7109	"	"	20L32	"	So 10/64 GE
DFT-1B	IHB*	7110	FM	(LD55)	20L18	7/48	Rt 3/66
"	IHB*	7111	"	"	20L19	"	Rt 3/66
"	IHB*	7112	"	"	20L20	"	Rt 3/66
"	IHB*	7113	"	"	20L21	"	Rt 3/66
"	IHB*	7114	"	"	20L22	"	Rt 3/66
DFT-1C	IHB@	7115	FM	(LD61)	20L35	9/48	So 6/64 GE
"	IHB@	7116	"	"	20L36	"	So 6/64 GE
DFT-1E	IHB*	7117	FM	(LD78)	20L49	4/49	Rt 3/66
"	IHB*	7118	"	"	20L50	5/49	Rt 3/66

* Acquired 2/50 by NYC. @ Acquired 11/49 by NYC.

Note: 7100 to 7107, 7110 to 7113, 7117, 7118 equipped for MU operation, both ends. 7108, 7109, 7115 and 7116 equipped for M.U. operation on No. 2 end only. 7114 not equipped for MU operation.

NYCSHS Collection

No. 7108 Class DFT-1D at Fairbanks-Morse in October1948. F-M was in such a rush to get the unit photographed that it had not even been stenciled with the road number and name, the only clue to its identity is the number board glass next to the classification lamp.

H. L. Vail Collection

No. 7113 Class DFT-1B was a 2000 HP "Transfer Switcher" built by Fairbanks-Morse in September 1948 for the Indiana Harbor Belt, it was purchased by the NYC in February 1950 and retired in March 1966. The paint scheme was "Pacemaker" green with an orange "lightning" stripe with red trim, orange lettering and pilot stripes with a black underframe and trucks.

CLASS DRS-1 and DRSP-1 (ARS-10m) Alco-GE 1000 HP Model RS-1

LOCOMOTIVE DESIGNED FOR 57.5° CURVE

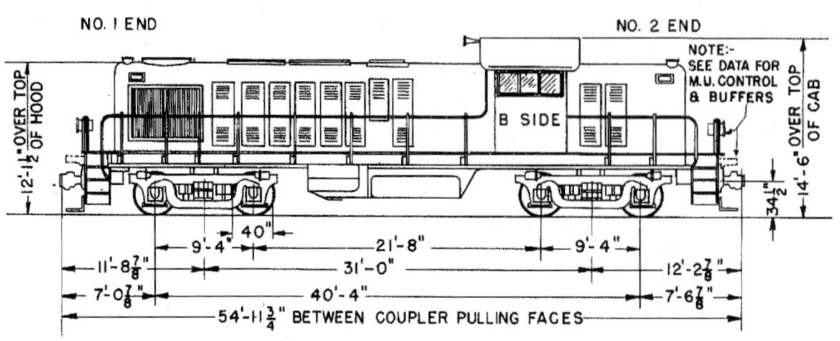

DIESEL ENGINE .... ALCO...MODEL 6-L-25
DIESEL ENGINE H.P. .... 1095 (1000 FOR TRACTION)
NUMBER OF CYLINDERS .... 6 IN LINE
BORE AND STROKE .... 12½x13"
ENGINE SPEED R.P.M. .... IDLING 270, FULL LOAD 740
MAIN GENERATOR .... G.E. CO. TYPE GT-553-C3 DIRECT DRIVEN
MAIN GENERATOR VOLTAGE .... MAX. 900V., FULL LOAD 750V.
MAIN GENERATOR CAPACITY .... 640 K.W.
NUMBER AND TYPE OF TRACTION MOTORS .... FOUR GE-731-D3
TRACTION MOTOR VENTILATION .... FORCED
GEAR RATIO 75/16 (4.6888)
CONTROL VOLTAGE .... 75 V.

MAXIMUM SPEED OF LOCOMOTIVE .... 60 M.P.H.
CONTINUOUS RATING - TRACTIVE EFFORT .... 34,000 LBS.
SPEED .... 8.0 M.P.H.
HORSEPOWER 725

PRINTED 5-1-53

CLASS DRS-1, DRSP-1

Class	Original Number	Renumber 1966	Builder	Order Number	c/n	Date	Disposition
DRSP-1A*	8100	9900	Alco-GE	(S-3058)	75825	2/48	PC Rt EMD
DRS-1B	8101	9901	"	(S-3052)	75680	"	PC
"	8102	9902	"	"	75681	"	PC
"	8103	9903	"	"	75682	"	PC
"	8104	9904	"	"	75683	"	PC
"	8105	9905	"	"	75684	"	PC
"	8106	9906	"	(S-3058)	75826	3/48	PC
"	8107	9907	"	"	75827	"	PC
"	8108	9908	"	"	75828	"	PC,CR
DRS-1C	8109	9909	"	(S-3133)	77986	4/50	PC Rt EMD
"	8110	9910	"	"	77987	"	PC
"	8111	9911	"	"	77988	"	PC
DRSP-1D*	8112	9912	"	(S-3139)	78090	5/50	PC
"	8113	9913	"	"	78091	"	PC

*Re-classified DRS-1A and DRS-ID a/c Steam Generator removed; ballast added
General Note: All built with Double End Train Control; 8100-8108 , 8112-8113 built with End Buffers and Air Signal; 8109-8111 built with Air Signal and no end buffers; 8100-8108 MU control both ends 8109-8113 MU control No 2 end only; 8100-8111 no platform gangway; 8112 8113 platform gangway No 2 end only; DRSP-1D built with Layover heating.

No 8109 Class DRS-1c was a 1000 HP Alco RS-1 built in April 1950. This locomotive was equipped with MU controls on the No. 2 or cab end only and was used mostly in New York state, after assignment to the B&A.

Both: NYCSHS Collection

No 8205 Class DRS-2B was a 1500 HP Model RS-2 built by Alco in January 1949. This locomotive was equipped with MU controls on both ends.

CLASS DRS-2 and DRSP-2 (ARS-16) Alco-GE 1500 HP Model RS-2

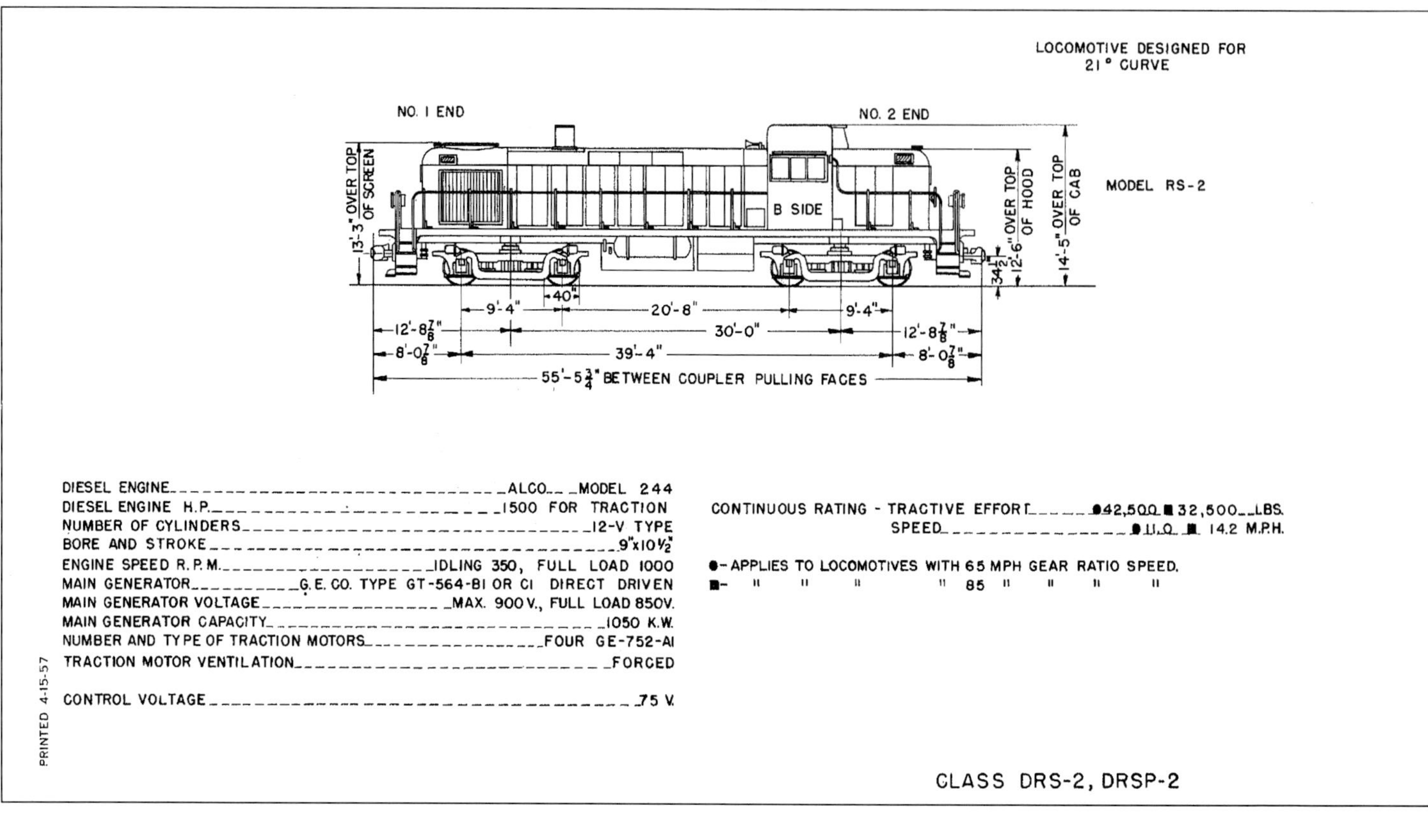

Class	Number	Re '66	Builder	Order Number	c/n	Date	Disposition
DRSP-2A*	8200		Alco-GE	(S-3053)	75685	2/48	Rt 2/65 So 3/65 GE
"	8201		"	"	75686	"	Rt 4/61, & 5/61
DRS-2B	8202		"	(S-3074)	76241	1/49	Rt 4/61, Sc 6/61
"	8203		"	"	76242	"	So 2/66 GE as 8355
"	8204		"	"	76243	"	Rt 9/65, So 10/65 GE
"	8205		"	"	76244	"	So 3/66 GE as 8357
"	8206		"	"	76245	"	Rt 2/65, So 3/65 GE
"	8207	5207	"	"	76246	"	PC Rt 7/68
"	8208		"	(S-3089)	76632	"	Rt 9/65, So 11/65 GE
DRSP-2C	*8209		"	(S-3122)	77900	2/50	So 2/65 GE
"	8210	5210	"	"	77901	"	PC
"	8211@	5229	"	"	77902	"	PC Rt 3/75
"	8212	5212	"	"	77903	"	PC
"	8213	5213	"	"	77904	"	Rt 10/67
"	8214	5214	"	"	77905	"	So 12/66 GE
"	8215	5215	"	"	77906	"	PC
"	8216		"	"	77907	"	So 1/65 GE
"	8217		"	"	77908	"	So 8/65 GE
"	8218		"	"	77909	"	So 8/65 GE
"	8219		"	"	77910	"	Rt 9/65, So 10/65 GE
"	8220		"	"	77911	"	Rt 2/65, So 3/65 GE
"	8221	5221	"	"	77912	"	So 11/67 Alco
"	8222		"	"	77913	"	Rt 2/65, So 3/65 GE

Note @8211 re '65 2nd 8229, then 5229.* Re DRS-2A and 2C when steam generator removed

General Note: Locomotives built with end buffers, Air Signal, and Double End Train Control; 8200-8208 built with MU control No. 1 and 2 ends; 8209-8222 built with MU controls No. 2 end only.

CLASS DRSP-3 (BRS-15as) BALDWIN 1500HP Model RS 4-4-15

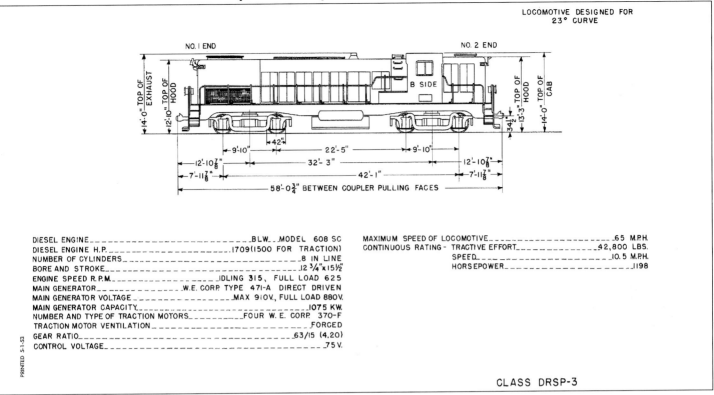

LOCOMOTIVE DESIGNED FOR 23° CURVE

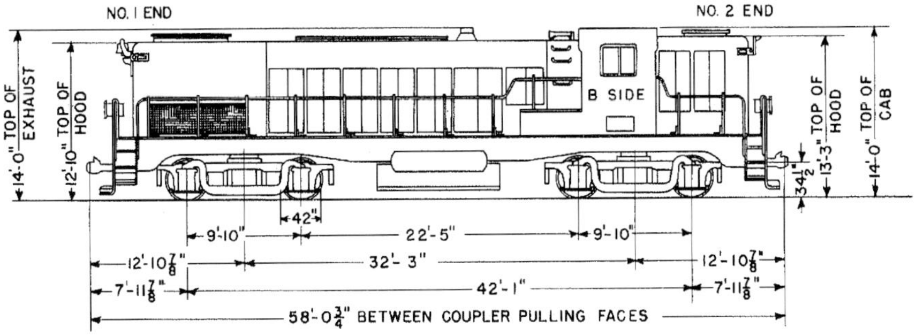

NO. 1 END — NO. 2 END — B SIDE

14'-0" TOP OF EXHAUST — 12'-10" TOP OF HOOD — 34½" — 13'-3" TOP OF HOOD — 14'-0" TOP OF CAB

9'-10" — 42" — 22'-5" — 9'-10"

12'-10⅞" — 32'-3" — 12'-10⅞"

7'-11⅞" — 42'-1" — 7'-11⅞"

58'-0¾" BETWEEN COUPLER PULLING FACES

DIESEL ENGINE — BLW. MODEL 608 SC
DIESEL ENGINE H.P. — 1709 (1500 FOR TRACTION)
NUMBER OF CYLINDERS — 8 IN LINE
BORE AND STROKE — 12 ¾" x 15½"
ENGINE SPEED R.P.M. — IDLING 315, FULL LOAD 625
MAIN GENERATOR — W.E. CORP. TYPE 471-A DIRECT DRIVEN
MAIN GENERATOR VOLTAGE — MAX 910V., FULL LOAD 880V.
MAIN GENERATOR CAPACITY — 1075 KW.
NUMBER AND TYPE OF TRACTION MOTORS — FOUR W. E. CORP. 370-F
TRACTION MOTOR VENTILATION — FORCED
GEAR RATIO — 63/15 (4.20)
CONTROL VOLTAGE — 75 V.

MAXIMUM SPEED OF LOCOMOTIVE — 65 M.P.H.
CONTINUOUS RATING - TRACTIVE EFFORT — 42,800 LBS.
SPEED — 10.5 M.P.H.
HORSEPOWER — 1198

PRINTED 5-1-53

CLASS DRSP-3

Class	Original Number	Re '51	Re '66	Builder	Order Number	c/n	Date	Re-Eng.	Disposition
DRSP-3A	8300	7300		BLW	(47512)	73479	7/48	5/56	Rt 2/66, Sc
"	8301	7301	(5991)	"	"	73480	"	4/56	Rt 8/67

*Re-engined Collinwood Diesel Loco Shop with EMD-567 C (V-16) set at 1500HP, using original WE electric equipment, and re-geared for 85 mph, Tractive Effort (max.) 66950, Weight 267800.
General Note: 1966 Class and number shown ( ) assigned but never put on locomotive. Locomotives built with Air Signal. End Buffers, MU control at both ends, Double End Train Control; and had "one piece" cast steel frame.

Another odd-ball road switcher assigned to the Chicago cowhide service was this Baldwin 1500 HP unit at La Salle Street in September 1961. It had been re-engined in May 1956 and lasted almost ten years more.

Louis A. Marre

CLASS DRS-4 and DRSP-4 (ERS-15, s) EMD 1500 HP Model GP7

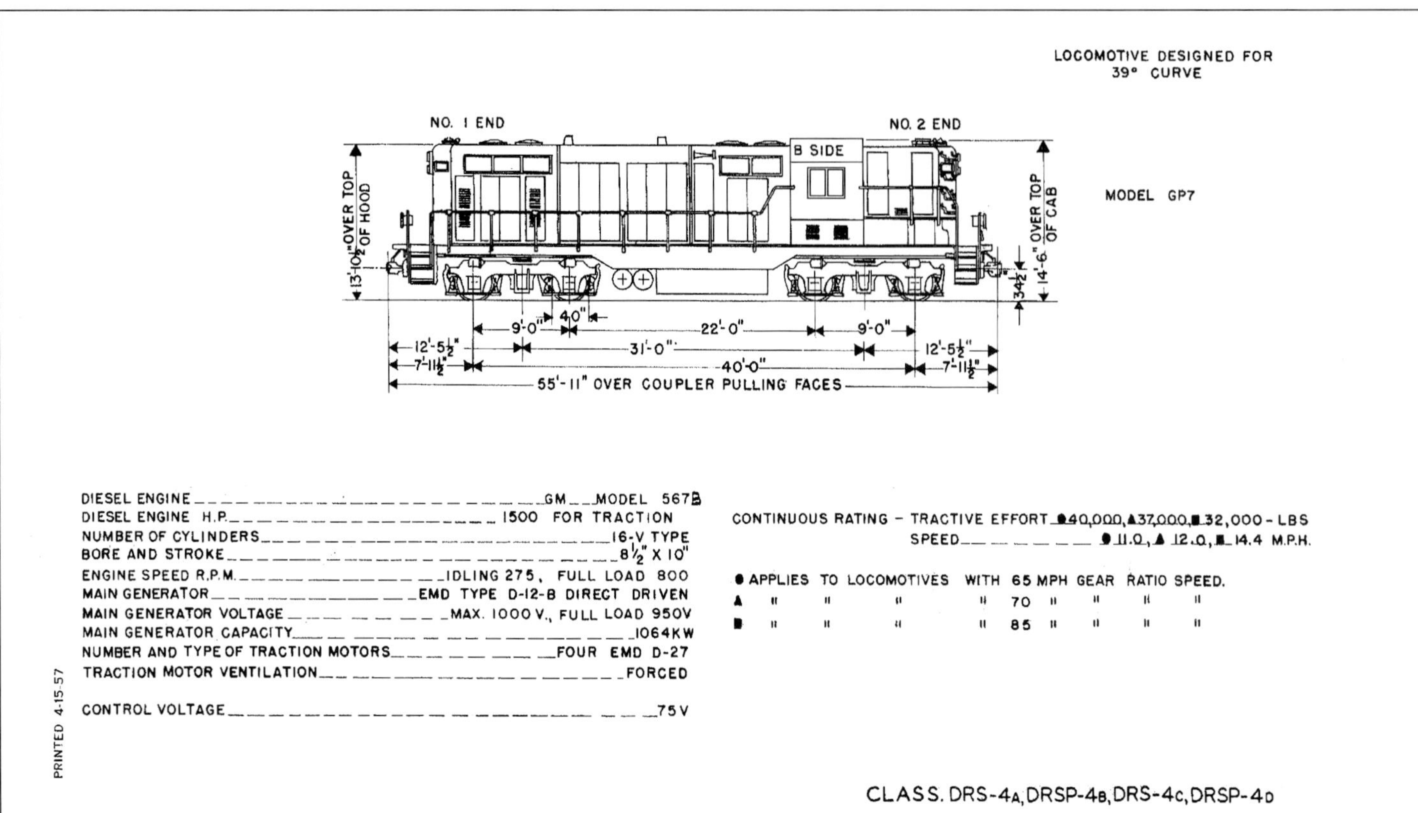

Class	Road	Original Number		Re '66	Builder	Order Number	c/n	Date	Disposition
DRS-4A		5600			EMD	(5012)	9227	8/50	PC, CR
"		5601			"	"	9228	"	PC, CR
"		5602			"	"	9229	"	PC, CR
"		5603			"	"	9230	"	PC, CR
"		5604			"	"	9231	"	PC, CR
"		5605			"	"	9232	"	PC, CR
"		5606			"	"	9233	"	PC, CR
"		5607			"	"	9234	"	PC, CR re '78 5450
DRSP-4B*		5608			EMD	(6125)	9235	"	So 12/66 GE
"		5609			"	"	9236	"	PC, CR
"		@5610	6052	7452	"	"	11772	"	PC, CR
"		5611			"	"	11773	"	PC, CR
DRS-4C	P&E	5612			EMD	(6173)	12998	11/50	PC, CR
"	"	5613			"	"	12999	"	PC, CR re 5722, 5402
"	"	5614			"	"	13000	"	PC, CR re 5725, 5405
"	"	5615			"	"	13001	"	PC, CR re 5438
"	"	5616			"	"	13002	12/50	PC, CR
"	"	5617			"	"	13003	"	PC, CR re 5451
"	"	5618			"	"	13004	"	PC, CR re 5437
"	"	5619			"	"	13005	"	PC, CR re 5723, 5403
"	"	5620	5686 @		"	"	13006	"	PC, CR
"	"	5621			"	"	13007	"	PC, CR re 5436
"	"	5622			"	"	13008	"	PC, CR re 5409
"	"	5623			"	"	13009	"	PC, CR
DRS-4D*	"	5624			EMD	(6196)	13010	12/50	PC, CR
"	"	5625			"	"	13011	"	PC, CR

Note : 5620 re 9/67 2nd 5686. 5610 re '65 2nd 6052
* DRSP-4b and 4d re DRS-4b and 4d when steam generators removed and ballast added.

No 5625 Class DRSP-4D along with 5624 were the two members of this sub-class lettered for the Peoria & Eastern when built in December 1950. When the steam generator was later removed they would be re-classified to DRS-4d.

Both: NYCSHS Collection

No 5635 Class DRS-4E was a EMD GP-7 built in August 1951 for Ohio Central service, maintained at Stanley.

Class	Original Number	Builder	Order Number	c/n	Date	Disposition
DRS-4E	5626	EMD	(5052)	14188	7/51	PC,CR
"	5627	"	"	14189	"	PC,CR
"	5628	"	"	14190	"	PC,CR re 5452
"	5629	"	"	14191	"	PC,CR
"	5630	"	"	14192	8/51	PC,CR
"	5631	"	"	14193	7/51	So 10/64 EMD as 5813
"	5632	"	"	14194	8/51	PC,CR
"	5633	"	"	14195	"	PC,CR
"	5634	"	"	14196	"	PC,CR
"	5635	"	"	14197	"	PC,CR
"	5636	"	"	14198	"	PC,CR
"	5637	"	"	14199	"	PC,CR
"	5638	"	"	14200	"	PC,CR
"	5639	"	"	14201	"	PC,CR re 5433
"	5640	"	"	14202	"	PC,CR
"	5641	"	"	14203	"	PC,CR
"	5642	"	"	14204	9/51	PC,CR
"	5643	"	"	14205	"	PC,CR
"	5644	"	"	14206	"	PC,CR
"	5645	"	"	14207	"	PC,CR
"	5646	"	"	14208	"	PC,CR
"	5647	"	"	14209	"	PC,CR
"	5648	"	"	14210	"	PC,CR
"	5649	"	"	14211	"	PC,CR
"	5650	"	"	14212	"	PC,CR
"	5651	"	"	14213	"	PC,CR
"	5652	"	"	14214	"	PC,CR
"	5653	"	"	14215	"	PC,CR
"	5654	"	"	14216	10/51	PC,CR
"	5655	"	"	14217	"	PC,CR
"	5656	"	"	14218	"	PC,CR
"	5657	"	"	14219	"	PC,CR
"	5658	"	"	14220	"	PC,CR
"	5659	"	"	14221	"	PC,CR
"	5660	"	"	14222	"	PC,CR re 5441
"	5661	"	"	14223	"	PC,CR
"	5662	"	"	14224	"	PC,CR re 5435
"	5663	"	"	14225	"	PC,CR
"	5664	"	"	14226	"	PC,CR
"	5665	"	"	14227	"	PC,CR
"	5666	"	"	14228	"	PC,CR
"	5667	"	"	14229	11/51	PC,CR
"	5668	"	"	14230	"	PC,CR
"	5669	"	"	14231	"	PC,CR
"	5670	"	"	14232	"	PC,CR
"	5671	"	"	14233	"	PC,CR
"	5672	"	"	14234	"	So 10/64 EMD as 5817
"	5673	"	"	14235	"	PC,CR
"	5674	"	"	14236	"	PC,CR
"	5675	"	"	14237	"	PC,CR

Class		Original Number		Builder	Order Number	c/n	Date	Disposition	
DRS-4F	P&LE	5676		EMD	(5120)	14573	9/51	P&LE 1533	So 12/75 Monga.1510
"	"	5677		"	"	14574	"	P&LE 1532	So 2/77 ICG 7746
"	"	5678		"	"	14575	"	P&LE 1531	So 2/77 ICG 7910
"	"	5679		"	"	14576	"	P&LE 1530	So 11/77 Morr.Knud.
"	"	5680		"	"	14577	"	P&LE 1529	So 11/77 Morr.Knud.
"	"	5681		"	"	14578	"	P&LE 1528	So 12/75 Monga.1508
DRSP-4G*	P&LE	5682		EMD	(6306)	14579	9/51	P&LE 1527	So 2/77 ICG 7954
"	"	5683		"	"	14580	"	P&LE 1526	So 12/73 ICG 7713
"	"	5684		"	"	14581	"	P&LE 1525	So 11/77 Morr.Knud.
"	"	5685		"	"	14582	"	P&LE 1524	So 12/75 Monga.
DRS-4H		@5686	5620	EMD	(5104)	15460	3/52	PC,CR	
"		5687		"	"	15461	"	PC,CR	
"		5688		"	"	15462	"	PC,CR	
"		5689		"	"	15463	"	PC,CR	
"		5690		"	"	15464	"	PC,CR	
"		5691		"	"	15465	"	PC,CR	
"		5692		"	"	15466	"	PC,CR	
"		5693		"	"	15467	"	PC,CR	
"		5694		"	"	15468	"	PC,CR	
"		5695		"	"	15469	"	PC,CR	
"		5696		"	"	15470	"	PC,CR	
"		5697		"	"	15471	"	PC,CR	
"		5698		"	"	15472	"	PC,CR	
"		5699		"	"	15473	"	PC,CR	
"		5700		"	"	15474	"	PC,CR	
"		5701		"	"	15475	"	PC,CR	
"		5702		"	"	15476	"	PC,CR	
"		5703		"	"	15477	"	PC,CR	
"		5704		"	"	15478	"	PC,CR	
"		5705		"	"	15479	"	PC,CR	
"		5706		"	"	15480	4/52	PC,CR	
"		5707		"	"	15481	"	PC,CR	
"		5708		"	"	15482	"	PC,CR	
DRSP-4J*		5709		EMD	(6345)	15483	3/52	PC,CR	
"		5710		"	"	15484	"	PC,CR	
"		5711		"	"	15485	"	PC,CR	
"		5712		"	"	15486	"	PC,CR	
DRS-4K	P&LE	5713		EMD	(6369)	16340	5/52	P&LE 1523	So 7/74 Monga.1505
"	"	5714		"	"	16341	"	P&LE 1522	So 2/77 ICG 7912
"	"	5715		"	"	16342	"	P&LE 1521	So 9/76 East.Kodak
"	"	5716		"	"	16343	"	P&LE 1520	So 7/74 Monga.1504
"	"	5717		"	"	16344	"	P&LE 1519	So 12/73 ICG 7712
"	"	5718		"	"	16345	"	P&LE 1518	So 12/73 ICG 7711
"	"	5719		"	"	16346	"	Wrck., So '66 NYC	PC,CR Rt '84.
"	"	5720		"	"	16347	"	P&LE 1517	So 7/74 Monga.1503
"	"	5721		"	"	16348	"	P&LE 1516	So 12/73 ICG 7710
"	"	5722		"	"	16349	"	P&LE 1515	So 12/73 ICG 7909
"	"	5723		"	"	16350	"	P&LE 1514	So 2/77 ICG 7903
"	"	5724		"	"	16351	"	P&LE 1513	So 6/74 Monga.1502

Note * : Re-classified DRS-4g, 4j when steam generator removed, ballast added. @5686 re 1967 to 2nd 5620.
All DRS-4 freight road switchers for P&LE were painted Pacemaker green with light grey lightining stripes, white lettering, black trucks and underbody. All DRSP-4 passenger road switchers for P&LE were painted 2-tone grey, as were Class DRSP-4Q NYC units.

Class	Road	Original Number	Re '66	Builder	Order Number	c/n	Date	Disposition	Disposition
DRS-4L	P&LE	5725		EMD	(5184)	17971	4/53	P&LE 1512	So 12/73 ICG 7708
"	"	5726		"	"	17972	"	P&LE 1511	So 12/73 ICG 7707
"	"	5727		"	"	17973	"	P&LE 1510	So 2/77 ICG 7965
"	"	5728		"	"	17974	"	P&LE 1509	So 12/73 ICG 7706
"	"	5729		"	"	17975	"	P&LE 1508	So 12/73 ICG 7705
"	"	5730		"	"	17976	"	P&LE 1507	So 2/77 ICG 7967
"	"	5731		"	"	17977	"	P&LE 1506	So 7/74 Monga.1501
"	"	5732		"	"	17978	"	P&LE 1505	So 2/77 ICG 7911
"	"	5733		"	"	17979	"	P&LE 1504	So 7/74 Monga.1500
"	"	5734		"	"	17980	"	P&LE 1503	So 7/77 ICG 7963
DRSP-4M*	P&LE	5735	5928	EMD	(5253)	17981	4/53	P&LE 1502	So 2/77 ICG 7800
"	"	5736	5929	"	"	17982	"	P&LE 1501	So 8/85 Yo.& Aus.
"	"	5737	5930	"	"	17983	"	P&LE 1500	Rt'85
DRSP-4N*		5738		EMD	(5183)	18442	5/53	PC,CR	
"		5739		"	"	18443	"	PC,CR	
"		5740		"	"	18444	"	PC,CR	
"		5741		"	"	18445	"	PC,CR	
"		5742		"	"	18446	"	PC,CR	
"		5743		"	"	18447	"	PC,CR	
"		5744		"	"	18448	"	PC,CR re 5411	
"		5745		"	"	18449	"	PC,CR	
"		5746		"	"	18550	"	PC,CR	
"		5747		"	"	18551	"	PC,CR	
"		5748		"	"	18552	"	PC,CR	
"		5749		"	"	18553	"	PC,CR	
"		5750		"	"	18554	"	PC,CR	
"		5751		"	"	18555	"	PC,CR	
"		5752		"	"	18556	"	PC	
"		5753	5900 +	"	"	18557	"	PC	
"		5754		"	"	18558	"	PC,CR	
"		5755		"	"	18559	"	PC,CR	
"		5756		"	"	18560	"	PC,CR	
"		5757		"	"	18561	"	PC,CR re 2nd 5752	
"		5758		"	"	18562	"	So 12/66 EMD as 5901	
"		5759		"	"	18563	"	PC,CR	
"		5760		"	"	18564	"	PC,CR	
"		5761		"	"	18565	6/53	PC,CR	
"		5762	5902 +	"	"	18566	"	PC	
"		5763	@7519	"	"	18567	"	PC	
"		5764		"	"	18568	"	PC,CR	
"		5765	5903	"	"	18569	"	PC,CR	
"		5766	5904 +	"	"	18570	"	PC	
"		5767	5905 +	"	"	18571	"	PC	
"		5768	5906 +	"	"	18572	"	PC	
"		5769	5907 +	"	"	18573	"	PC	
"		5770	5908 +	"	"	18574	"	PC re 5432	
"		5771	5909	"	"	18575	"	PC,CR	
"		5772	5910 +	"	"	18576	"	PC	
"		5773	5911 +	"	"	18577	"	PC	
"		5774	5912	"	"	18578	"	PC,CR re 5453	
"		5775	5913 +	"	"	18579	"	PC	
"		5776		"	"	18580	"	PC,CR	

Note *: Many 5700's were reclassified DRS-4M and DRS-4N when converted to freight service (Steam Generator removed, ballast added., 65 mph gearing). In 1966, remianing DRSP units were renumbered in 5900 series as listed, then renumbered back to original 5700's when converted to freight service. + Original number restored. @5763 re '65 to 2nd 5948, then 7519.

Class	Original Number	Re '66	Builder	Order Number	c/n	Date	Disposition
DRSP-4N*	5777		EMD	(5183)	18481	6/53	PC, CR
"	5778		"	"	18482	"	PC, CR
"	5779		"	"	18483	"	Wreck, So 11/65 GE
"	5780		"	"	18484	"	PC, CR
"	5781		"	"	18485	"	PC, CR
"	5782	5914	"	"	18486	"	PC, CR
"	5783	5915+	"	"	18487	"	PC
"	5784	5916	"	"	18488	"	PC, CR
"	5785	5917	"	"	18489	"	PC, CR
"	5786		"	"	18490	"	PC, CR re 5440
"	5787		"	"	18491	"	
"	5788		"	"	18492	"	PC, CR
"	5789	5918+	"	"	18493	"	PC
"	5790	5919+	"	"	18494	"	PC
"	5791	5920	"	"	18495	"	PC
"	5792		"	"	18496	"	PC, CR
"	5793		"	"	18497	"	PC, CR
"	5794	5921+	"	"	18498	"	PC
"	5795	5922+	"	"	18499	"	PC
"	5796		"	"	18500	"	So 10/64 EMD
"	5797	5923	"	"	18501	"	PC, CR
"	5798		"	"	18502	"	So 10/64, EMD
"	5799	5924	"	"	18503	"	PC
"	5800		"	"	18504	"	PC, CR
"	5801	5925+	"	"	18505	"	PC
"	5802		"	"	18506	"	PC, CR
"	5803		"	"	18507	"	PC, CR
"	5804		"	"	18508	"	PC, CR re 5412
"	5805		"	"	18509	"	PC, CR
"	5806	5926	"	"	18510	"	PC re 5765
"	5807	5927+	"	"	18511	"	PC

Note * Re-classed DRS-4N when steam generator removed and ballast added, re-geared to 65 mph
+ Previous number restored.

NYCSHS Collection

No 5690 Class DRS-4H note the dynamic braking and winterization hatch on top. This class was first assigned to Ashtabula-Youngstown service.

Class	Original Number	Re '64	Re '66	Builder	Order Number	c/n	Date	Disposition
DRS-4P	5808			EMD	(5280)	18512	5/53	PC, CR
"	5809			"	"	18513	"	PC, CR
"	5810			"	"	18514	"	PC, CR
"	5811			"	"	18515	"	PC, CR
"	5812			"	"	18516	"	PC, CR
"	5813@	5631		"	"	18517	6/53	PC, CR re 5434
"	5814@	6020	7420	"	"	18518	"	PC, CR
"	5815@	5980	7380	"	"	18519	"	PC
"	5816@	5969	7369	"	"	18520	"	PC
"	5817@	5672		"	"	18521	"	PC

Class	Original Number	Former	Builder	Order Number	c/n	Date	Date Acquired	Disposition
DRS-4Q	5818	C&O 5720	GMD	(6109)	A154	3/51	1/56	PC, CR
"	5819	" 5721	"	"	A155	"	"	PC, CR
"	5820	" 5722	"	"	A156	"	"	PC, CR
"	5821	" 5723	"	"	A157	"	"	PC, CR
"	5822	" 5724	"	"	A158	"	"	PC, CR
"	5823	" 5725	"	"	A159	"	"	PC, CR
"	5824	" 5726	"	"	A160	"	"	PC, CR
"	5825	" 5727	"	"	A161	"	"	PC, CR
"	5826	" 5728	"	"	A162	"	"	PC, CR
"	5827	" 5729	"	"	A163	"	"	PC, CR

@ 5813-5817 re '64 to 2nd 5631,etc.

General Note: Gear ratio on all DRSP-4N except 5739, 5741, 5743, 5766, 5769 changed by NYC to 59:18 for 85 mph by 4/1957. DRSP-4N units re-numbered to 5900-5927 in 1966 retained 85 mph gear ratio until again re-built and re-numbered as above. General Notes on entire Class DRS/DRSP-4 as originally built: Geared speed 65 mph on all except DRSP- 4D-71 mph and DRSP-4N- 71 mph.

All built with Air Signal; Platform Gangway and MU control on No 1 and 2 ends on Sub Class E, H, J, L, M, N, P, Q platform gangway and MU control on No. 2 end only on Sub Classes A, B, C, D, G, K; End Buffers on Sub Classes A, B, D, E, G, J, M, N ; Double End Train Control on all except DRS-4C none ; DRSP-4D none; Layover Heating on DRS-4C and DRS-4D only; DRS-4H built with Dynamic Brake.

NYCSHS Collection

No 5735 Class DRSP-4M as built in April 1953 for the P&LE, later renumbered 1502. This unit was painted in the two tone grey scheme. Also of interest is the train control motor-generator located on the side of the short hood.

5690
5690

CLASS DRSP-5 (LRS-12as) Lima 1200 HP Road Switcher

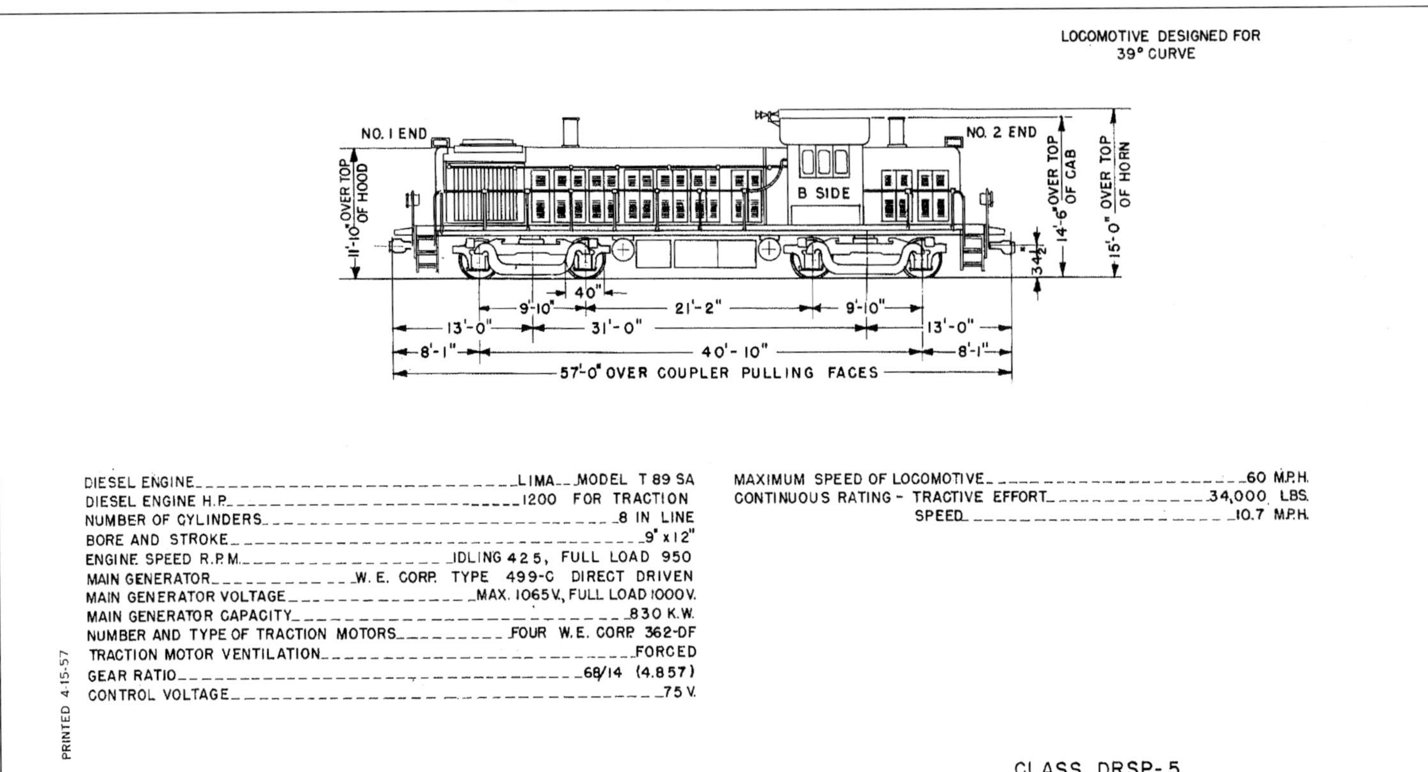

Class	Number	Re '53	Re '66	Builder	Order Number	c/n	Date	Disposition
DRSP-5A*	5800	6200		Lima	(1217)	9423	8/50	Rt 2/65, SS
"	5801	6201		"	"	9424	9/50	Rt 2/65, SS
"	5802	6202		"	"	9425	"	Rt 2/65, SS
"	5803	6203		"	"	9426	"	Rt 1/65, SS
"	5804	6204		"	"	9427	"	Rt 2/65
"	5805	6205		"	"	9428	"	Rt 2/65, SS
"	5806	6206		"	"	9429	"	Rt 8/65
"	5807	6207		"	"	9430	"	Rt 2/65
"	5808	6208		"	"	9431	"	Rt 2/65, SS
"	5809	6209		"	"	9432	"	Rt 8/65, SS
"	5810	6210	8062	"	"	9433	"	@ PC re 8398
"	5811	6211	8063	"	"	9434	"	@ PC re 8399
"	5812	6212		"	"	9435	10/50	Rt 2/65, SS
"	5813	6213		"	"	9436	"	Rt 1/66, SS
"	5814	6214		"	"	9437	11/50	Rt 1/66, SS
"	5815	6215		"	"	9438	"	Rt 1/66, SS

* Re-classified DRS-5A a/c Steam Generator removed, ballast added.
@ Note: 5810 Re-engined 2/56 and 5811 re-engined 6/55 at Collinwood Diesel Locomotive Shop with EMD 12-567B, V12, 1200HP and EMD D-4 generator, using original WE 362 Traction Motors. Tractive effort (Max) 6210-63250, 6211-62500; Weight - 6210 - 253000, 6211 - 250000.

General Note: All locomotives built with End Buffers, Air Signal, MU Control No. 2 end only, Platform Gangway No. 2 end only and Double End Train Control.

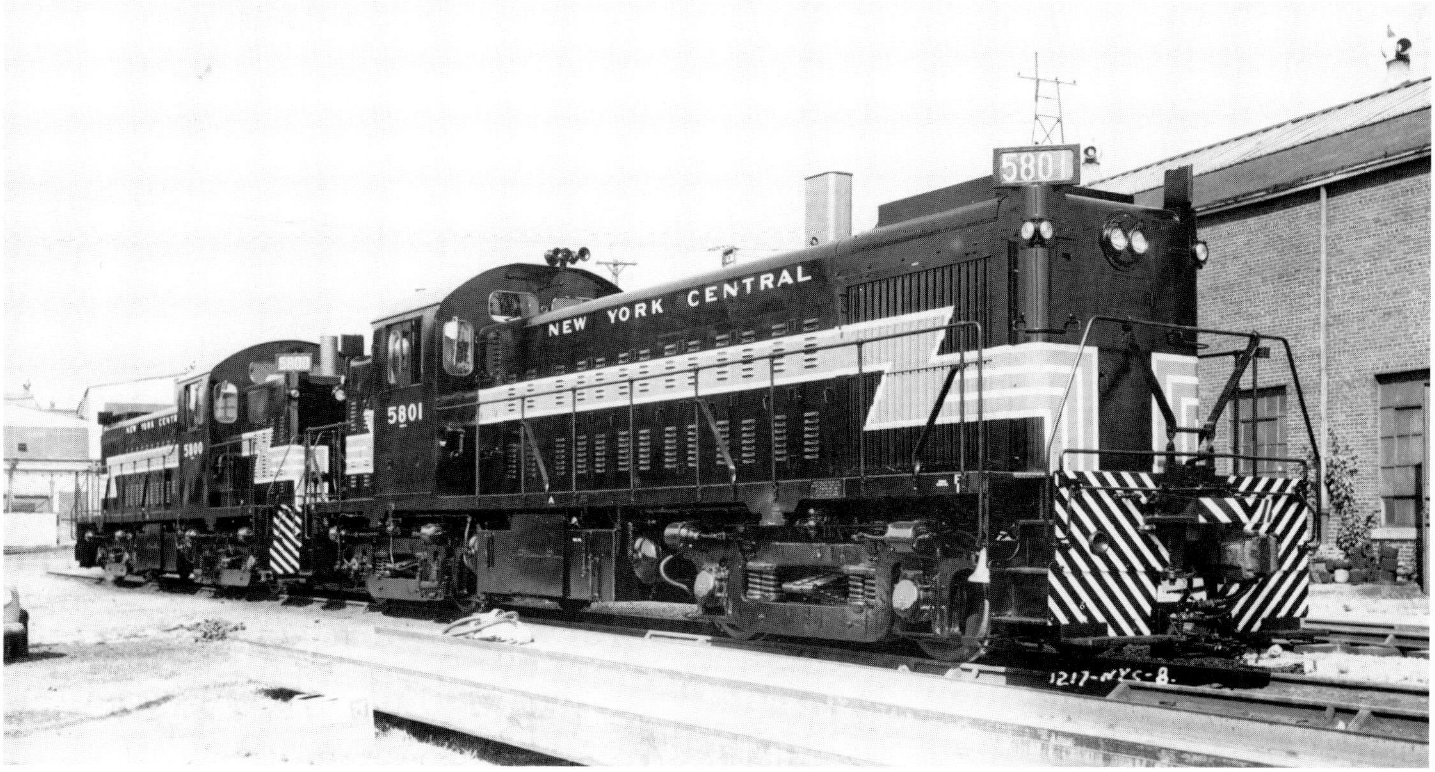

NYCSHS Collection

Nos 5800 and 5801 Class DRSP-5A pose new at Lima, Ohio in September 1950, before entering passenger service on the B&A. Note the stack for the steam generator on the short hood end.

Louis A. Marre

No 6211 Class DRS-5A. One of two Lima products fixed up for Chicago cowhide service. Photo at Englewood November 11, 1964.

CLASS DRS-6 and DRSP-6 (ARS-16,s) ALCO-GE 1600HP Model RS-3

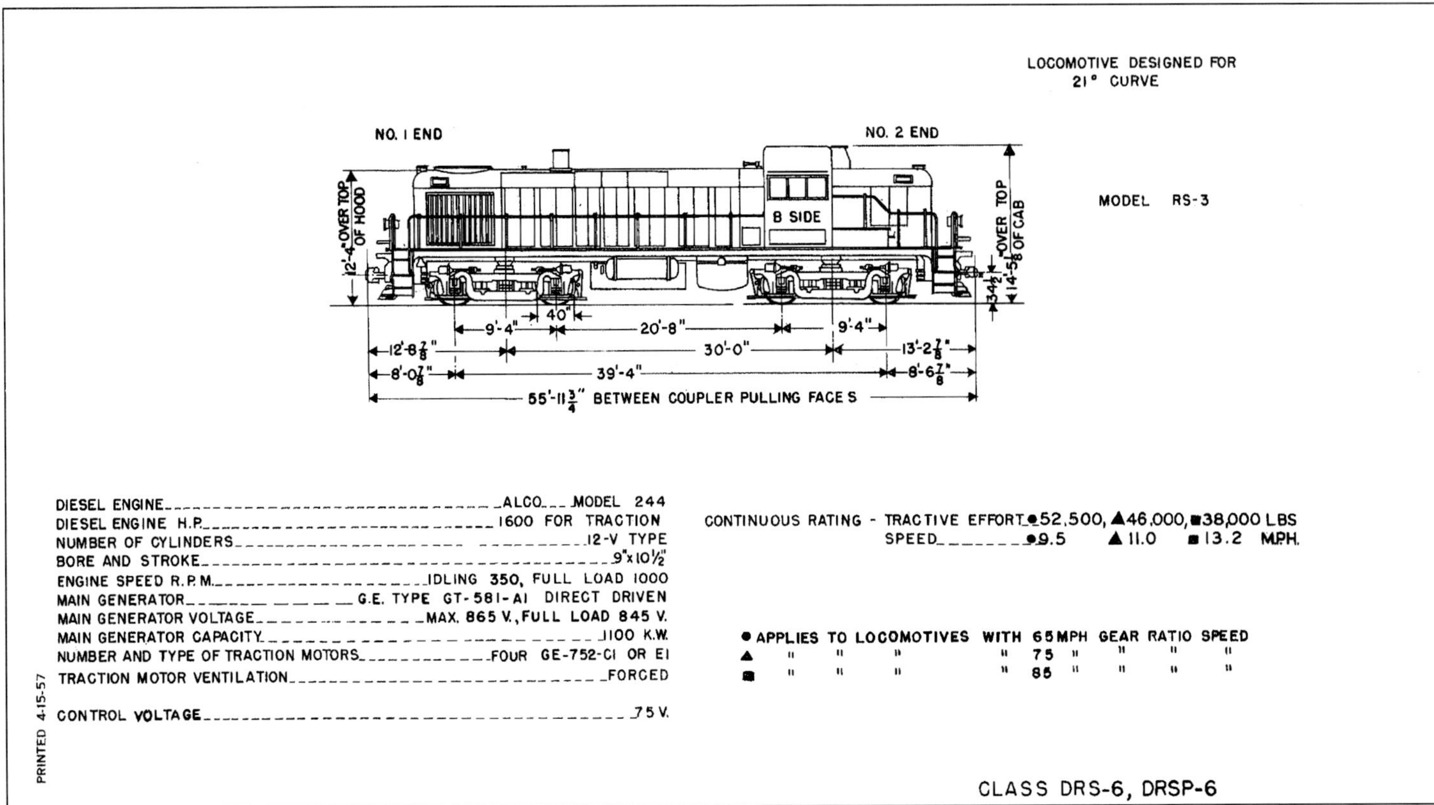

Class	Number	Re '66	Builder	Order Number	c/n	Date	Disposition
DRSP-6A*	8223	5223	Alco-GE	(S-3134)	78080	8/50	PC AM 100
"	8224	5224	"	"	78081	"	PC
"	8225		"	"	78082	"	So 9/65 GE
"	8226	5226	"	"	78083	"	PC, Rt 7/68
"	8227	5227	"	"	78084	"	PC, CR re 9954
"	8228	5228	"	"	78085	"	PC
"	8229				78086		So 2/65 GE as 8211
"	8230	5230	"	"	78087	"	PC, CR re 9951
DRS-6B	8231	5231	Alco GE	(S-3160)	78595	5/51	PC
"	8232	5232	"	"	78596	"	PC AM 101
"	8233	5233	"	"	78597	"	PC AM 102
"	8234	5234	"	"	78598	"	PC
"	8235		"	"	78599	"	So 2/66 GE as 8353
"	8236	5236	"	"	78600	"	PC AM 103
"	8237	5237	"	"	78601	"	PC
"	8238	5238	"	"	78602	"	PC, CR re 9971
"	8239	5239	"	"	78603	"	PC, CR
"	8240	5540	"	"	78604	"	PC CR re 9952
"	8241	5241	"	"	78605	"	PC,CR re 9965
"	8242	5242	"	"	78751	"	PC,CR re 9953
"	8243	5243	"	"	78752	"	PC,CR re 9964

Note * Reclassified DRS-6a when steam generator removed, ballast added.
General Notes on entire Class DRS/DRSP-6 as originally built: Air Signal in all except Sub Class D and J; End Buffers on Sub Class A, C, E, F, G, H, J; Platform Gangway and MU control on No. 1 and 2 ends on Sub Class F, G,H J, Platform Gangway and MU control No. 2 end only on Sub Class A, B, C, D, E; Double End Train Control on all except DRSP-6G - none. Various DRSP units re-geared by NYC to 85 mph by 1957, then re-geared back to 65 mph when steam generator equipment removed.

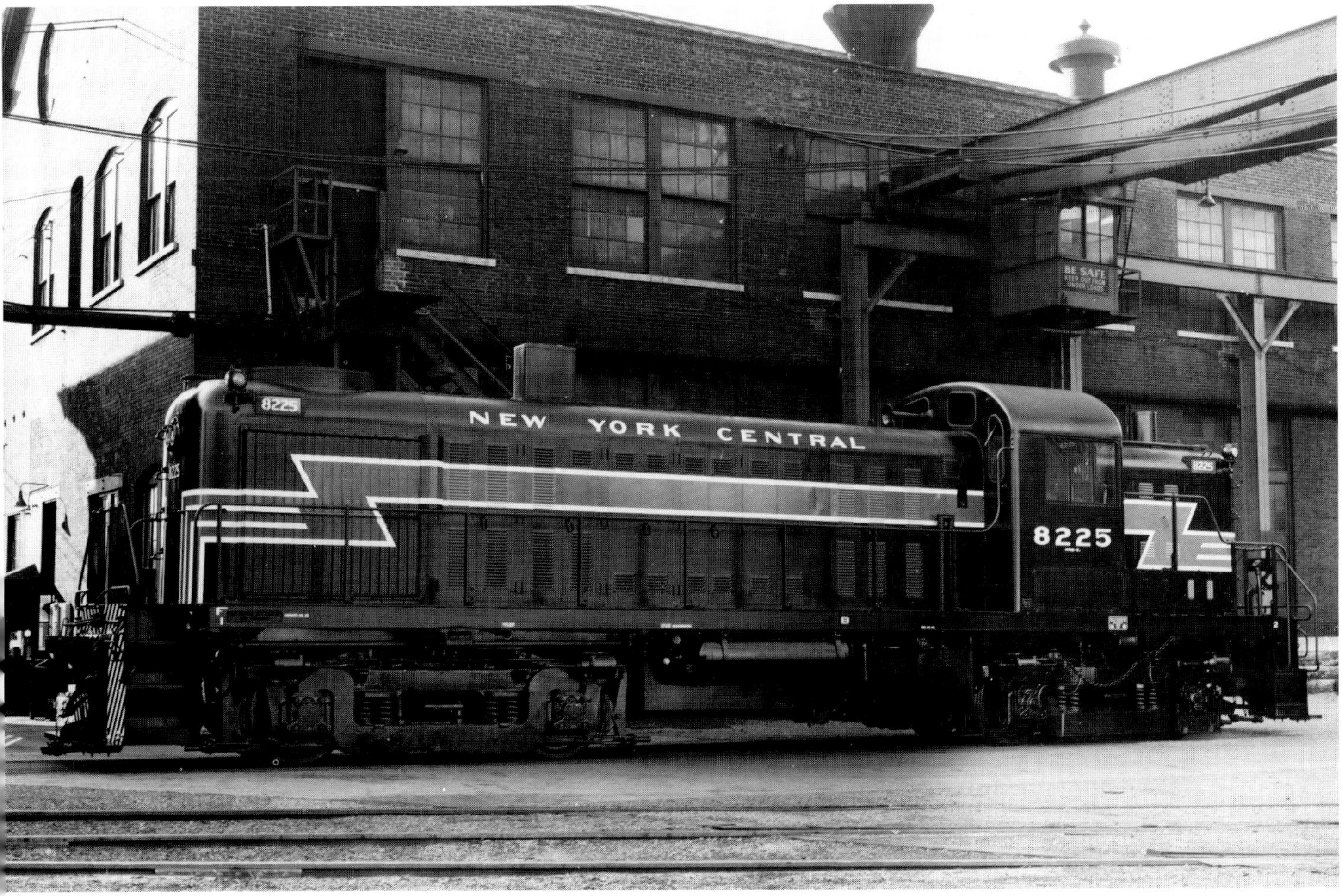

No 8225 Class DRSP-6A in a rather unusual location at the Alco plant for a builder's photo.

Both: NYCSHS Collection

No 8246 Class DRSP-6C. One of the twenty six RS-3s that were sold to Amtrak. When Conrail was formed this unit became Amtrak 104. Notice the unfinished RS-3 next to the building at left.

Class	Number	Re '66	Builder	Order Number	c/n	Date	Disposition
DRSP-6C*	8244	5244	Alco-GE	(S-3168)	78860	5/51	PC Rt 7/68
"	8245	5245	"	"	78861	"	PC Rt 7/68
"	8246	5246	"	"	78862	6/51	PC,AM 104
"	8247	5500	"	"	78863	5/51	PC,CR
"	8248	5522	"	"	78864	6/51	PC Rt GE
"	8249	5249	"	"	78865	5/51	PC Rt 7/68
"	8250	5523	"	"	78866	"	PC Rt GE
"	8251	5524	"	"	78867	6/51	PC
"	8252	5501	"	"	78868	"	PC,AM 124
"	8253	5502	"	"	78869	"	PC,AM 125
"	8254	5503	"	"	78870	"	PC,AM 126
"	8255	5504	"	"	78871	"	PC,AM 127
"	8256	5525-5256	"	"	78872	"	PC Rt GE
"	8257	5257	"	"	78873	"	PC re 9963
"	8258	5526-5258	"	"	78874	"	PC,AM 105
"	8259	5505	"	"	78875	"	PC
"	8260	5260	"	"	78876	"	PC,CR re 9984
"	8261	5261	"	"	78877	"	
"	8262	5262	"	"	78878	"	PC Rt GE
"	8263	5263	"	"	78879	"	PC,AM 106
"	8264	5506	"	"	78900	"	PC,AM 128
"	8265	5507	"	"	78901	"	PC,CR
"	8266	5508	"	"	78903	"	PC,CR re 9976
"	8267	5509	"	"	78904	"	PC,CR
"	8268	5510	"	"	78905	"	PC,AM 129
"	8269	5511	"	"	78906	7/51	PC,AM 130
"	8270	5512	"	"	78907	"	PC,AM 131
"	8271	5513	"	"	78908	"	PC
"	8272	5272	"	"	78909	"	PC
"	8273	5514	"	"	78910	"	PC,CR
"	8274	5515	"	"	78911	"	PC,CR
"	8275	5516	"	"	78912	"	PC,AM 132
"	8276	5517	"	"	78913	"	PC Rt GE
"	8277	5518	"	"	78914	"	PC,AM 133
"	8278	5519	"	"	78915	"	PC Rt GE
"	8279	5520	"	"	78916	"	PC,CR
"	8280	5521	"	"	78917	"	PC,AM 134
DRS-6D	8281	5281	Alco-GE	(S-3178)	79240	10/51	PC, Rt 7/68
"	8282	5282	"	"	79241	"	PC,AM 107
"	8283	5283	"	"	79242	"	
"	8284	5284	"	"	79243	"	PC, Rt 4/68
DRSP-6E*	8285	5527	Alco-GE	(S-3174)	79097	9/51	PC,AM 135
"	8286	5528	"	"	79098	"	PC
"	8287	5287	"	"	79099	"	PC Rt 7/68
"	8288	5288	"	"	79100	"	PC,CR re 9969
"	8289	5529	"	"	79101	"	PC,CR
"	8290	5290	"	"	79102	"	PC,CR re 9977
"	8291	5530	"	"	79103	"	PC,AM 136
"	8292	5292	"	"	79104	"	PC,CR
"	8293	5293	"	"	79105	"	PC
"	8294	5294	"	"	79106	"	PC,CR
"	8295	5295	"	"	79107	"	PC Rt GE
"	8296	5296	"	"	79108	"	
"	8297	5297	"	"	79109	"	PC,CR
"	8298	5298	"	"	79110	"	PC,CR
"	8299	5299	"	"	79111	"	PC Rt GE
"	8300	5300	"	"	79112	"	PC Rt 7/68

Class	Number	Re '66	Builder	Order Number	c/n	Date	Disposition
DRSP-6E*	8301		Alco-GE	(S-3174)	79113	9/51	So 3/66 GE as 8356
"	8302	5302	"	"	79114	"	PC,AM 108
"	8303	5303	"	"	79115	10/51	Rt 11/67 Alco
"	8304	5304	"	(S-3178)	79236	"	PC
"	8305	5305	"	"	79237	"	Wreck, Rt 6/67
"	8306	5306	"	"	79238	"	PC,CR
"	8307	5307	"	"	79239	"	PC,CR
DRSP-6F*	8308	5308	Alco-GE	(S-3189)	79675	3/52	PC Rt GE
"	8309	5309	"	"	79676	"	PC Rt GE
"	8310	5310	"	"	79677	"	PC
"	8311	5311	"	"	79678	"	PC
"	8312	5312	"	"	79679	"	PC Rt GE
"	8313	5313	"	(S-3197)	79852	4/52	PC,CR re 9997
"	8314	5314	"	"	79853	"	PC
"	8315	5315	"	"	79854	"	PC
"	8316	5316	"	"	79855	"	PC,AM 109
"	8317	5317	"	"	79856	"	PC Rt GE
"	8318	5318	"	"	79857	"	PC,CR re 9966
"	8319	5319	"	"	79858	"	PC
DRSP-6G*	8320	5320	Alco-GE	(S-3197)	79879	5/52	PC,AM 110
"	8321	5321	"	"	79880	"	
"	8322	5322	"	"	79881	"	PC Rt GE
"	8323	5323	"	"	79882	"	PC
"	8324	5324	"	"	79883	"	PC Rt 4/68
"	8325	5325	"	"	79884	"	PC,CR
"	8326	5326	"	"	79885	"	PC,CR
"	8327	5327	"	"	79886	"	PC
"	8328	5328	"	"	79887	"	PC,CR re 9974
"	8329	5329	"	"	79889	"	PC,CR
"	8330	5330	"	"	79890	"	PC Rt GE
"	8331	5331	"	"	79892	"	PC Rt 6/68
"	8332	5332	"	"	79893	"	PC,Cr
"	8333	5333	"	"	79894	"	PC,CR re 9968
"	8334	5334	"	"	79896	"	PC Rt 7/68
"	8335	5335	"	"	79897	"	Rt 5/67 GE
"	8336	5336	"	"	79898	"	PC,CR
"	8337	5337	"	"	79900	"	
"	8338	5338	"	"	79901	"	
"	8339	5339	"	"	79902	"	PC,CR re 9989
"	8340	5340	"	"	79904	"	PC,AM 111
"	8341	5341	"	"	79905	"	
"	8342	5342	"	"	79906	"	PC,CR re 9957

Class	Number	Re '66	Builder	Order Number	c/n	Date	Disposition
DRSP-6H*	8343	5343	Alco-GE	(S-3218)	80535	9/53	PC
"	8344	5344	"	"	80536	"	PC Rt 7/68
"	8345	5345	"	"	80537	"	PC Rt GE
"	8346	5346	"	"	80538	"	PC
"	8347	5347	"	"	80539	"	
"	8348	5348	"	"	80540	"	PC,AM 112
	8349	5349	"	"	80541	"	PC,CR
"	8350	5350	"	"	80542	"	PC Rt 7/68
"	8351	5351	"	"	80543	10/53	PC,CR
	8352	5352	"	"	80544	"	PC,CR
DRS-6J P&LE	8353	5235	Alco-GE	(S-3218)	80545	10/53	PC Rt 8/70 GE
" "	8354		"	"	80546	"	So 8/65 Truax-Traer
" "	8355	5203	"	"	80547	"	PC Rt 4/71 GE
" "	8356	5301	"	"	80549	"	PC Rt /71 GE
" "	8357	5205	"	"	80550	"	PC Rt 4/71 GE

* Note: Reclassified DRS when steam generator removed and ballast added.
P&LE class DRS-6J painted Pacemaker green with grey lighting stripes.

Jerry Pinkepank, Collection of Louis A. Marre

Alco RS-3 No. 8253 arriving at White Plains North Station with a Harlem Division commuter train on February 1, 1965.

H. L. Vail

Alco RS-3 No. 5298 formerly No. 8298 at Harmon, after the Alco road switchers had been renumbered about 1968.

Ronald F. Amberger

Alco RS-3 No. 8331 has an eastbound River Division commuter run in hand at Dumont, New Jersey.

CLASS DRS-7 (FRS-16) Fairbanks-Morse 1600HP Model H16-44

LOCOMOTIVE DESIGNED FOR
23° CURVE

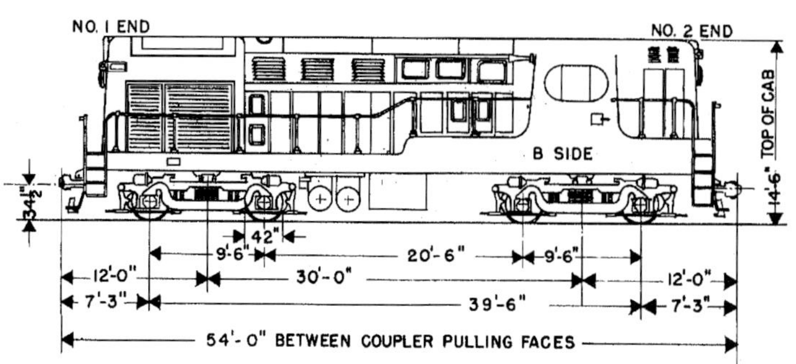

DIESEL ENGINE — F. M. MODEL 38 D 8 1/8
DIESEL ENGINE H. P. — (1600 FOR TRACTION)
NUMBER OF CYLINDERS — 8 IN LINE (O.P.)
BORE AND STROKE — 8 1/8" X 10"
ENGINE SPEED R. P. M. — IDLING 300, FULL LOAD 850
MAIN GENERATOR — W. E. CORP. TYPE 472-A OR 472-AZ DIRECT DRIVEN
MAIN GENERATOR VOLTAGE — MAX. 870V, FULL LOAD 820V.
MAIN GENERATOR CAPACITY
NUMBER AND TYPE OF TRACTION MOTORS — FOUR W.E.CORP. 370-DE OR DEZ
TRACTION MOTOR VENTILATION — FORCED
GEAR RATIO — 63/15 (4.20)
CONTROL VOLTAGE — 75V

MAXIMUM SPEED OF LOCOMOTIVE — 70 M.P.H.
CONTINUOUS RATING - TRACTIVE EFFORT — 48,600 LBS.
SPEED — 9.9 M.P.H.
HORSEPOWER — 1283

PRINTED 5-1-53

CLASS DRS-7A

Class	Number	Re '66	Builder	Order Number	c/n	Date	Disposition
DRS-7A	7000	5100	FM	(LD118)	16L414	7/51	Rt 5/67 GE
"	7001	5101	"	"	16L415	"	Rt 5/67 GE
"	7002	5102	"	"	16L416	"	Rt 9/66 SS
"	7003	5103	"	"	16L417	"	Rt 9/66 SS
"	7004	5104	"	"	16L418	"	Rt 9/66 SS
"	7005	5105	"	"	16L419	"	Rt 5/67 GE
"	7006	5106	"	"	16L420	"	Rt 9/66 SS
"	7007	5107	"	"	16L421	"	Rt 5/67 GE
"	7008		"	"	16L422	"	Rt 3/57 Sc
"	7009	5109	"	"	16L423	10/51	Rt 9/66 SS
"	7010	5110	"	"	16L424	"	Rt 9/66 SS
"	7011	5111	"	"	16L425	"	Rt 5/67 GE
"	7012	5112	"	"	16L426	11/51	Rt 9/66 SS

General Note: All locomotives built with Air Signal, No Buffers, MU Control No. 2 end only and Double End Train Control; 7000-7003 equipped by NYC with Layover Heating in 1952-1953.

NYCSHS Collection

No. 7000 Class DRS-7a was built by Fairbanks-Morse as a 1600 HP model H16-44 in July 1951. In just a few short years, the rounded window styling in the cab side would be dropped from the production models by F-M.

No. 7002 one of 13 such units on the NYC is shown here at Terre Haute, Indiana on September 2, 1963. All thirteen of these units would be retired 1965-1966.

Louis A. Marre

CLASS DRS-8 and DRSP-8 (BRS-12m) BALDWIN 1200HP Model RS-12

LOCOMOTIVE DESIGNED FOR 39° CURVE

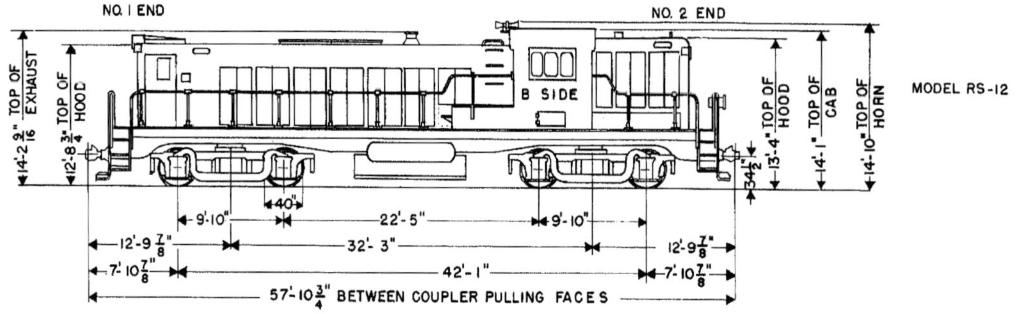

NO. 1 END — NO. 2 END — B SIDE — MODEL RS-12

14'-2 2/16" TOP OF EXHAUST — 12'-8 3/4" TOP OF HOOD — 34 1/2" — 13'-4" TOP OF HOOD — 14'-1" TOP OF CAB — 14'-10" TOP OF HORN

9'-10" — 40" — 22'-5" — 9'-10"

12'-9 7/8" — 32'-3" — 12'-9 7/8"

7'-10 7/8" — 42'-1" — 7'-10 7/8"

57'-10 3/4" BETWEEN COUPLER PULLING FACES

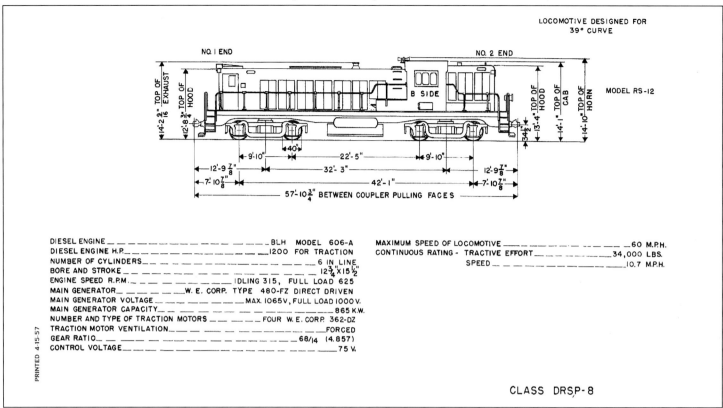

DIESEL ENGINE — BLH MODEL 606-A
DIESEL ENGINE H.P. — 1200 FOR TRACTION
NUMBER OF CYLINDERS — 6 IN LINE
BORE AND STROKE — 12 3/4" X 15 1/2"
ENGINE SPEED R.P.M. — IDLING 315, FULL LOAD 625
MAIN GENERATOR — W. E. CORP. TYPE 480-FZ DIRECT DRIVEN
MAIN GENERATOR VOLTAGE — MAX. 1065V, FULL LOAD 1000 V.
MAIN GENERATOR CAPACITY — 865 K.W.
NUMBER AND TYPE OF TRACTION MOTORS — FOUR W. E. CORP. 362-DZ
TRACTION MOTOR VENTILATION — FORCED
GEAR RATIO — 68/14 (4.857)
CONTROL VOLTAGE — 75 V.

MAXIMUM SPEED OF LOCOMOTIVE — 60 M.P.H.
CONTINUOUS RATING - TRACTIVE EFFORT — 34,000 LBS.
SPEED — 10.7 M.P.H.

PRINTED 4-15-57

CLASS DRSP-8

Class	Number	Re '53	Re '66	Order Builder	Number	c/n	Date	Disposition
DRSP-8A*	5820	6220	8067	BLH	(50544)	75256	11/51	PC Rt EMD
"	5821	6221	8068	"	"	75257	"	PC, Rt 6/68
"	5822	6222	8069	"	"	75258	"	PC
"	5823	6223	8070	"	"	75259	"	PC Rt 4/68
"	5824	6224	8071	"	"	75260	"	PC
"	5825	6225	8072	"	"	75261	"	PC
"	5826	6226	8073	"	"	75262	"	PC
"	5827	6227	8074	"	"	75263	"	PC Rt EMD
"	5828	6228	8075	"	"	75264	"	PC
"	5829	6229	8076	"	"	75265	"	PC
"	5830	6230	8077	"	"	75266	12/51	PC
"	5831	6231	8078	"	"	75267	"	Rt 5/67 GE
"	5832	6232	8079	"	"	75268	"	PC
"	5833	6233	8080	"	"	75269	"	PC, Rt EMD
"	5834	6234	8081	"	"	75270	"	PC, Rt EMD
"	5835	6235	8082	"	"	75271	1/52	PC
"	5836	6236	8083	"	"	75272	"	PC, Rt 7/68

* Re-classified DRS-8A a/c Steam Generator removed, ballast added.
General Note: All locomotives built with Air Signal, End Buffers, MU Control No. 2 end only, and Double End Train Control; 6230, 6231, 6233, 6234, 6236 equipped by NYC with layover heating in 1953.

No. 5828 looks good from either end at Baldwin. Notice that the MU connections and the gangway or drop step is at the rear of the unit only. There is also a light fixture to light the gangway for safety. These units handled Putnam and River Division commuter trains at first.

Both: NYCSHS Collection

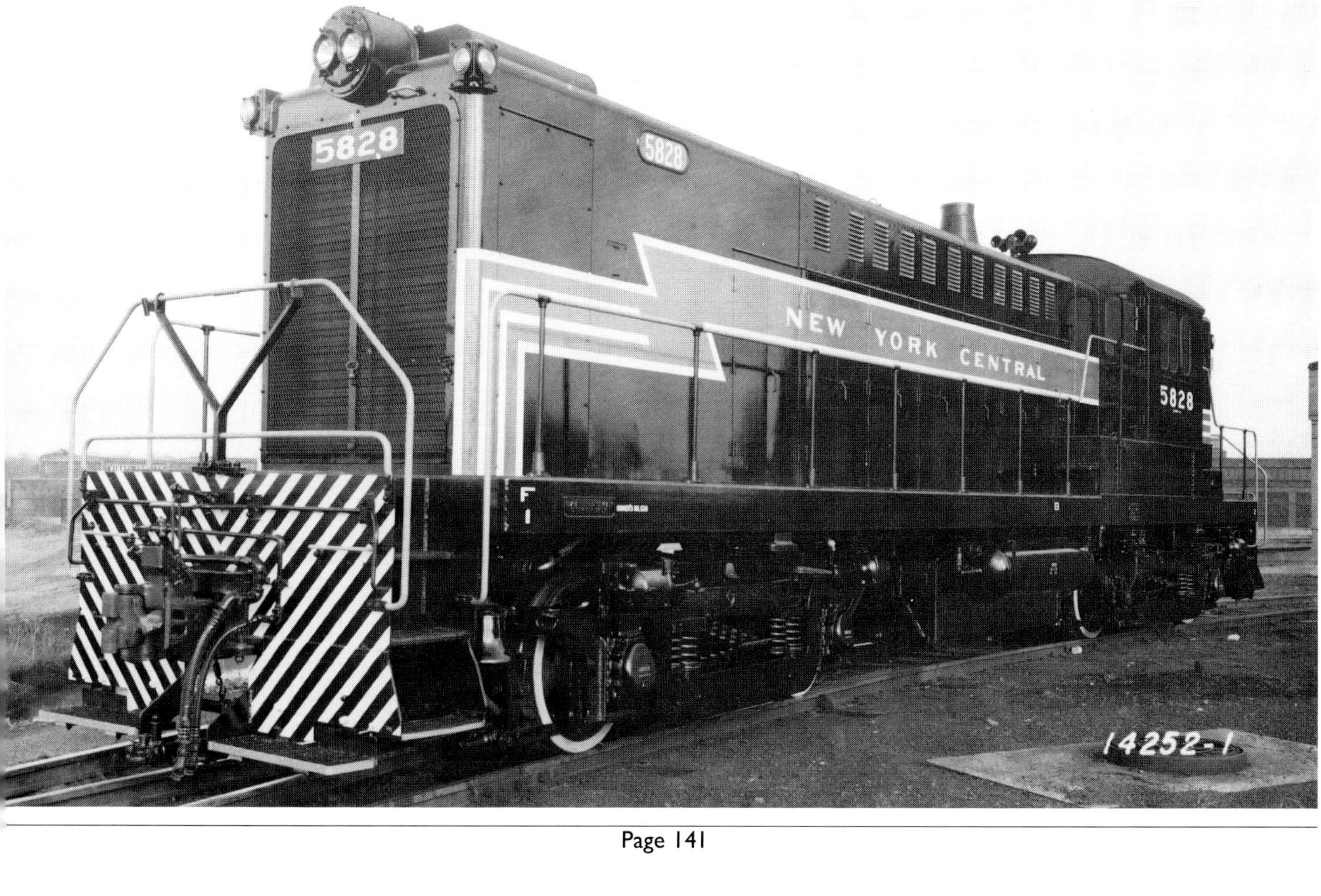

CLASS DRS-9 and DRSP-9 (ERS-17,s) EMD 1750HP Model GP9

Class	Road	Number	Re '66	Builder	Order Number	c/n	Date	Disposition
DRSP-9A*	CUT	5900	7300	EMD	(5340)	19521	4/54	PC,CR
"	"	5901	7301	"	"	19522	"	PC,CR
"	"	5902	7302	"	"	19523	"	PC,CR
"	"	5903	7303	"	"	19524	"	PC,CR
DRS-9B		5904	7304	EMD	(5415)	20893	4/56	PC,CR
"		5905	7305	"	"	20894	"	PC,CR
"		5906	7306	"	"	20895	"	PC,CR
"		5907	7307	"	"	20896	"	PC,CR re 7548
"		5908	7308	"	"	20897	"	PC,CR
"		5909	7309	"	"	20898	"	PC,CR
"		5910	7310	"	"	20899	"	PC,CR
"		5911	7311	"	"	20900	"	PC,CR re 7566
"		5912	7312	"	"	20901	"	PC,CR
"		5913	7313	"	"	20902	"	PC,CR re 7530
"		5914	7314	"	"	20903	"	PC,CR
"		5915		"	"	20904	"	Wreck, So 11/65 EMD
"		5916	7316	"	"	20905	"	PC,CR
"		5917	7317	"	"	20906	"	PC,CR
"		5918	7318	"	"	20907	"	PC,CR
"		5919	7319	"	"	20908	"	PC,CR
"		5920	7320	"	"	20909	"	PC,CR
"		5921		"	"	20910	"	Wreck, So 11/65 EMD
"		5922	7322	"	"	20911	"	PC,CR re 7547
"		5923	7323	"	"	20912	"	PC
"		5924	7324	"	"	20913	"	PC
"		5925	7325	"	"	20914	"	PC,CR
"		5926	7326	"	"	20915	"	PC,CR
"		5927	7327	"	"	20916	"	PC,CR
DRSP-9C*		5928	7500	"	"	20917	12/55	PC,CR
"		5929	7501	"	"	20918	"	PC,CR re 7301 re 7329
"		5930	7502	"	"	20919	"	PC
"		5931	7503	"	"	20920	"	PC,CR re 7331
"		5932	7504	"	"	20921	"	PC,CR re 7332
"		5933	7505	"	"	20922	"	Rt 10/67
"		5934	7506	"	"	20923	"	PC,CR
"		5935	7507	"	"	20924	"	PC,CR re 7335
"		5936	7508	"	"	20925	"	PC,CR
"		5937	7509	"	"	20926	"	PC,CR re 7337
"		5938	7510	"	"	20927	"	PC,CR re 7338, 7564
"		5939	7511	"	"	20928	"	PC,CR re 7339
"		5940	7512	"	"	20929	"	PC,CR re 7571
"		5941	7513	"	"	20930	"	Wreck, Rt 5/67 EMD
"		5942	7514	"	"	20931	"	PC,CR re 7342
"		5943	7515	"	"	20932	"	PC,CR re 7343, 7549
"		5944	7516	"	"	20933	"	PC,CR re 7344
"		5945	7517	"	"	20934	"	PC,CR re 7345
"		5946	7346	"	"	20951	"	PC,CR
"		5947	7518	"	"	20952	"	PC re 7347
"		5948		"	"	20953	"	So 6/65 EMD as 5763

Note * - Re DRS-9A and 9C when steam generator removed, ballast added.
General Notes on entire class DRS/DRSP-9 as originally built: Geared speed-DRSP-9A; 71 mph, DRS-9B, -9D, -9F, 9H; 65 mph - DRSP-9C, DRS-9E, DRSP-9G, 85 mph; All locomotives built with MU No. I and No. 2 ends, Double end Train Control, Air Signal; Buffers on DRSP-9A, -9C, -9G only; Layover Heating on: DRS-9D 5974-5998 only, DRS-9E 5999-6010 only, and DRS-9F; DRS-9F and DRSP-9G short hood is No. 1 end (arranged to run short hood forward), all others long hood is No. 1 end.

LOCOMOTIVE DESIGNED FOR
39° CURVE

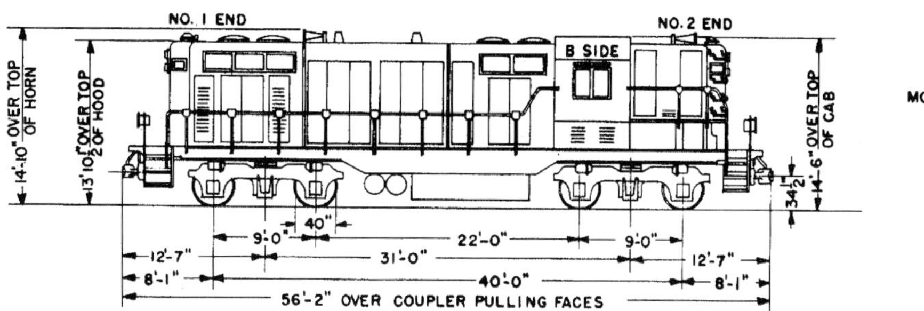

MODEL GP9

DIESEL ENGINE	GM MODEL 567C
DIESEL ENGINE H.P.	1750 FOR TRACTION
NUMBER OF CYLINDERS	16-V TYPE
BORE AND STROKE	8 1/2" X 10"
ENGINE SPEED R.P.M.	IDLING 275, FULL LOAD 835
MAIN GENERATOR	EMD TYPE D-12B DIRECT DRIVEN
MAIN GENERATOR VOLTAGE	MAX. 1070 V, FULL LOAD 1020 V
MAIN GENERATOR CAPACITY	1240 KW
NUMBER AND TYPE OF TRACTION MOTORS	FOUR EMD D-37
TRACTION MOTOR VENTILATION	FORCED
CONTROL VOLTAGE	75V

PRINTED 4-15-57

CLASS DRS-9D, DRS-9E

Class	Road	Number	Re '66	Builder	Order Number	c/n	Date	Disposition
DRS-9D		5949	7349	EMD	(5417)	20962	1/56	PC,CR
"		5950	7350	"	"	20963	"	PC,CR
"		5951	7351	"	"	20964	"	PC,CR
"		5952	7352	"	"	20965	"	PC,CR
"		5953	7353	"	"	20966	2/56	PC,CR
"		5954	7354	"	"	20967	"	PC,CR
"		5955	7355	"	"	20968	"	PC,CR
"		5956	7356	"	"	20969	"	PC,CR
"		5957	7357	"	"	20970	"	PC,CR
"		5958	7358	"	"	20971	"	PC,CR re 7529
"		5959	7359	"	"	20972	"	PC,CR
"		5960		"	"	20973	"	Rt 4/66 GE, to SJ&LC 200
"		5961	7361	"	"	20974	"	PC,CR
"		5962	7362	"	"	20975	"	PC
"		5963	7363	"	"	20976	"	PC
"		5964	7364	"	"	20977	"	PC,CR
"		5965		"	"	20978	"	Wreck; So 11/65 EMD
"		5966	7366	"	"	20979	"	PC,CR
"		5967	7367	"	"	20980	"	PC,CR re 7528
"		5968	7368	"	"	20981	"	PC,CR
"		5969		"	"	20982	"	So 10/64 EMD as 5816
"		5970	7370	"	"	20983	"	PC,CR
"		5971	7371	"	"	20984	"	PC,CR
"		5972	7372	"	"	20985	"	PC,CR re 7527
"		5973	7373	"	"	20986	"	PC,CR re 7531
"		5974	7374	"	"	20987	"	PC,CR
"		5975	7375	"	"	20988	"	PC,CR
"		5976	7376	"	"	20989	"	PC,CR
"		5977	7377	"	"	20990	"	PC,CR re 7546
"		5978	7378	"	"	20991	"	PC,CR

Class	Road	Number	Re '66	Builder	Order Number	c/n	Date	Disposition
DRS-9D		5979	7379	EMD	(5417)	20992	2/55	PC,CR
“		5980		“	“	20993	“	So 10/64 EMD as 5815
“		5981	7381	“	“	20994	“	PC,CR
“		5982	7382	“	“	20995	“	PC,CR
“		5983	7383	“	“	20996	“	PC,CR
“		5984	7384	“	“	20997	“	PC,CR re 7560
“		5985	7385	“	“	20998	“	PC,CR re 7533
“		5986	7386	“	“	20999	“	PC,CR
“		5987	7387	“	“	21000	“	PC,CR
“		5988	7388	“	“	21001	“	PC,CR
“		5989	7389	“	“	21002	“	PC,CR
“		5990	7390	“	“	21003	“	PC,CR
“		5991	7391	“	“	21004	“	PC,CR
“		5992	7392	“	“	21005	“	PC,CR
“		5993	7393	“	“	21006	“	PC,CR
“		5994	7394	“	“	21007	“	PC,CR re 7513
“		5995	7395	“	“	21008	“	PC,CR
“		5996	7396	“	“	21009	“	PC,CR re 7553
“		5997	7397	“	“	21010	“	PC,CR re 7554
“		5998	7398	“	“	21011	“	PC,CR
DRS-9E		5999	7399	EMD	(5500)	22666	10/56	PC,CR re 7534
“		6000	7400	“	“	22667	“	PC,CR re 7524
“		6001	7401	“	“	22668	“	PC,CR
“		6002	7402	“	“	22669	“	PC,CR re 7561
“		6003	7403	“	“	22670	“	PC,CR
“		6004	7404	“	“	22671	“	PC,CR
“		6005	7405	“	“	22672	“	PC,CR
“		6006	7406	“	“	22673	“	PC,CR re 7525
“		6007	7407	“	“	22674	“	PC,CR
“		6008	7408	“	“	22675	“	PC,CR re 7555
“		6009	7409	“	“	22676	“	PC,CR re 7552
“		6010	7410	“	“	22677	“	PC Rt 7/68
“		6011	7411	“	(5520)	22678	12/56	PC,CR
“		6012	7412	“	“	22679	“	PC,CR
“		6013	7413	“	“	22680	“	PC,CR
“		6014	7414	“	“	22681	“	PC,CR
“		6015	7415	“	“	22682	“	PC,CR
“		6016	7416	“	“	22683	“	PC,CR
“		6017	7417	“	“	22684	“	PC,CR
“		6018	7418	“	“	22685	“	PC,CR
“		6019	7419	“	“	22686	“	PC,CR
“		6020		“	“	22687	“	So 10/64 EMD as 5814
“		6021	7421	“	“	22688	“	PC,CR re 7526
“		6022	7422	“		22689	“	PC,CR
“		6023	7423	“	“	22690	“	PC,CR
“		6024	7424	“	“	22691	“	PC,CR
“		6025	7425	“	“	22692	“	PC,CR
“		6026	7426	“	“	22693	“	PC,CR
“		6027	7427	“		22694	“	PC,CR
“		6028	7428	“	“	22695	“	PC,CR

Note: Subclasses A, E, F, G, H painted black with grey lighting stripes, subclasses B, C, D were two-tone grey.

Both: NYCSHS Collection

No. 5903, one of four GP9s built for Cleveland Union Terminal service. These units are painted in the black with the grey stripe scheme and replaced the P-1A electrics.

No. 5979 Class DRS-9D wears the two tone grey paint scheme in the February 1956 builders photo.

Class	Road	Number	Re '66	Builder	Order Number	c/n	Date	Disposition
DRS-9F		6029	7429	GMD	(C221)	A1074	4/57	PC,CR
		6030	7430	"	"	A1075	"	PC,CR
"		6031	7431	"	"	A1076	"	PC,CR
"		6032	7432	"	"	A1077	"	PC,CR
"		6033	7433	"	"	A1078	"	PC,CR
"		6034	7434	"	"	A1079	"	PC,CR
"		6035	7435	"	"	A1080	"	PC,CR
"		6036	7436	"	"	A1081	"	PC,CR
"		6037	7437	"	"	A1082	"	PC,CR
"		6038	7438	"	"	A1083	"	PC,CR
DRSP-9G*		6039	7439	GMD	(C222)	A1084	5/57	PC,CR
"		6040	7440	"	"	A1085	"	PC,CR

Note * - Re DRS-9g when steam generator removed, ballast added, 65mph gears.

W. D. Edson

A pair of matching grey GP9 units leaving Cleveland Union Terminal with matching cars on train No. 401 the Cincinnati *Mercury* in June 1956. For a few months this train covered a 5:00 pm departure from CUT while the Explorer left town in the morning.

Class	Road	Number	Re '66	Builder	Order Number	c/n	Date	Disposition
DRS-9H		6041	7441	EMD	(5548)	23644	4/57	PC,CR re 7551
"		6042	7442	"	"	23645	"	Rt 11/67
"		6043	7443	"	"	23646	"	PC,CR re 7550
"		6044	7444	"	"	23647	"	PC,CR
"		6045	7445	"	"	23648	"	PC,CR
"		6046	7446	"	(5546)	23579	8/57	PC,CR
"		6047	7447	"	"	23580	"	PC
"		6048	7448	"	"	23581	"	PC,CR
"		6049	7449	"	"	23582	"	PC,CR
"		6050	7450	"	"	23583	"	PC,CR re 7563
"		6051	7451	"	"	23584	"	PC,CR
"		6052		"	"	23585	"	So 6/65 EMD as 5610
"		6053	7453	"	"	23586	"	PC,CR
"		6054	7454	"	"	23587	"	PC,CR
"		6055	7455	"	"	23588	"	PC,CR
"		6056		"	"	23589	"	So 4/66 GE as 5970@
"		6057	7457	"	"	23590	"	PC,CR re 7535
"		6058	7458	"	"	23591	"	PC,CR
"		6059	7459	"	"	23592	"	PC,CR
"		6060	7460	"	"	23593	"	PC,CR
"		6061	7461	"	"	23594	"	PC,CR
"		6062	7462	"	"	23595	"	PC,CR
"		6063	7463	"	"	23596	"	PC,CR
"		6064	7464	"	"	23597	"	Rt 5/67 EMD
"		6065	7465	"	"	23598	"	PC,CR re 7545
"		6066	7466	"	"	23599	8/57	PC, CR
"		6067	7467	"	"	23600	"	PC Rt 4/68
"		6068	7468	"	"	23601	9/57	PC,CR
"		6069	7469	"	"	23602	"	PC,CR
"		6070	7470	"	"	23603	"	PC,CR
"		6071	7471	"	"	23604	"	PC,CR
"		6072	7472	"	"	23605	"	PC,CR
"		6073	7473	"	"	23606	"	PC,CR
"		6074	7474	"	"	23607	"	PC,CR
"		6075	7475	"	"	23608	"	PC,CR

Louis A. Marre

This GP9 was at Notre Dame at South Bend, Indiana on March 17, 1958. It would later become the 7325.

CLASS DRS-10 (ARS-18) ALCO 1800 HP Model RS-11 (DL-701)

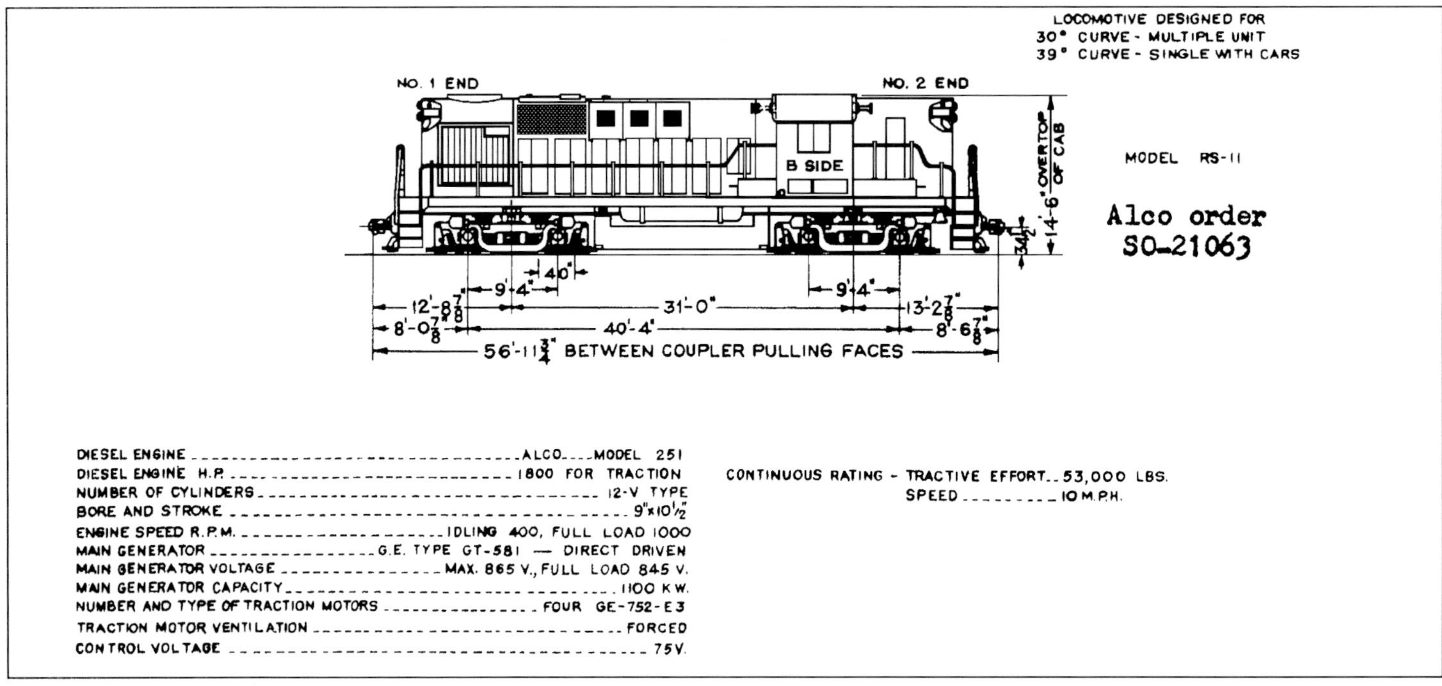

Class	Number	Re ' 66	Builder	Order Number	c/n	Date	Disposition
DRS-10A	8000	7600	Alco-GE	(S-3284)	82361	6/57	PC, CR
"	8001	7601	"	"	82362	"	PC, CR
"	8002	7602	"	"	82363	"	PC, CR
"	8003	7603	"	"	82364	"	PC, CR
"	8004	7604	"	"	82365	"	PC, CR
"	8005	7605	"	"	82366	7/57	PC, CR
"	8006	7606	"	"	82367	"	PC, CR
"	8007	7607	"	"	82368	"	PC, CR
"	8008	7608	"	"	82369	"	PC, CR

NYCSHS Collection

Alco RS-11 No. 8000 was the first road switcher to be delivered in the later "standard" solid black paint scheme with the larger lettering. Note the use of the "script" style herald on the cab side.

CLASS DRS-11 (EF-20) ELECTRO-MOTIVE 2000HP Model GP20

LOCOMOTIVE DESIGNED FOR
21° CURVE - MULTIPLE UNIT
39° CURVE - SINGLE WITH CARS

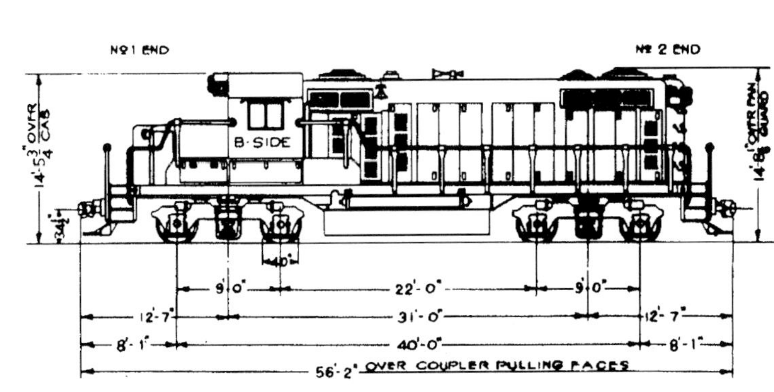

MODEL GP-20

EMD orders:

2100-2103 = 7606
2104-2112 = 7607

DIESEL ENGINE — GM MODEL 567D2
DIESEL ENGINE H.P. — 2000 FOR TRACTION
NUMBER OF CYLINDERS — 16-V TYPE
BORE AND STROKE — 8½" × 10"
ENGINE SPEED R.P.M. — IDLING 275, FULL LOAD 835
MAIN GENERATOR — EMD TYPE D-22 DIRECT DRIVEN
MAIN GENERATOR VOLTAGE — MAX. 1110 V., FULL LOAD 1008 V
MAIN GENERATOR CAPACITY — 1416 KW
NUMBER AND TYPE OF TRACTION MOTORS — FOUR EMD D47
TRACTION MOTOR VENTILATION — FORCED
CONTROL VOLTAGE — 74V

Class	Number	Re '66	Builder	Order Number	c/n	Date	Disposition
DRS-11A	6100	2100	EMD	(7606)	26815	7/61	PC,CR
"	6101	2101	"	"	26816	"	PC,CR
"	6102	2102	"	"	26817	"	PC,CR
"	6103	2103	"	"	26818	"	PC,CR
"	6104	2104	"	(7607)	26819	"	PC,CR
"	6105	2105	"	"	26820	"	PC,CR
"	6106		"	"	26821	"	So 8/65 EMD
"	6107	2106	"	"	26822	"	PC,CR
"	6108	2107	"	"	26823	"	PC,CR
"	6109		"	"	26824	"	Wrecked; So 12/63 EMD
"	6110	2108	"	"	26825	8/61	PC,CR
"	6111	2109	"	"	26826	"	PC,CR
"	6112	2110	"	"	26827	"	PC,CR
"	6113	2111	"	"	26828	"	PC,CR
"	6114	2112	"	"	26829	"	PC,CR

No. 6110 Class DRS-11A was a 2000 HP Model GP-20 built by EMD in August 1961. It was renumbered to 2108 and reclassified to EF-20 in 1966. The hood-side mounted bell and a lack of dynamic brakes are easily spotted. The white safety striping is quite vivid in this view.

NYCSHS Collection

CLASS DRS-12 (AF-20) ALCO 2000HP Model RS-32 (DL-721)

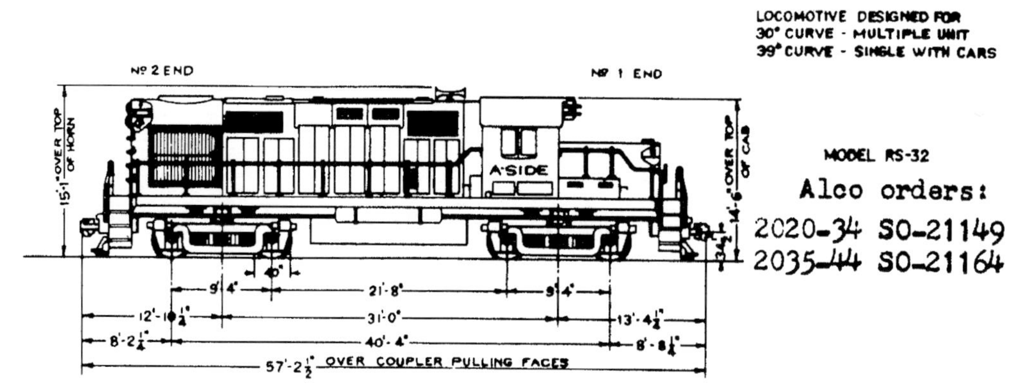

DIESEL ENGINE — ALCO — MODEL 251
DIESEL ENGINE H.P. — 2000 FOR TRACTION
NUMBER OF CYLINDERS — 12-V TYPE
BORE AND STROKE — 9" x 10½"
ENGINE SPEED R.P.M. — IDLING 400, FULL LOAD 1025
MAIN GENERATOR — G.E.CO., TYPE 5GT564C1, 566E1 & 581D1 DIRECT DRIVEN
MAIN GENERATOR VOLTAGE — MAX. 920 V., FULL LOAD 640 V.
MAIN GENERATOR CAPACITY — 1410 KW.
NUMBER AND TYPE OF TRACTION MOTORS — FOUR GE-752 A1, B-1 OR C-1
TRACTION MOTOR VENTILATION — FORCED
CONTROL VOLTAGE — 75 V.

CONTINUOUS RATING - TRACTIVE EFFORT — 53000 LBS.
SPEED — 11.25 M.P.H.

Class	Number	Re '66	Builder	Order Number	c/n	Date	Disposition
DRS-12A	8020	2020	Alco	(3341)	83981	6/61	Wreck; Rt 6/67
"	8021	2021	"	"	83982	"	PC,CR
"	8022	2022	"	"	83983	"	PC,CR
"	8023	2023	"	"	83984	"	PC,CR
"	8024	2024	"	"	83985	"	PC,CR
"	8025	2025	"	"	83986	"	PC,CR
"	8026	2026	"	"	83987	"	PC,CR
"	8027	2027	"	"	83988	"	PC,CR
"	8028	2028	"	"	83989	"	PC,CR
"	8029	2029	"	"	83990	"	PC,CR
"	8030	2030	"	"	83991	"	PC,CR
"	8031	2031	"	"	83992	"	PC,CR
"	8032	2032	"	"	83993	7/61	PC,CR
"	8033	2033	"	"	83994	"	PC,CR
"	8034	2034	"	"	83995	"	PC,CR
DRS-12B	8035	2035	"	(3344)	84035	6/62	PC,CR
"	8036	2036	"	"	84036	"	PC,CR
"	8037	2037	"	"	84037	"	PC,CR
"	8038	2038	"	"	84038	"	PC,CR
"	8039	2039	"	"	84039	"	PC,CR
"	8040	2040	"	(3349)	84183	"	PC,CR
"	8041	2041	"	"	84184	"	PC,CR
"	8042	2042	"	"	84185	"	PC,CR
"	8043	2043	"	"	84186	"	PC,CR
"	8044	2044	"	"	84187	"	PC,CR

General Note: Locomotives built with MU Control No. 1 and 2 ends, single end train control.

NYCSHS Collection

No. 8022 Class DRS-12A was a 2000 HP Model RS-32 built by Alco in June 1961. It was to be renumbered 2022 in 1966 and re-classified to AF-20.

Louis A. Marre

No. 8024 Class DRS-12A one of the twenty-five Alco RS-32 freight units delivered in 1961-62. Shown here at Dearborn, Michigan.

CLASS DRS-13 (EF-22) ELECTRO-MOTIVE 2250HP Model GP30

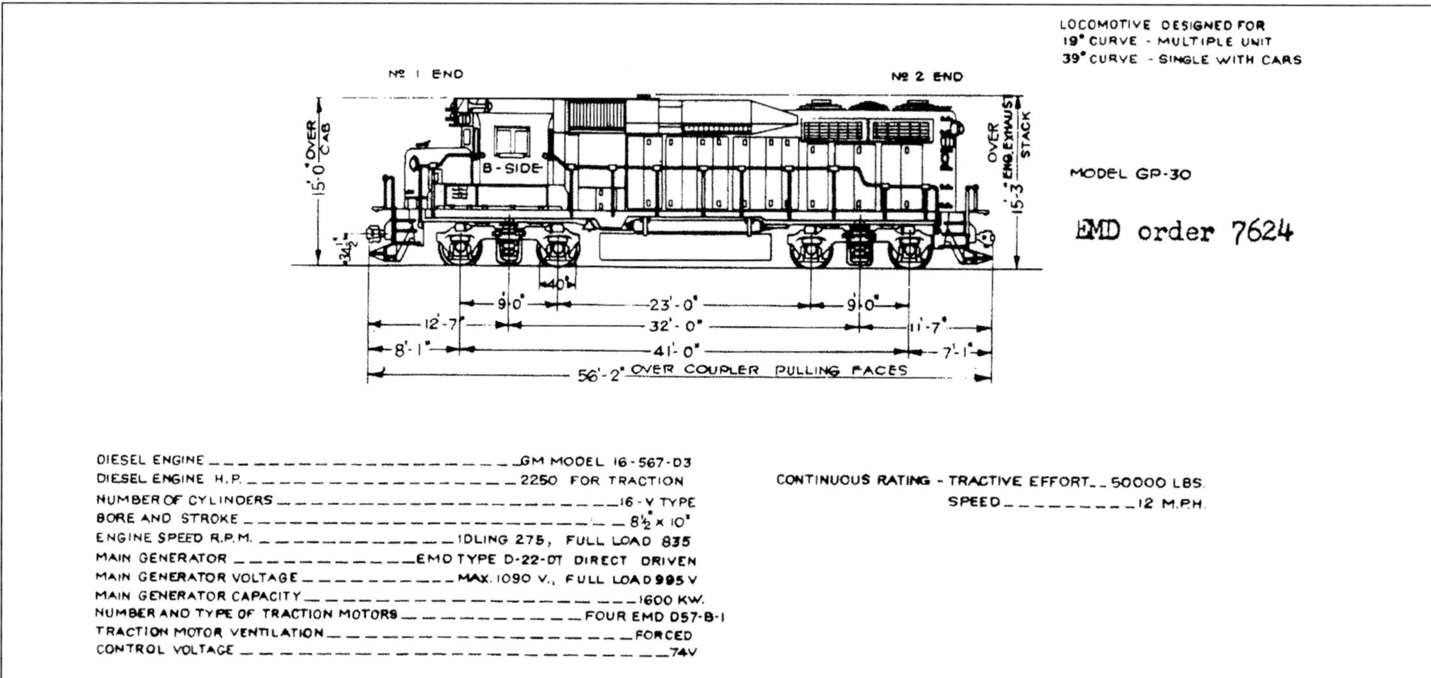

Class	Number	Re '66	Builder	Order Number	c/n	Date	Disposition
DRS-13A	6115	2188	EMD	(7624)	27979	8/62	PC,CR
"	6116	2189	"	"	27980	"	PC, CR
"	6117	2190	"	"	27981	"	PC,CR
"	6118	2191	"	"	27982	"	PC,CR
"	6119	2192	"	"	27983	"	PC,CR
"	6120	2193	"	"	27984	"	PC,CR
"	6121	2194	"	"	27985	"	PC,CR
"	6122	2195	"	"	27986	"	PC,CR
"	6123	2196	"	"	27987	"	PC,CR
"	6124	2197	"	"	27988	"	PC,CR

General Note: Locomotive built with MU No. 1 and 2 ends, single end train control.

ROAD TO THE FUTURE

Louis A. Marre

No. 6118 Class DRS-13A one of the ten GP-30s that EMD built and delivered for the NYC in August of 1962.

Louis A. Marre

No. 6119 Class DRS-13A and 6118 above show the lack of white safety striping on the pilot.

CLASS DRS-14 (EF-25) ELECTRO-MOTIVE 2500HP Model GP35

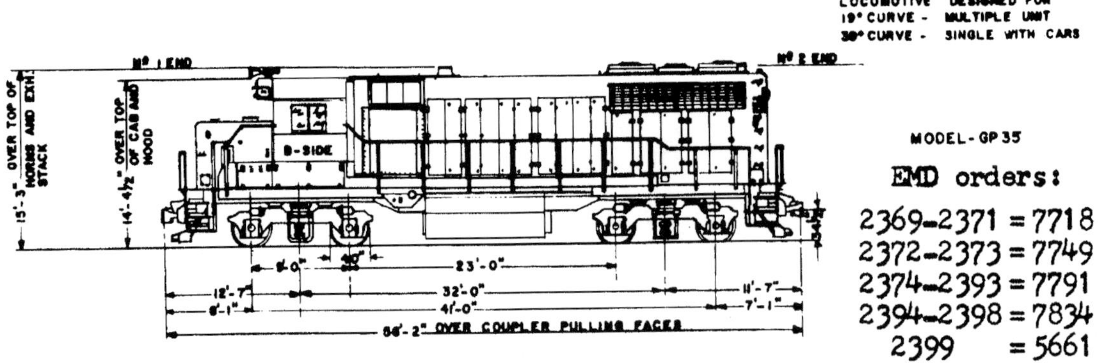

DIESEL ENGINE .... GM-MODEL 16-567 D3A
DIESEL ENGINE H.P. .... 2500 FOR TRACTION
NUMBER OF CYLINDERS .... 16-V TYPE
BORE AND STROKE .... 8½" X 10"
ENGINE SPEED R.P.M. .... IDLING 315, FULL LOAD 900
MAIN GENERATOR .... E.M.D. TYPE-D32 DIRECT DRIVEN
MAIN GENERATOR VOLTAGE .... MAX. 1160 V. FULL LOAD 1060 V.
MAIN GENERATOR CAPACITY .... 1725 KW
NUMBER AND TYPE OF TRACTION MOTORS FOUR-E.M.D.-D67
TRACTION MOTOR VENTILATION .... FORCED
CONTROL VOLTAGE .... 74 V.

2399 is Dynamic Brake Equipped

Class	Number	re '66	Builder	Order Number	c/n	Date	Disposition
DRS-14A	6125	2369	EMD	(7718)	29130	12/63	PC,CR
"	6126	2370	"	"	29131	"	PC,CR
"	6127	2371	"	"	29132	"	PC,CR
DRS-14B	6128	2372	EMD	(7749)	29668	12/64	PC,CR
"	6129	2373	"	"	29669	"	PC,CR
DRS-14C	6130	2374	EMD	(7781)	29670	12/64	PC,CR
"	6131	2375	"	"	29671	"	PC,CR
"	6132	2376	"	"	29672	"	PC,CR
"	6133	2377	"	"	29673	"	PC,CR
"	6134	2378	"	"	29674	"	PC,CR
"	6135	2379	"	"	29675	"	PC,CR
"	6136	2380	"	"	29676	"	PC,CR
"	6137	2381	"	"	29677	"	PC,CR
"	6138	2382	"	"	29678	"	PC,CR
"	6139	2383	"	"	29679	"	PC,CR
"	6140	2384	"	"	29680	"	Wrecked; Rt 8/67
"	6141	2385	"	"	29681	"	PC,CR
"	6142	2386	"	"	29682	"	PC,CR
"	6143	2387	"	"	29683	"	PC,CR
"	6144	2388	"	"	29684	"	PC,CR
"	6145	2389	"	"	29685	"	PC,CR
"	6146	2390	"	"	29686	"	PC,CR
"	6147	2391	"	"	29687	"	PC,CR
"	6148	2392	"	"	29688	1/65	PC,CR
"	6149	2393	"	"	29689	"	PC,CR
DRS-14D	6150	2394	EMD	(7834)	30791	8/65	PC,CR
"	6151	2395	"	"	30792	"	PC,CR
"	6152	2396	"	"	30793	"	PC,CR
"	6153	2397	"	"	30794	"	PC,CR
"	6154	2398	"	"	30795	"	PC,CR
DRS-14E	6155	2399	EMD	(5661)	28906	11/63	PC,CR

Note: 6155 exhibited at New York World's Fair: acquired 1965.
Note: DRS-14a, b, c and e geared for 70 mph. DRS-14d geared for 85 mph. 2384 wrecked New York 5/22/67,Scrapped.
General Note: All locomotives built with MU No. 1 and 2 ends, single end train control; DRS-14e 6155 built with Dynamic Brake.

No. 6148 Class DRS-14C one of the thirty-one GP-35s. Only the last, 6155 was equipped with dynamic brakes.

Both: NYCSHS Collection

No. 2501 Class DRS-15A was a 2500 HP U-25B locomotive built by General Electric in January 1964.

CLASS DRS-15 (GF-25) GENERAL ELECTRIC 2500HP Model U-25B

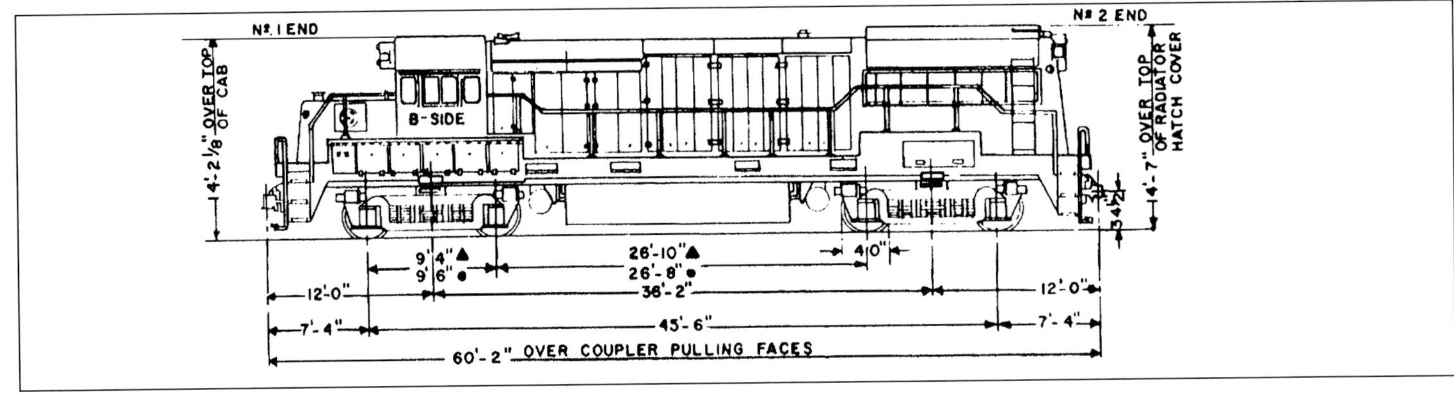

Class	Number	Builder	Order Number	c/n	Date	Disposition
DRS-15A	2500	GE	300-88359	34986	1/64	PC,CR
"	2501	"	"	34987	"	PC,CR
"	2502	"	"	34988	"	PC,CR
"	2503	"	"	34989	"	PC,CR
"	2504	"	"	34990	2/64	PC,CR
"	2505	"	"	34991	"	PC,CR
"	2506	"	"	34992	"	PC,CR
"	2507	"	"	34993	"	PC,CR
"	2508	"	"	34994	4/64	PC,CR
"	2509	"	"	34995	"	PC,CR
"	2510	"	"	34996	"	PC,CR
"	2511	"	"	34997	"	PC,CR
"	2512	"	"	34998	5/64	PC,CR
"	2513	"	"	34999	"	PC,CR
"	2514	"	"	35000	6/64	PC,CR
"	2515	"	"	35001	"	PC,CR
"	2516	"	"	35002	"	PC,CR
"	2517	"	"	35003	7/64	PC,CR
"	2518	"	"	35004	"	PC,CR
"	2519	"	"	35005	8/64	PC,CR
"	2520	"	"	35006	"	PC,CR
"	2521	"	"	35007	"	PC,CR
"	2522	"	"	35008	"	PC,CR
"	2523	"	"	35009	"	PC,CR
"	2524	"	"	35010	"	PC,CR
"	2525	"	"	35011	"	PC,CR
"	2526	"	"	35012	9/64	PC,CR
"	2527	"	"	35013	"	PC,CR
"	2528	"	"	35014	"	PC,CR
"	2529	"	"	35015	"	PC,CR
DRS-15B	2530	GE	300-88412	35423	11/64	PC,CR
"	2531	"	"	35424	"	PC,CR
"	2532	"	"	35425	"	PC,CR
"	2533	"	"	35426	12/64	PC,CR
"	2534	"	"	35427	"	PC,CR
"	2535	"	"	35428	12/64	PC,CR
"	2536	"	"	35429	"	PC,CR
"	2537	"	"	35430	"	PC
"	2538	"	"	35431	"	PC,CR
"	2539	"	"	35432	"	PC,CR
"	2540	"	"	35433	"	PC,CR
"	2541	"	"	35434	"	PC,CR
"	2542	"	"	35435	"	PC,CR

Class	Number	Builder	Order Number	c/n	Date	Disposition
DRS-15B	2543	GE	300-88412	35436	1/65	PC,CR
"	2544	"	"	35437	"	PC,CR
"	2545	"	"	35438	"	PC,CR
"	2546	"	"	35439	"	PC,CR
"	2547	"	"	35440	"	PC,CR
"	2548	"	"	35441	"	PC,CR
"	2549	"	"	35442	"	PC,CR
"	2550	"	"	35443	"	PC,CR
"	2551	"	"	35444	"	PC,CR
"	2552	"	"	35445	"	PC,CR
"	2553	"	"	35446	"	PC,CR
"	2554	"	"	35447	"	PC,CR
"	2555	"	"	35448	"	PC,CR
DRS-15C	2556	GE	300-88412	35449	"	PC,CR
"	*2557	"	"	35450	2/65	PC,CR
"	*2558	"	"	35451	"	PC,CR
"	*2559	"	"	35452	"	PC,CR
DRS-15D	2560	GE	300-88429	35691	9/65	PC,CR
"	2561	"	"	35692	7/65	PC
"	2562	"	"	35693	"	PC,CR
"	2563	"	"	35694	"	PC,CR
"	2564	"	"	35695	"	PC,CR
"	2565	"	"	35696	"	PC,CR
"	2566	"	"	35697	"	PC,CR
"	2567	"	"	35698	8/65	PC,CR
"	2568	"	"	35699	"	PC,CR
"	2569	"	"	35700	"	PC,CR

* 2557-2559 rated at 2800 HP.
Note: 2553-2560 built with 9"-6" wheelbase trucks from Fairbanks Morse trade ins, later replaced with 9' 4" Alco trucks.
General Note: Locomotives built with MU No. 1 and 2 ends, single end train control, dynamic brake.

Louis A. Marre

No. 2539 leads a group of four GE units at Dearborn, Michigan on August 29, 1965. Note the bay window caboose behind the units.

CLASS DRS-16 (EF-25) Electro-Motive 3000HP Model GP40

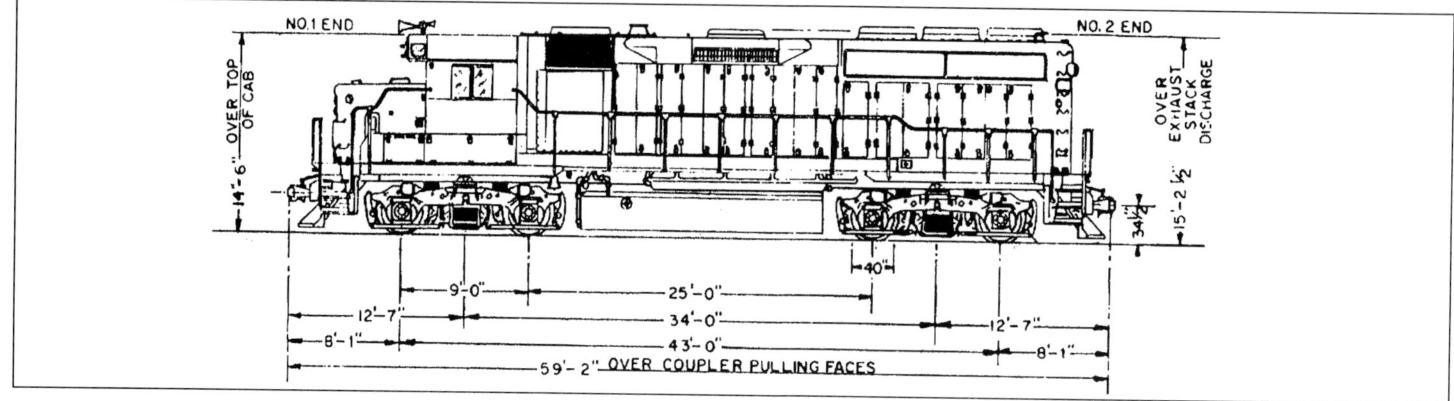

Class	Number	Builder	Order Number	c/n	Date	Disposition
DRS-16A	3000	EMD	A-7831	30937	12/65	PC,CR
"	3001	"	"	30938	"	PC,CR
"	3002	"	"	30939	"	PC,CR
"	3003	"	"	30940	"	PC,CR
"	3004	"	"	30941	"	PC,CR
"	3005	"	"	30942	"	PC,CR
"	3006	"	"	30943	"	PC,CR
"	3007	"	"	30944	"	PC,CR
"	3008	"	"	30945	"	PC,CR
"	3009	"	"	30946	"	PC,CR
"	3010	"	"	30947	"	PC,CR
"	3011	"	"	30948	"	PC,CR
"	3012	"	"	30949	"	PC,CR
"	3013	"	"	30950	"	PC,CR
"	3014	"	"	30951	"	PC,CR
"	3015	"	"	30952	"	PC,CR
"	3016	"	"	30953	"	PC,CR
"	3017	"	"	30954	"	PC,CR
"	3018	"	"	30955	"	PC,CR
"	3019	"	"	30956	"	PC,CR
"	3020	"	"	30957	"	PC,CR
"	3021	"	"	30958	"	PC,CR
"	3022	"	"	30959	"	PC,CR
"	3023	"	"	30960	"	PC,CR
"	3024	"	"	30961	"	PC,CR
"	3025	"	"	30962	"	PC,CR
"	3026	"	"	30963	"	PC,CR
"	3027	"	"	30964	"	PC,CR
"	3028	"	"	30965	"	PC,CR
"	3029	"	"	30966	"	PC,CR
"	3030	"	"	30967	"	PC,CR
"	3031	"	"	30968	"	PC,CR
"	3032	"	"	30969	"	PC,CR
"	3033	"	"	30970	"	PC,CR
"	3034	"	"	30971	"	PC,CR
"	3035	"	"	30972	"	PC,CR

All units built with MU both ends, train control single end, dynamic brake.

Class	Number	Builder	Order Number	c/n	Date	Disposition
DRS-16A	3036	EMD	7851	30973	11/65	PC,CR
"	3037	"	"	30974	"	PC,CR
"	3038	"	"	30975	"	PC,CR
"	3039	"	"	30976	"	PC,CR
"	3040	"	"	30977	"	PC,CR
"	3041	"	"	30978	"	PC,CR
"	3042	"	"	30979	"	PC,CR
"	3043	"	"	30980	"	PC,CR
"	3044	"	"	30981	"	PC,CR
"	3045	"	"	30982	"	PC,CR
"	3046	"	"	30983	"	PC,CR
"	3047	"	"	30984	"	PC,CR
"	3048	"	"	30985	12/65	PC,CR
"	3049	"	"	30986	"	PC,CR
EF-30	3050	EMD	7987	33214	7/67	PC,CR
"	3051	"	"	33215	"	PC,CR
"	3052	"	"	33216	"	PC,CR
"	3053	"	"	33217	"	PC,CR
"	3054	"	"	33218	"	PC,CR
"	3055	"	"	33219	"	PC,CR
"	3056	"	"	33220	"	PC,CR
"	3057	"	"	33221	"	PC,CR
"	3058	"	"	33222	"	PC,CR
"	3059	"	"	33223	"	PC,CR
"	3060	"	"	33224	"	PC,CR
"	3061	"	"	33225	"	PC,CR
"	3062	"	"	33226	"	PC,CR
"	3063	"	"	33227	"	PC,CR
"	3064	"	"	33228	"	PC,CR
"	3065	"	"	33229	8/67	PC,CR
"	3066	"	"	33230	"	PC,CR
"	3067	"	"	33231	9/67	PC,CR
"	3068	"	"	33232	"	PC,CR
"	3069	"	"	33233	"	PC,CR
"	3070	"	"	33234	"	PC,CR
"	3071	"	"	33235	"	PC,CR
"	3072	"	"	33236	"	PC,CR
"	3073	"	"	33237	"	PC,CR
"	3074	"	"	33238	"	PC,CR
"	3075	"	"	33239	"	PC,CR
"	3076	"	"	33240	"	PC,CR
"	3077	"	"	33241	"	PC,CR
"	3078	"	"	33242	"	PC,CR
"	3079	"	"	33243	"	PC,CR
"	3080	EMD	7064	33491	10/67	PC,CR
"	3081	"	"	33492	"	PC,CR
"	3082	"	"	33493	"	PC,CR
"	3083	"	"	33494	"	PC,CR
"	3084	"	"	33495	"	PC,CR
"	3085	"	"	33496	"	PC,CR
"	3086	"	"	33497	"	PC,CR
"	3087	"	"	33498	"	PC,CR
"	3088	"	"	33499	"	PC,CR

All units built with MU both ends, train control single end, dynamic brake.

Class	Number	Builder	Order Number	c/n	Date	Disposition
EF-30	3089	"	"	33500	11/67	PC,CR
"	3090	"	"	33501	"	PC,CR
"	3091	"	"	33502	"	PC,CR
"	3092	"	"	33503	"	PC,CR
"	3093	"	"	33504	"	PC,CR
"	3094	"	"	33505	"	PC,CR
"	3095	"	"	33506	"	PC,CR
"	3096	"	"	33507	"	PC,CR
"	3097	"	"	33508	"	PC,CR
"	3098	"	"	33509	"	PC,CR
"	3099	"	"	33510	"	PC,CR
"	3100	"	"	33511	"	PC,CR
"	3101	"	"	33512	"	PC,CR
"	3102	"	"	33513	"	PC,CR
"	3103	"	"	33514	"	PC,CR
"	3104	"	"	33515	"	PC,CR

All units built with MU both ends, train control single end, dynamic brake.

Bob Pennisi, Railroad Avenue Enterprises

No. 3019 heads train ML-12 at Iona Island, New York near the Bear Mountain Bridge on January 1, 1968.

NYCSHS Collection

No. 3046 Class DRS-16A built by EMD in November of 1965. It would be reclassified the following year to EF-30.

Louis A. Marre

No. 3057 an EMD GP-40 at East Syracuse, New York was only three months old when this view was made on October 3, 1967.

CLASS DRS-17 (GF-28) General Electric 2800HP Model U-28B

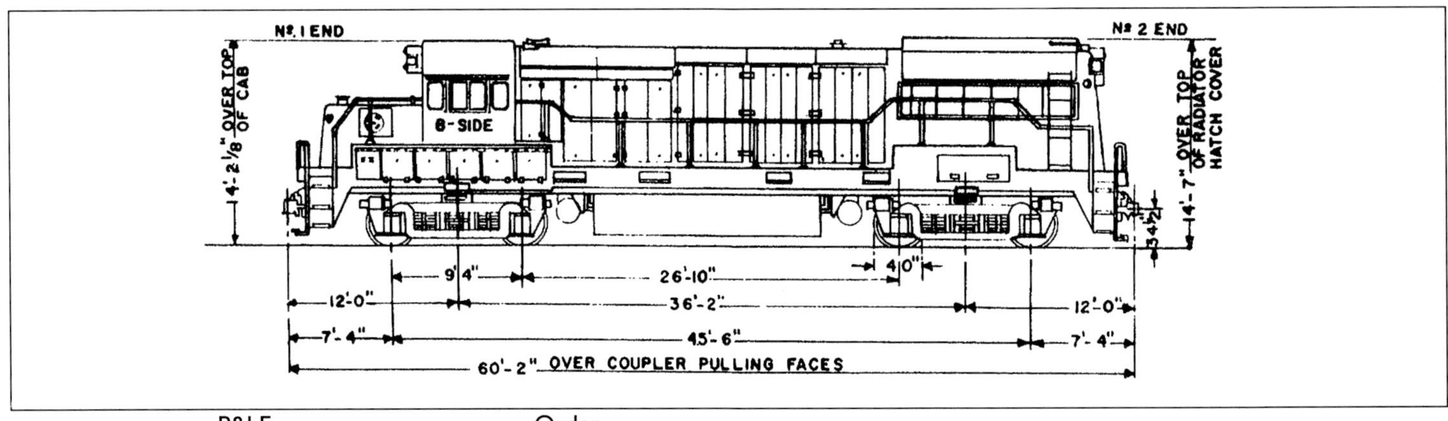

Class	P&LE Number	Builder	Order Number	c/n	Date	Disposition
DRS-17a	2800	GE	300-88467	35856	2/66	P&LE Rt 10/84
"	2801	"	"	35857	"	P&LE
"	2802	"	"	35858	"	P&LE
"	2803	"	"	35859	"	P&LE
"	2804	"	"	35860	"	P&LE
"	2805	"	"	35861	"	P&LE
"	2806	"	"	35862	"	P&LE Rt 10/84
"	2807	"	"	35863	"	P&LE
"	2808	"	"	35864	"	P&LE Note a
"	2809	"	"	35865	"	P&LE Note a
"	2810	"	"	35866	"	P&LE Note a
"	2811	"	"	35867	"	P&LE
"	2812	"	"	35868	2/66	P&LE
"	2813	"	"	35869	"	P&LE
"	2814	"	"	35870	"	P&LE Rt 10/84
"	2815	"	"	35871	"	P&LE
"	2816	"	"	35872	3/66	P&LE Sc '81
"	2817	"	"	35873	"	P&LE
"	2818	"	"	35874	"	P&LE
"	2819	"	"	35875	"	P&LE
"	2820	"	"	35876	"	P&LE Note a
"	2821	"	"	35877	"	P&LE Rt 10/84

Class	NYC Number	Builder	Order Number	c/n	Date	Disposition
GF-28	2822	GE	300-80530	35878	5/66	PC,CR
"	2823	"	"	35879	"	PC,CR

Note: 2808-2810, 2820 leased 5/85 to Transkentucky Transp.RR 245, 247, 249, 250. 2800-2821 built with MU both ends, train control single end. 2822-2823 built with dynamic brake, in addition, and used U-28 carbody.

No. 2802 a DRS-17A was a U-28B at McKees Rocks terminal in September, 1966. The 22 units in this sub class were built with U-25B type carbodies.

Both: Louis A. Marre Collection

No. 2822 along with 2823 were the only class GF-28s to be built with the U-28B carbody. The units were only five months old when this view at West Detroit was made October 24, 1966

CLASS GF-30 GENERAL ELECTRIC 3000HP Model U-30B

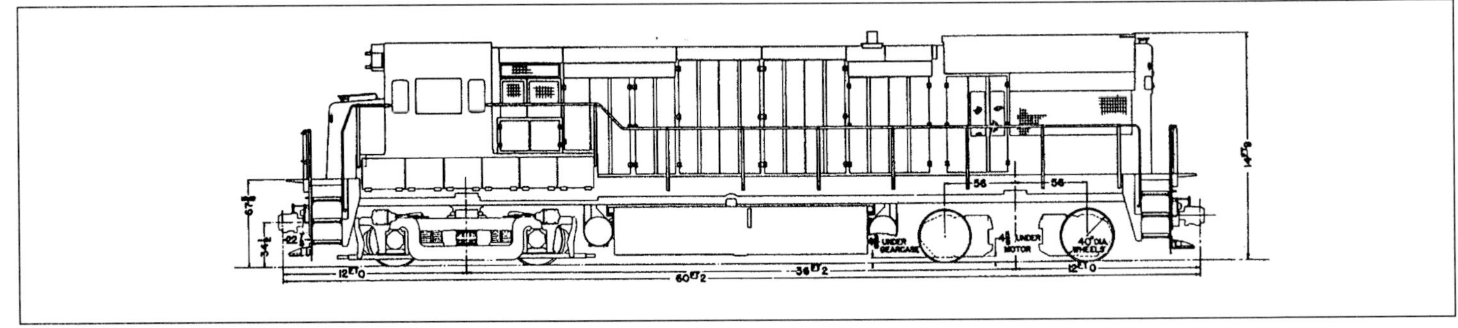

Class	Number	Builder	Order Number	c/n	Date	Disposition
GF-30	2830	GE	300-80890	36246	1/67	PC,CR
"	2831	"	"	36247	"	PC,CR
"	2832	"	"	36248	"	PC,CR
"	2833	"	"	36249	"	PC,CR
"	2834	"	"	36250	"	PC,CR
"	2835	"	"	36251	"	PC,CR
"	2836	"	"	36252	"	PC,CR
"	2837	"	"	36253	"	PC,CR
"	2838	"	"	36254	"	PC,CR
"	2839	"	"	36255	"	PC,CR
"	2840	GE	300-81060	36256	"	PC,CR
"	2841	"	"	36257	"	PC,CR
"	2842	"	"	36258	"	PC,CR
"	2843	"	"	36259	"	PC,CR
"	2844	"	"	36260	"	PC,CR
"	2845	"	"	36261	"	PC,CR
"	2846	"	"	36262	"	PC,CR
"	2847	"	"	36263	"	PC,CR
"	2848	"	"	36264	"	PC,CR
"	2849	"	"	36265	"	PC,CR
"	2850	"	"	36266	"	PC,CR
"	2851	"	"	36267	"	PC,CR
"	2852	"	"	36268	"	PC,CR
"	2853	"	"	36269	"	PC,CR
"	2854	"	"	36270	"	PC,CR
"	2855	"	"	36271	"	PC,CR
"	2856	"	"	36272	"	PC,CR
"	2857	"	"	36273	"	PC,CR
"	2858	"	"	36274	"	PC,CR
"	2859	"	"	36275	"	PC,CR
GF-30	2860	GE	300-81120	36411	9/67	PC,CR
"	2861	"	"	36412	"	PC,CR
"	2862	"	"	36413	"	PC,CR
"	2863	"	"	36414	"	PC,CR
"	2864	"	"	36415	"	PC,CR
"	2865	"	"	36416	"	PC,CR
"	2866	"	"	36417	10/67	PC,CR
"	2867	"	"	36418	"	PC,CR
"	2868	"	"	36419	"	PC,CR
"	2869	"	"	36420	"	PC,CR
"	2870	"	"	36421	"	PC,CR
"	2871	"	"	36422	"	PC,CR
"	2872	"	"	36423	"	PC,CR
"	2873	"	"	36424	"	PC,CR
"	2874	"	"	36425	"	PC,CR

Class	Number	Builder	Order Number	c/n	Date	Disposition
GF-30	2875	GE	300-81145	36426	10/67	PC,CR
"	2876	"	"	36427	"	PC,CR
"	2877	"	"	36428	"	PC,CR
"	2878	"	"	36429	"	PC,CR
"	2879	"	"	36430	"	PC,CR
"	2880	"	"	36431	11/67	PC,CR
"	2881	"	"	36432	"	PC,CR
"	2882	"	"	36433	"	PC,CR
"	2883	"	"	36434	"	PC,CR
"	2884	"	"	36435	"	PC,CR
"	2885	"	"	36436	"	PC,CR
"	2886	"	"	36437	"	PC,CR
"	2887	"	"	36438	"	PC,CR
"	2888	"	"	36439	"	PC,CR
"	2889	"	"	36440	"	PC,CR

General Note: Locomotives built with MU No. 1 and 2 ends. single end train control, dynamic brake.

Locos. 2830-2839 originally built using 9'-6" wheelbase Fairbanks-Morse trucks received on trade in, replaced with standard 9'-4" wheelbase Alco-GE trucks after PC merger.

Locos. 2858 and 2859 built with extended radiator and internal modifications. Set up at 3300hp. Official designation remained U-30B.

No. 2858 and 2859 were ordered and paid for by the NYC as U30Bs, but in a special deal with GE were delivered as field test units of a U-33B configuration. They were later changed and re-rated to 3000 HP units to better blend with the other 58 units of the class.

NYCSHS Collection

CLASS AF-30 ALCO 3000HP Model C-430

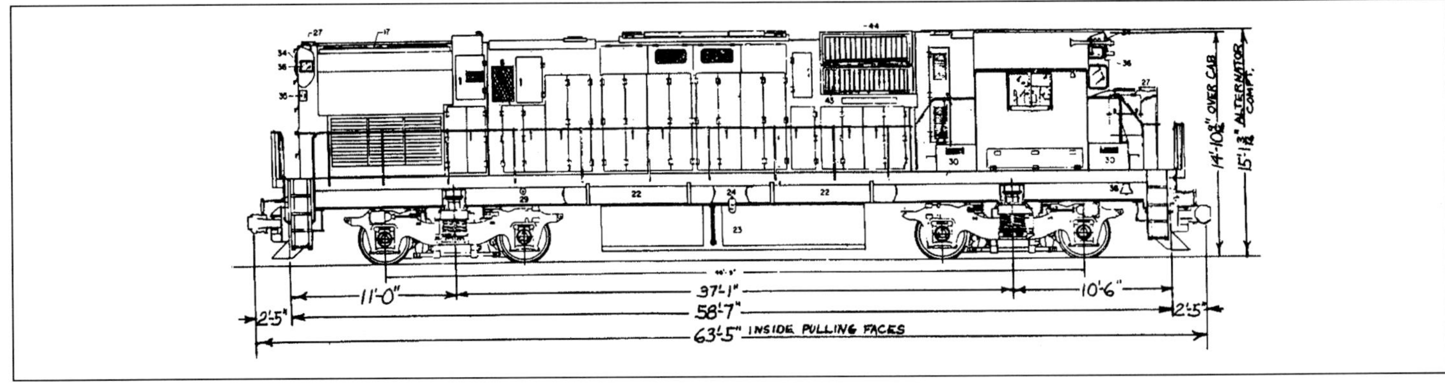

Class	Number	Builder	Order Number	c/n	Date	Disposition
AF-30	2050	Alco	(S0-21295)	3494-01	11/67	PC,CR
"	2051	"	"	3494-02	"	PC,CR
"	2052	"	"	3494-03	"	PC,CR
"	2053	"	"	3494-04	"	PC,CR
"	2054	"	"	3494-05	"	PC,CR
"	2055	"	"	3494-06	"	PC,CR
"	2056	"	"	3494-07	"	PC,CR
"	2057	"	"	3494-08	"	PC,CR
"	2058	"	"	3494-09	"	PC,CR
"	2059	"	"	3494-10	"	PC,CR

Note: All units built with MU both ends, train control single end, and dynamic brake.

No. 2058 Class AF-30 was a 3000 HP Alco C-430 "Century" locomotive built in November 1967. These ten Alco units would be the New York Central System's last locomotives acquired before the Penn Central Merger in 1968. This unit is lacking the white frame stripe standard on the last paint scheme.

NYCSHS Collection

LOCOMOTIVE WEIGHT AND TRACTIVE EFFORT

In preparing this roster of New York Central Diesel Locomotives, the general specifications have been included which shows the maximum Tractive Effort available for each unit. This maximum Tractive Effort is a calculated figure, based on 25% of the weight on driving wheels of the unit, is available only when starting and for a "short time". An additional' characteristic of diesel units by which their performance can be judged and compared is the continuous Tractive Effort.
Continuous Tractive Effort is the maximum which can be developed by the unit continuously, and is stated "at a given speed". Gear ratio or maximum speed rating of the unit is also a factor in the continuous rating, and therefore is stated when this is pertinent. This is particularly true with the DRS/DRSP units which were furnished with various gear ratios, and some of which were changed by the NYC at various times to suit the requirements.

Continuous Tractive Effort

Early Diesel Units

Class	Notes	Continuous TE Lbs	@	MPH
DEP		13,500	@	16.5
DEF		20,800	@	9.0
DES-A	30 minute	11,720	@	5.5
	60 minute	7,800	@	6.5
DES-2	external power (1 hour)	34,100	@	18
	internal power (1 hour)	34,100	@	8
DES-3	External power FS-1	24, 600	@	19.8 MPH
	(600 volts)			

(A) Internal power Locos. w/ 400 a.h. battery FS-1, series parallel

	Notes	TE	@	MPH
(1)	30 minutes	20. 800	@	7.5 MPH
(2)	60 minutes	16,000	@	8.3 MPH

(B) Internal power Locos. w/ 600 a. h. battery FS-1

(1) Series parallel

	Notes	TE	@	MPH
	(a) 30 minutes	29,600	@	6.5 MPH
	(b) 60 minutes	21,600	@	7.4 MPH

(2) Parallel

	Notes	TE	@	MPH
	(a) 30 minutes	11,200	@	17 MPH
	(b) 60 minutes	8, 000	@	20.0 MPH

Diesel Hump Trailers

Class	Geared Speed	Continuous TE	@	MPH	Average Weight
DHT-1A					
w/one DES-7	(FS-l)	41000	@	2.95	---
w/one DES-11	(FS-3)	29900	@	5. 4	---
w/two DES-11	(FS-3)	44000	@	7.58	---
w/one DES-13 or 16.	(FS-3)	36000	@	5.38	---
DHT-2A, B, C, D, E					
w/one DES-11	(FS-3)	29900	@	5.4	---
w/two DES-11	(FS-3)	44000	@	7. 58	---
w/one DES-13 or 16	(FS-3)	36000	@	5. 38	---
DHT-2F					
w/one DES-16		31200	@	6. 0	

Freight Transfer Units

Class	Geared Speed	Continuous TE	@	MPH	Average Weight
DFT-1	(65)	42800	@	14. 7	255890

Switching Units

Class	Notes	Continuous TE	@	MPH	Average Weight
DES-1A	FS-1	14600	@	7.1	140000
	FS-2	8600	@	11.9	
DES-1B, C	FS-1	17000	@	5.0	144500
	FS-2	10360	@	9.4	
DES-4	FS-1	22800	@	7.6	202000
	FS-2	11,200	@	16.2	
DES-5		23400	@	7.5	201200
DES-6		23400	@	7.5	223400
DES-7		28000	@	6.0	216700
DES-8 A, C, D, E, F		29200	@	6.3	198300
DES-8B, Nos. 693-707		29200	@	5.3	
DES-8B, Nos. 708-729		29200	@	6.3	
DES-9		29,200	@	6.3	215600
DES-10		29200	@	6.3	207050
DES-11		34000	@	8.0	230500
DES-12		34000	@	8.3	239950
DES-13		31200	@	10.0	247500
DES-14A, B		34600	@	8.3	240500
DES-14 C, D, E		34000	@	8.9	251000
DES-15A		34000	@	8.9	240400
DES-15B		34000	@	10.7	247100
DES-16		31200	@	12.0	247100
DES-17		34000	@	11.3	247800
DES-18		31200	@	7.0	234900
DES-19		34000	@	6.5	228800
DES-20		34000	@	10.8	240750
DES-21		44600	@	5.5	247600
ES-15		58000	@	7.2	248300

Combination Freight and Passenger Units

Class	Geared Speed	Continuous TE	@	MPH	Average Weight
DCA-1	100	21000	@	22.5	249300
DCB-1	100	21000	@	22.5	252000
DCA-2A	100	25400	@	18.1	334800
DCB-2A	100	25400	@	18.1	342000
DCA-3A	100	25400	@	18.1	342000
DCB-3A	100	25400	@	18.1	335000

Freight Units

Class	Geared Speed	Continuous TE	MPH	Average Weight
DFA-1	65	32500	@ 14.5	234000
DFB-1	65	32500	@ 14.5	227000
DFA-2 A, B, J	65	32500	@ 14.2	235100
DFA2 C-H	65	40000	@ 11.5	241400
DFB-2 A, B, H	65	32500	@ 14.2	237800
DFB-2 C-G	65	40000	@ 11.5	239900
DFA-3	65	42500	@ 11.0	239900
DFB-3	65	42500	@ 11.0	241500
DFA-4	65	42500	@ 10.5	258000
DFB-4	65	42500	@ 10.5	254700
DFA-5	79	41000	@ 15.5	347900
DFB-5	79	41000	@ 15.5	349700
DFA-6	65	42800	@ 14.7	259400
rebuilt with 567A	65	42800	@ 10.8	
rebuilt with 567C	65	42800	@ 12.6	
DFB-6	65	42800	@ 14.7	257300
rebuilt with 567C	65	42800	@ 12.6	
DFA-7	65	52500	@ 9.4	248100
DFB-7	65	52500	@ 9.4	247700
DFA-8	70	48600	@ 9.9	255000
DFB-8	70	48600	@ 9.9	250400
DFA-9	70	48600	@ 9.9	255000
DFB-9	70	48600	@ 9.9	253500

Passenger Units

Class	Geared Speed	Continuous TE	MPH	Average Weight
DPA-1A-D	98	18400	@ 35	324400
4003, 4020 mod.	98	23500	@ 29.5	340300
DPB-1A-C	98	18400	@ 35	310000
DPA-2	100	27000	@ 23	309800
DPB-2	100	27000	@ 23	306800
rebuilt with 567C	100	27000	@ 20	2993
DPA-3A	103	27500	@ 23	3333
	97	29000	@ 21.9	3333
DPA-4	100	33000	@ 21.8	3149
DPB-4	100	3300	@ 21.8	3140
DPA-5	98	23500	@ 29.5	3337
DPA-6	100	32000	@ 23 3	30054
rebuilt with 567C	100	32000	@ 16.8	30601
DH-1	120	21000	@ 12	1983

Road Switcher Units

Class	Geared Speed	Continuous TE	MPH	Average Weight
DRS/DRSP-1	60	34000	@ 8. 0	243400
DRS-2	65	42500	@ 11.0	245400
DRSP-2	65	42500	@ 11.0	245400
DRSP-2	85	32500	@ 14.2	245500
DRSP-3	65	42800	@ 10.5	265800
rebuilt with 567C	85	37200	@ 12.4	267800
DRS-4	65	40000	@ 11.0	248400
DRSP-4	65	40000	@ 11.0	248400
DRSP-4	71	37000	@ 12.0	248400
DRSP-4	85	32000	@ 14.4	248400
DRSP-5	60	34000	@ 10.7	247500
DRS-6	65	52500	@ 9.5	248200
DRSP-6	65	52500	@ 9.5	248200
DRSP-6	75	46000	@ 11.0	248200
DRSP-6 (re-geared)	85	38000	@ 13.2	248200
DRS-7	70	48600	@ 9.9	248000
DRSP-8	60	34000	@ 10.7	248800
DRSP-9A	70	42200	@ 12.8	253200
DRS-9	65	44600	@ 11.8	253200
DRS-9	85	35400	@ 15.3	253200
DRSP-9	85	35400	@ 15.3	253200
DRS-10	65	53000	@ 10.0	245000
DRS-11	65	44800	@ 13.7	254600
DRS-12	65	53000	@ 11.25	245847
	85	40000	@ 15.65	254000
DRS-13	71*	50000	@ 12.0	257700
	65*	50000	@ 12.0	257700
	85	44000	@ 15.2	257700
DRS-14 A, B, C, E	70	51700	@ 12.0	258740
DRS-14D	85	47000	@ 15.1	261400
DRS-15	70	53000	@ 14.9	268300
DRS-16 (EF-30)	77	51250	@ 11.3	276600
DRS-17 (GF-28)	75	55100	@ 15.5	272790
GF-30	75	55100	@ 17.0	274900
AF-30	75	55100	@ 17.0	277400

*Reduced permissible speed - same gear ratio.

ROAD TO THE FUTURE

No. 1083 with two "B" units are developing their full tractive effort as they head out of Dearborn, Michigan on August 20, 1966. Note that the first car is one of the 86 foot long box cars.

A Portrait Gallery Diesel Locomotives of the New York Central System

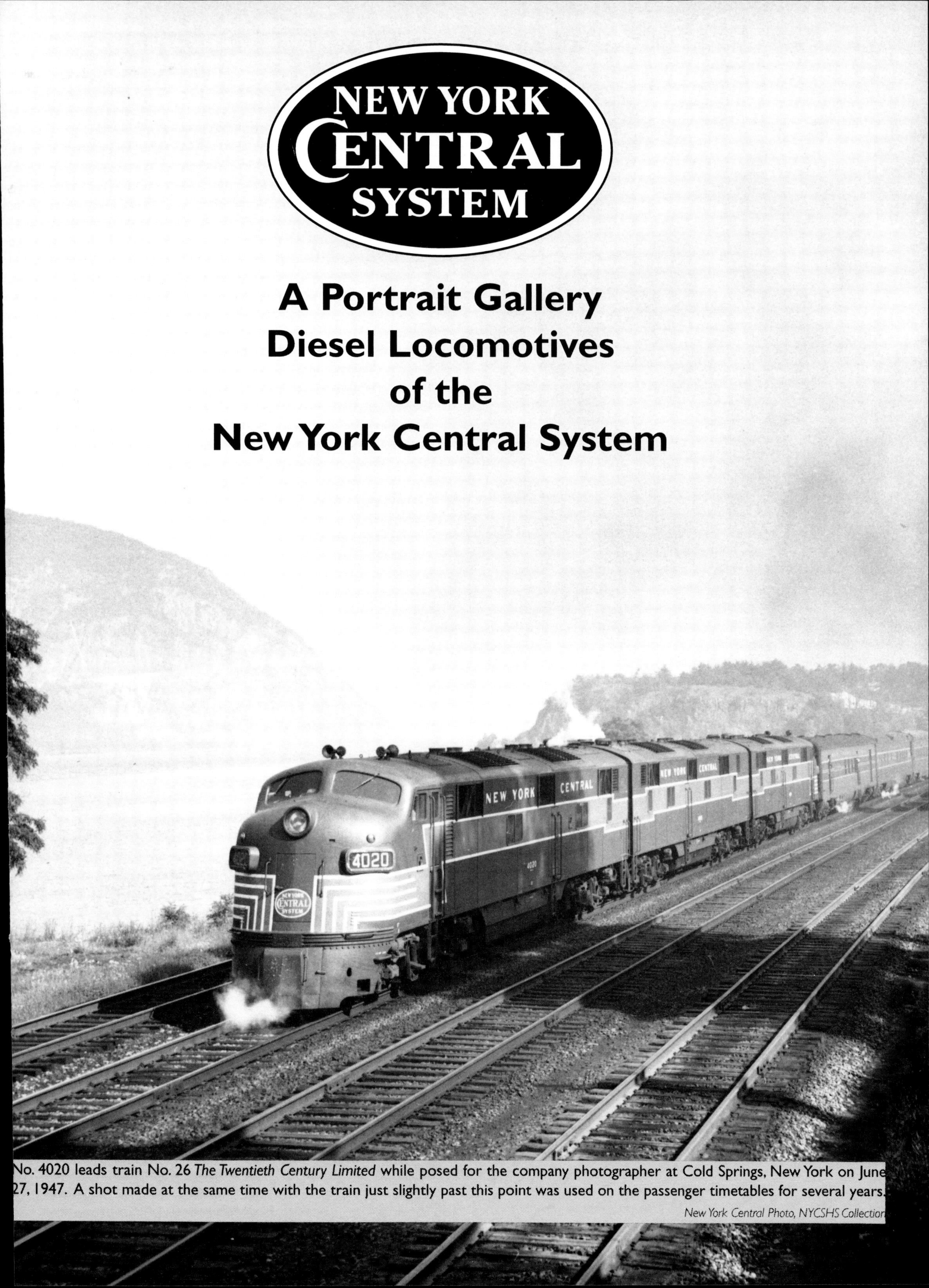

No. 4020 leads train No. 26 *The Twentieth Century Limited* while posed for the company photographer at Cold Springs, New York on June 27, 1947. A shot made at the same time with the train just slightly past this point was used on the passenger timetables for several years.

New York Central Photo, NYCSHS Collection

Al Staufe

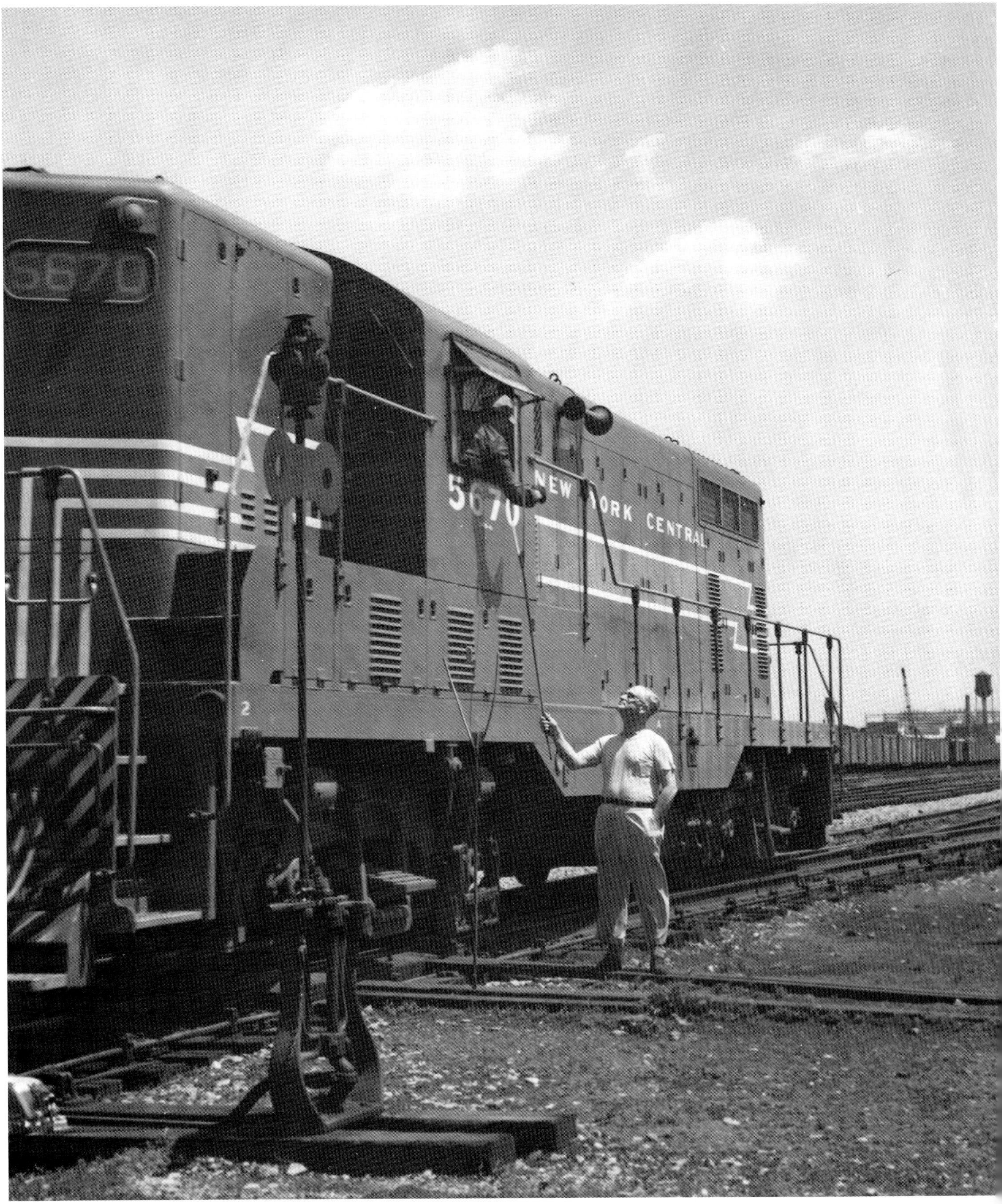

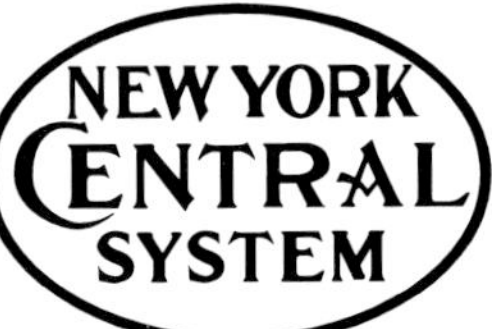
NEW YORK
CENTRAL
SYSTEM

Louis A. Marre

Baldwin heaven! Riverside yard in Cincinnati, Ohio, January 23, 1966.

Louis A. Marre Collection

This E-7 plus two more EMD's handled the last special out of Notre Dame, Indiana on October 13, 1958. Note the unusual application of the script herald with the lightning stripes.

Louis A. Marre Collection

Nos. 1657 and 1658 are invading steam territory at Bellfontaine, Ohio in March 1951.

Louis A. Marre

There were 26 of the Baldwin freight units; 18 "A" and 8 "B". At first they were all based at DeWitt, but later were moved to the Big Four. Shown here at Cincinnati's Riverside yard in January 1966.

W. D. Edson

Four month old Nos. 1601, 2401, 2400 and 1600 (A-B-B-A) at Batavia, New York on October 22, 1944.

W. D. Edson

No. 4010 will not be scooping water from the track pans here in steam territory with a coal dock in the background. Also of interest in the middle hopper from the Interstate; a small southwestrn Virginia shortline. This is train No. 41 *The Knickerbocker* at Scotia, New York in April 1948.

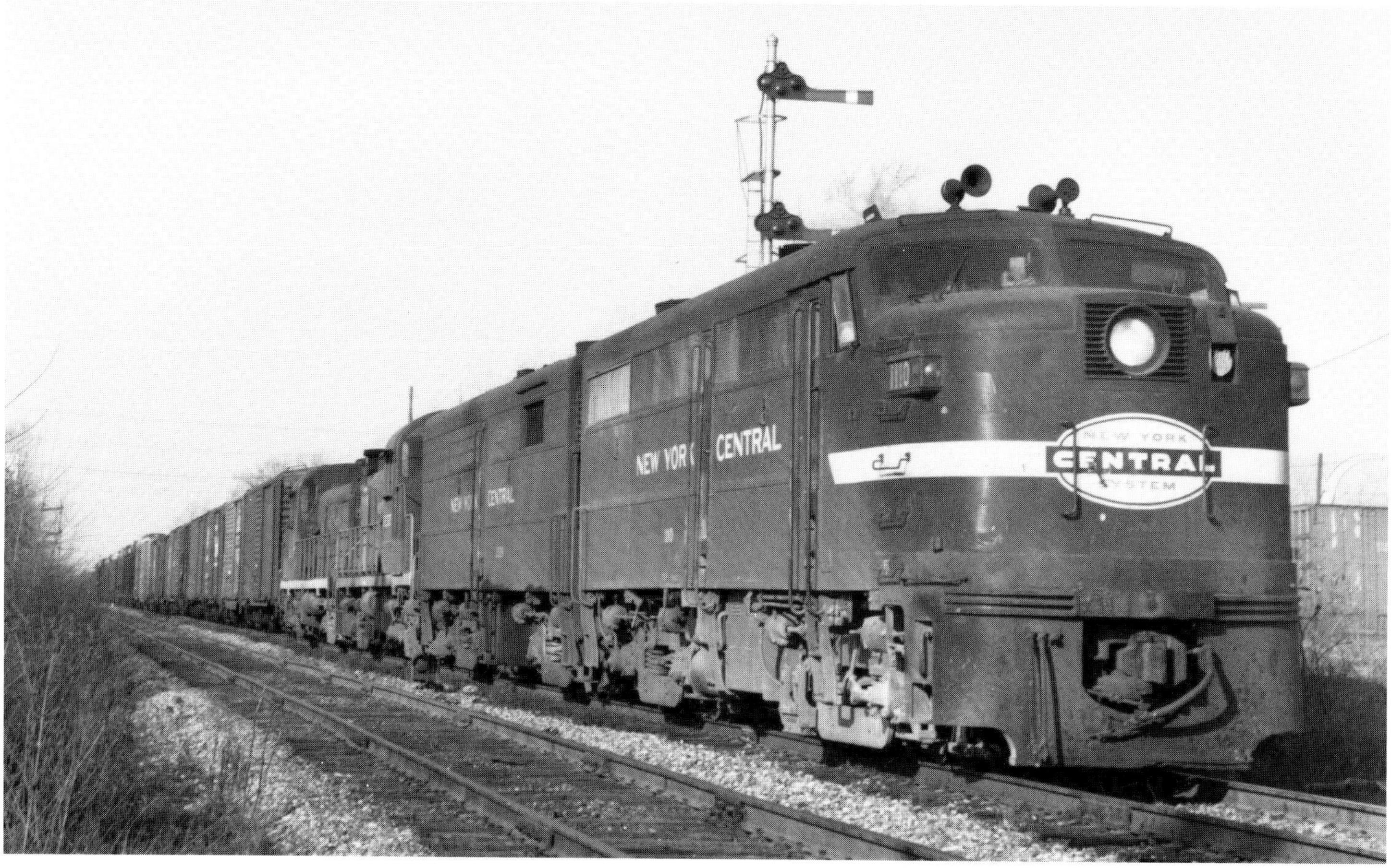

J. D. Ingles, Louis A. Marre Collection

DFA-3d No. 1110 renumbered from 1033 in 1964 leads three other Alco products in this view at Dearborn, Michigan on December 22, 1965.

Louis A. Marre

Another odd-ball road switcher assigned to the Chicago cowhide service was this Baldwin 1500 HP unit. It was re-engined with EMD power in May 1956. Shown at LaSalle Street in September 1961.

Railroad Avenue Enterprises

A pod of sharks at Williamsport, Pennsylvania in October 1952. They were less than a year old.

Louis A. Marre Collection

Diesel hump trailer No 453 working the hump yard in multiple with FM transfer until 7112 at Elkhart, Indiana in March 1959.

NYCSHS Collection

A variety of builders is represented here including Fairbanks-Morse, EMD and Baldwin, at Collinwood diesel terminal.

With thirteen cars on train 40, *The Missourian*, the 4009 and 4008 are making 60 MPH going through East Lancaster, New York, November, 1948.

Harold K. Vollrath Collection

Harold K. Vollrath Collection

Rare indeed is this view of steam and diesel cooperating at Lancaster, New York in November 1948.

W. D. Edson

No. 4022 gets boiler water while surrounded by the trappings of steam as passengers crowd the platform at Terre Haute, Indiana while waiting to board train No. 41 *The Knickerbocker* on May 30, 1947.

The railroad takes on a special aura at night. Lima switcher No. 6201 is seen here in February, 1965 at Sharonville, Ohio just before retirement.

Louis A. Marre Collection

W. D. Edson

Albany, New York, April 1968.

Diesel exhaust on a foggy afternoon in Boston makes for an intersting photo as commuter trains wait at signal bridge No. 2 in South Station, June 1953.

Bob Lorenz Collection

Louis A. Marre Collection

No. 4063 leads the *South Shore Express* at South Bend, Indiana on April 18, 1960.

W. D. Edson

No. 8323 at Lake Mahopac, New York in this May 1956 scene.

Al Staufer

No. 3502 and and F-M are set to leave the Cleveland Union Terminal with No. 257, just as Nickel Plate N o. 6, the *Nickel Plate Limited*, arrives from Chicago.

COLOR GALLERY

Louis A. Marre

No. 1670 at Elkhart, Indiana, April 29, 1961

Louis A. Marre

No. 6601 at West Detroit, Michigan, October, 1963

Louis A. Marre

In an unusual paint scheme with "Century" green the No. 4053 is shown at West Detroit, Michigan, December 4, 1961. Units 4083 and 4107 were also painted this color for a short time.

Louis A. Marre

Class GF-30, No. 2844. Only a few months old at Elkhart, Indiana, July 30, 1967

Louis A. Marre

No. 1049 at Fostoria Ohio, May 25, 1961

Louis A. Marr

No. 3804 at Paris, Illinois, April 20, 1956

Louis A. Marre

Train X "The X-Plorer" shortly after entering service between Cleveland and Cincinnati is shown here at Columbus, Ohio, July 10, 1956

Louis A. Marre

First of the high hood Alcos, built in 1938 as No. 614. Buffalo, New York, August 18, 1962.

Nos. 8043, 8020, and 8034 at Elkhart, Indiana, April 23, 1963

Both: Louis A. Marre

Alco's answer to the GP9, class DRS-10a, No. 8000, once again at Elkhart, Indiana, November 3, 1964

Louis A. Marre

Class DFA-6a, No. 5012 in the lead through South Bend, Indiana, on April 26, 1962

Louis A. Marre

Class DPA-2a, No. 4201, the Central's second Alco PA at Cincinnati Ohio, August 11, 1956

Louis A. Marre

No. 5645 at Lansing, Michigan April 25, 1962

No. 4056 in an experimental all grey scheme at South Bend, Indiana, May 25, 1961

Both: Louis A. Marre

No. 4031 also at South Bend, November 29, 1962

Louis A. Marre

Class DRS-3a No. 7300 and 7301 after being rebuilt with EMD engines at Englewood, New Jersey, November 8, 1964

Class DRS-5a, No. 6207 a Lima 1200 HP road switcher at Cincinnati, Ohio, August 8, 1965

Both: Louis A. Marre

Chicago River & Indiana No. 9803 at Chicago, Illinois, October 13, 1963

With an experimental all black with gold band paint scheme, No. 1608 is shown at Elkhart, Indiana, August 2, 1965

Louis A. Marre

At Dayton, Ohio, this 3 unit set is crossing the Great Miami River, September 8, 1965.

Louis A. Marre Collection

Once again at Dayton, a Chesapeake and Ohio train passes No. 9328 a DES-20b in this September 1965 view.

A Buick Special and friend at Elkhart, April 25, 1964.

Louis A. Marre

DES-5c No. 604 was equipped with swing link couplers, radial buffers and a cab operated front coupler release by the NYC for use as a helper for passenger train service on Albany Hill. This view was made August 18, 1957 at Rensselaer, New York.

Jay Williams, H. L. Vail Jr. Collection

One of the seven EMD SW1 units in the subclass DES-5e were delivered to the CR&I, then brought back to the NYC after only one year, in 1951. The 616 is at the Muncie, Indiana passenger station in October, 1963.

H. N. Proctor, Louis A. Marre Collection

Louis A. Marre Collection

An EMD F7 heading a westbound freight through South Bend, Indiana on September 30, 1959.

Alco FA-1 units eventually wandered all over the system, this one on the Big Four leading four other Alco products in a view made from inside the partially abandoned station shed at the Indianapolis Union Station in September, 1963.

Louis A. Marre

General Electric's "More Power to America" special units 8375A and 8375B became New York Central DPA-4B No 4212 and DPB-4A No. 4304

H. L. Vail Jr. Collection

NYCSHS Collection

Definitely a different beast here, as almost new DH-1a No. 20 is posed next to F7 No. 1643 at Collinwood on May 15, 1956.

Louis A. Marre

An EMD E7 No 4026 is in need of a visit to the paint shop in this March 28, 1963 scene at South Bend, Indiana with train No. 59 *The Chicagoan.*

Louis A. Marre Collection

Two EMD E8s led by No. 4049 power train No. 35 the *Iroquois,* once again at South Bend, Indiana on April 29, 1961.

Bob Pennisi, Railroad Avenue Enterprises

Super-Van train SV-2 nearing the FlexiVan terminal at High Bridge, snaking through Spuyten Duyvil New York behind four second generation diesels with a General Electric U25B in the lead on January 6, 1968.

Bob Pennisi, Railroad Avenue Enterprises

This GP9 was renumbered from 5940 and headed a Poughkeepsie local at Manitou, New York on July 29, 1967. This station building was surely one of the smallest on line.

No. 4021 on train No. 26 passing Bannerman's Island on the Hudson Division June 1947.

NYCSHS Collection

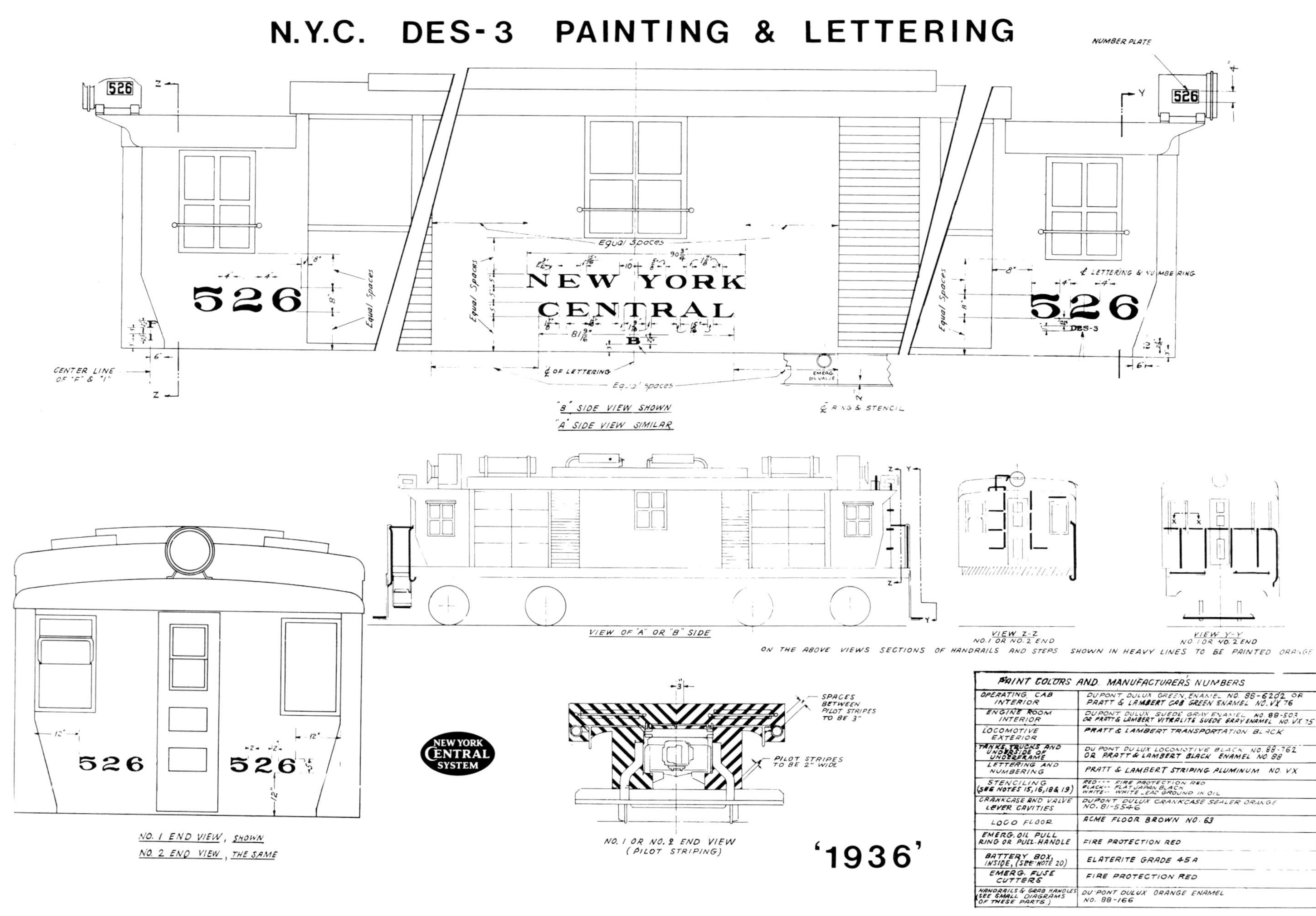

PAINT COLORS AND MANUFACTURER'S NUMBERS	
OPERATING CAB INTERIOR	DU PONT DULUX GREEN ENAMEL NO. 86-6202 OR PRATT & LAMBERT CAB GREEN ENAMEL NO. VX 76
ENGINE ROOM INTERIOR	DU PONT DULUX SUEDE GRAY ENAMEL NO. 88-503 OR PRATT & LAMBERT VITRALITE SUEDE GRAY ENAMEL NO. VX 75
LOCOMOTIVE EXTERIOR	PRATT & LAMBERT TRANSPORTATION BLACK
TANKS, TRUCKS AND UNDERSIDE OF UNDERFRAME	DU PONT DULUX LOCOMOTIVE BLACK NO. 88-762 OR PRATT & LAMBERT BLACK ENAMEL NO. 88
LETTERING AND NUMBERING	PRATT & LAMBERT STRIPING ALUMINUM NO. VX
STENCILING (SEE NOTES 15, 16, 18 & 19)	RED -- FIRE PROTECTION RED BLACK -- FLAT JAPAN BLACK WHITE -- WHITE LEAD GROUND IN OIL
CRANKCASE AND VALVE LEVER CAVITIES	DU PONT DULUX CRANKCASE SEALER ORANGE NO. 81-5546
LOCO FLOOR	ACME FLOOR BROWN NO. 63
EMERG. OIL PULL RING OR PULL HANDLE	FIRE PROTECTION RED
BATTERY BOX, INSIDE, (SEE NOTE 20)	ELATERITE GRADE 45A
EMERG. FUSE CUTTERS	FIRE PROTECTION RED
HANDRAILS & GRAB HANDLES (SEE SMALL DIAGRAMS OF THESE PARTS)	DU PONT DULUX ORANGE ENAMEL NO. 88-166

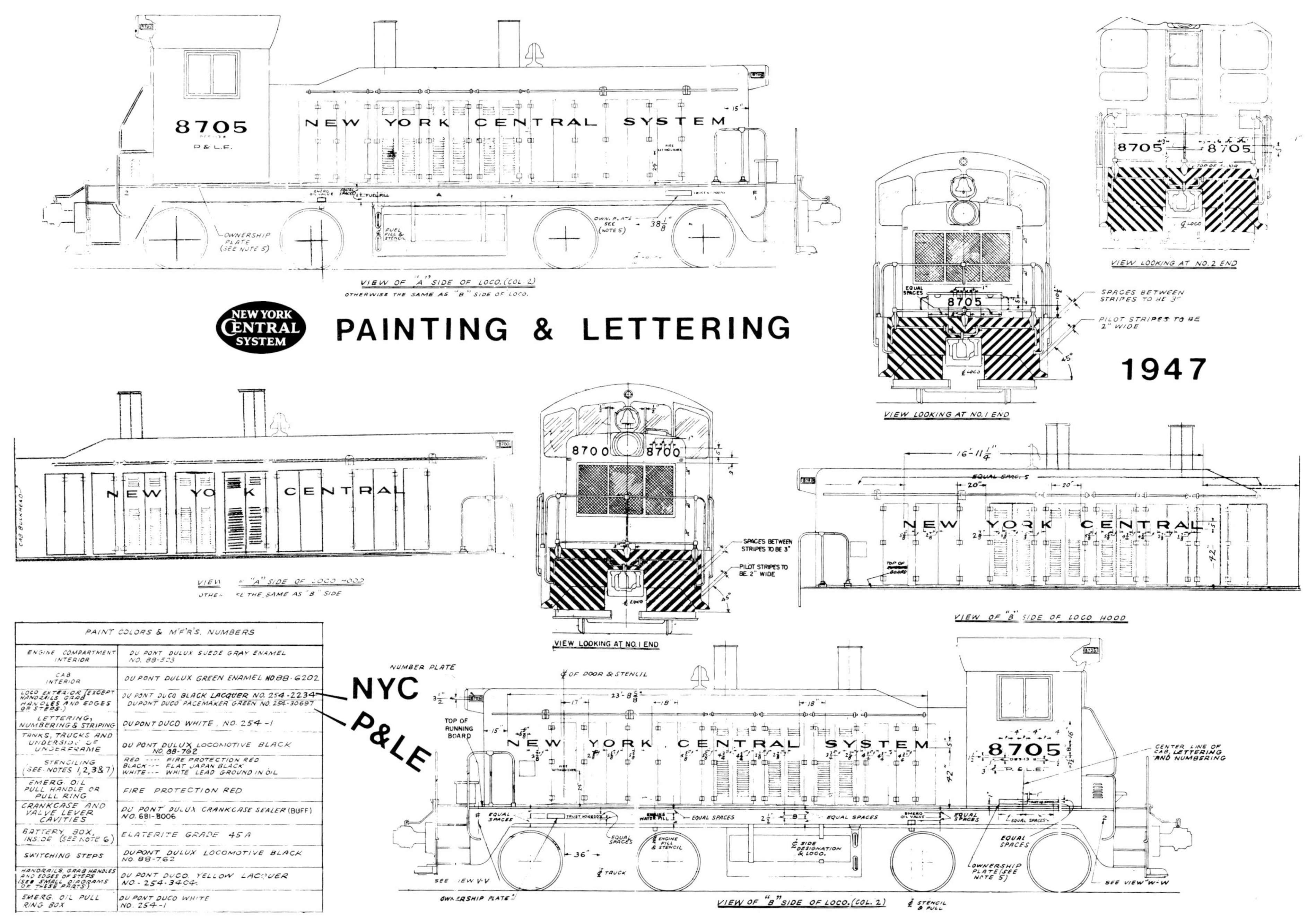

PAINT COLORS & M'F'R'S. NUMBERS	
ENGINE COMPARTMENT INTERIOR	DU PONT DULUX SUEDE GRAY ENAMEL NO. 88-503
CAB INTERIOR	DU PONT DULUX GREEN ENAMEL NO 88-6202
LOCO EXTERIOR (EXCEPT HANDRAILS, GRAB HANDLES AND EDGES OF STEPS)	DU PONT DUCO BLACK LACQUER NO. 254-2234 DUPONT DUCO PACEMAKER GREEN NO. 254-30697
LETTERING, NUMBERING & STRIPING	DU PONT DUCO WHITE, NO. 254-1
TANKS, TRUCKS AND UNDERSIDE OF UNDERFRAME	DU PONT DULUX LOCOMOTIVE BLACK NO. 88-762
STENCILING (SEE NOTES 1, 2, 3 & 7)	RED ---- FIRE PROTECTION RED BLACK --- FLAT JAPAN BLACK WHITE --- WHITE LEAD GROUND IN OIL
EMERG. OIL PULL HANDLE OR PULL RING	FIRE PROTECTION RED
CRANKCASE AND VALVE LEVER CAVITIES	DU PONT DULUX CRANKCASE SEALER (BUFF) NO. 681-8006
BATTERY BOX, INSIDE (SEE NOTE 6)	ELATERITE GRADE 45A
SWITCHING STEPS	DUPONT DULUX LOCOMOTIVE BLACK NO. 88-762
HANDRAILS, GRAB HANDLES AND EDGES OF STEPS (SEE SMALL DIAGRAMS OF THESE PARTS)	DU PONT DUCO YELLOW LACQUER NO. 254-3404
EMERG. OIL PULL RING BOX	DU PONT DUCO WHITE NO. 254-1

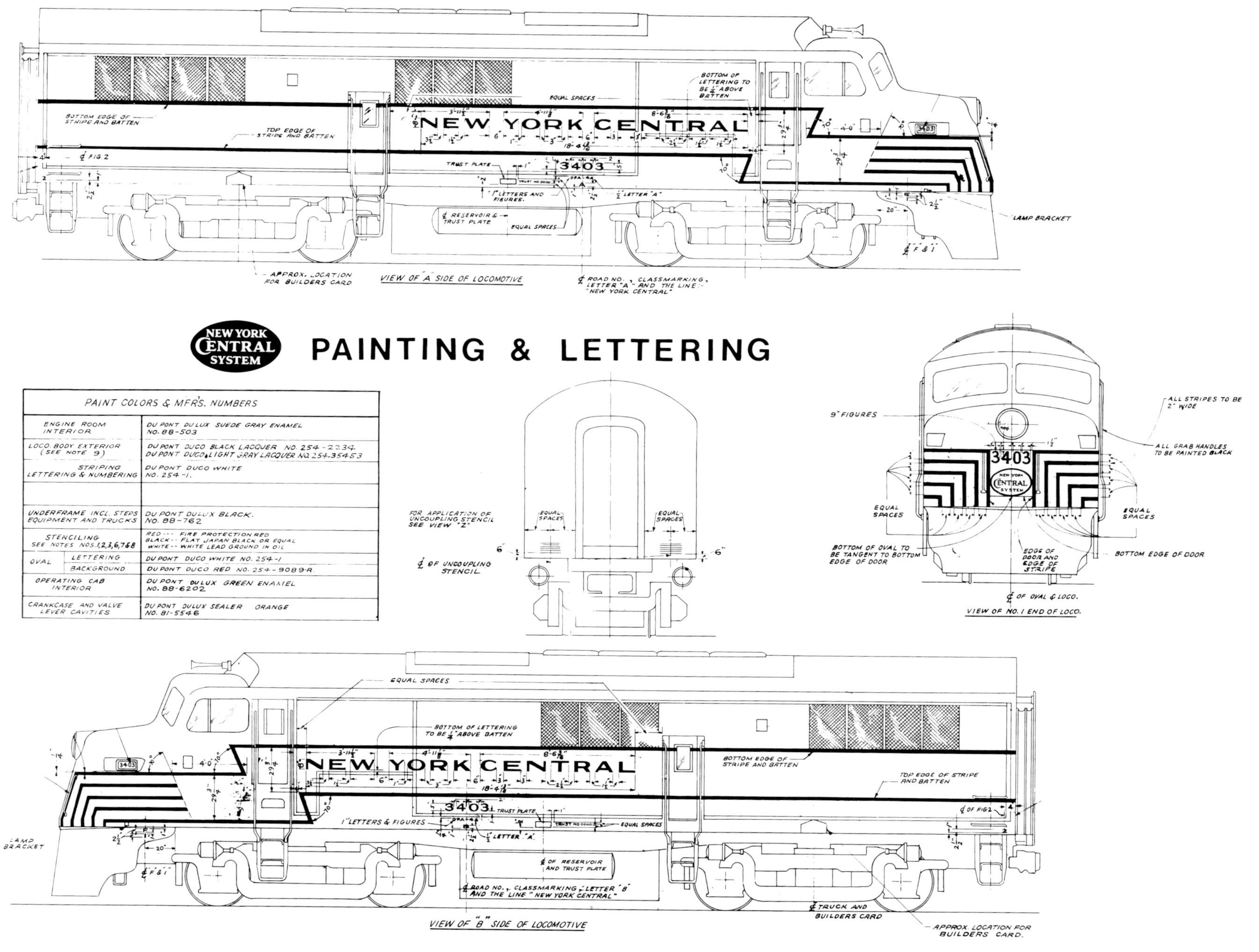

PAINT COLORS & MFR'S. NUMBERS		
ENGINE ROOM INTERIOR		DU PONT DULUX SUEDE GRAY ENAMEL NO. 88-503
LOCO. BODY EXTERIOR (SEE NOTE 9)		DU PONT DUCO BLACK LACQUER NO. 254-2234 DU PONT DUCO LIGHT GRAY LACQUER NO. 254-35453
STRIPING LETTERING & NUMBERING		DU PONT DUCO WHITE NO. 254-1.
UNDERFRAME INCL. STEPS EQUIPMENT AND TRUCKS		DU PONT DULUX BLACK. NO. 88-762
STENCILING SEE NOTES NOS. 1,2,3,6,7 & 8		RED --- FIRE PROTECTION RED BLACK -- FLAT JAPAN BLACK OR EQUAL WHITE -- WHITE LEAD GROUND IN OIL
OVAL	LETTERING	DU PONT DUCO WHITE NO. 254-1
	BACKGROUND	DU PONT DUCO RED NO. 254-9089-R.
OPERATING CAB INTERIOR		DU PONT DULUX GREEN ENAMEL NO. 88-6202
CRANKCASE AND VALVE LEVER CAVITIES		DU PONT DULUX SEALER ORANGE NO. 81-5546

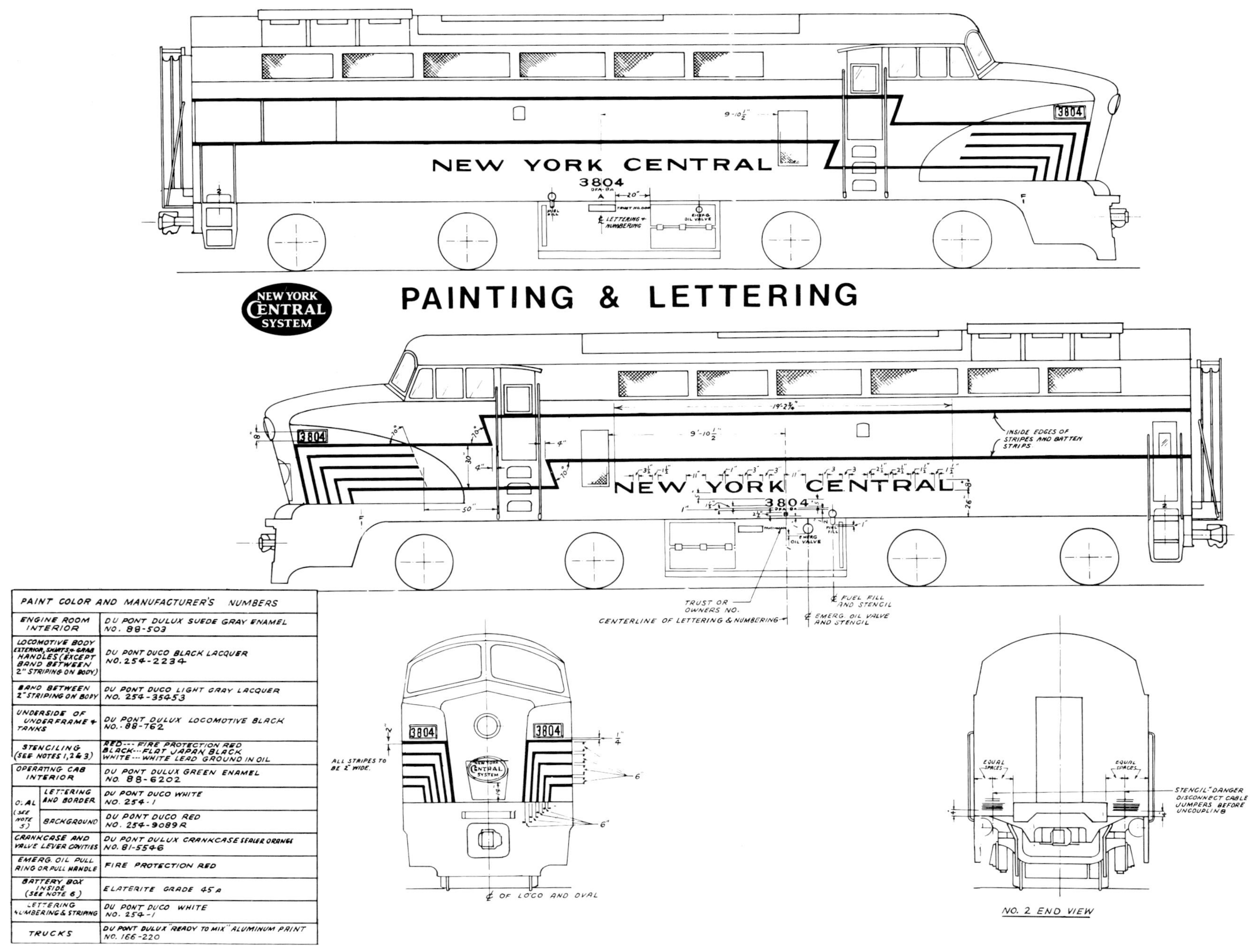

PAINT COLOR AND MANUFACTURER'S NUMBERS	
ENGINE ROOM INTERIOR	DU PONT DULUX SUEDE GRAY ENAMEL NO. 88-503
LOCOMOTIVE BODY EXTERIOR, SHAFTS & GRAB HANDLES (EXCEPT BAND BETWEEN 2" STRIPING ON BODY)	DU PONT DUCO BLACK LACQUER NO. 254-2234
BAND BETWEEN 2" STRIPING ON BODY	DU PONT DUCO LIGHT GRAY LACQUER NO. 254-35453
UNDERSIDE OF UNDERFRAME + TANKS	DU PONT DULUX LOCOMOTIVE BLACK NO. 88-762
STENCILING (SEE NOTES 1, 2 & 3)	RED --- FIRE PROTECTION RED BLACK --- FLAT JAPAN BLACK WHITE --- WHITE LEAD GROUND IN OIL
OPERATING CAB INTERIOR	DU PONT DULUX GREEN ENAMEL NO. 88-6202
OVAL (SEE NOTE 5) — LETTERING AND BORDER	DU PONT DUCO WHITE NO. 254-1
OVAL (SEE NOTE 5) — BACKGROUND	DU PONT DUCO RED NO. 254-9089R
CRANKCASE AND VALVE LEVER CAVITIES	DU PONT DULUX CRANKCASE SEALER ORANGE NO. 81-5546
EMERG. OIL PULL RING OR PULL HANDLE	FIRE PROTECTION RED
BATTERY BOX INSIDE (SEE NOTE 6)	ELATERITE GRADE 45A
LETTERING NUMBERING & STRIPING	DU PONT DUCO WHITE NO. 254-1
TRUCKS	DU PONT DULUX "READY TO MIX" ALUMINUM PRINT NO. 166-220

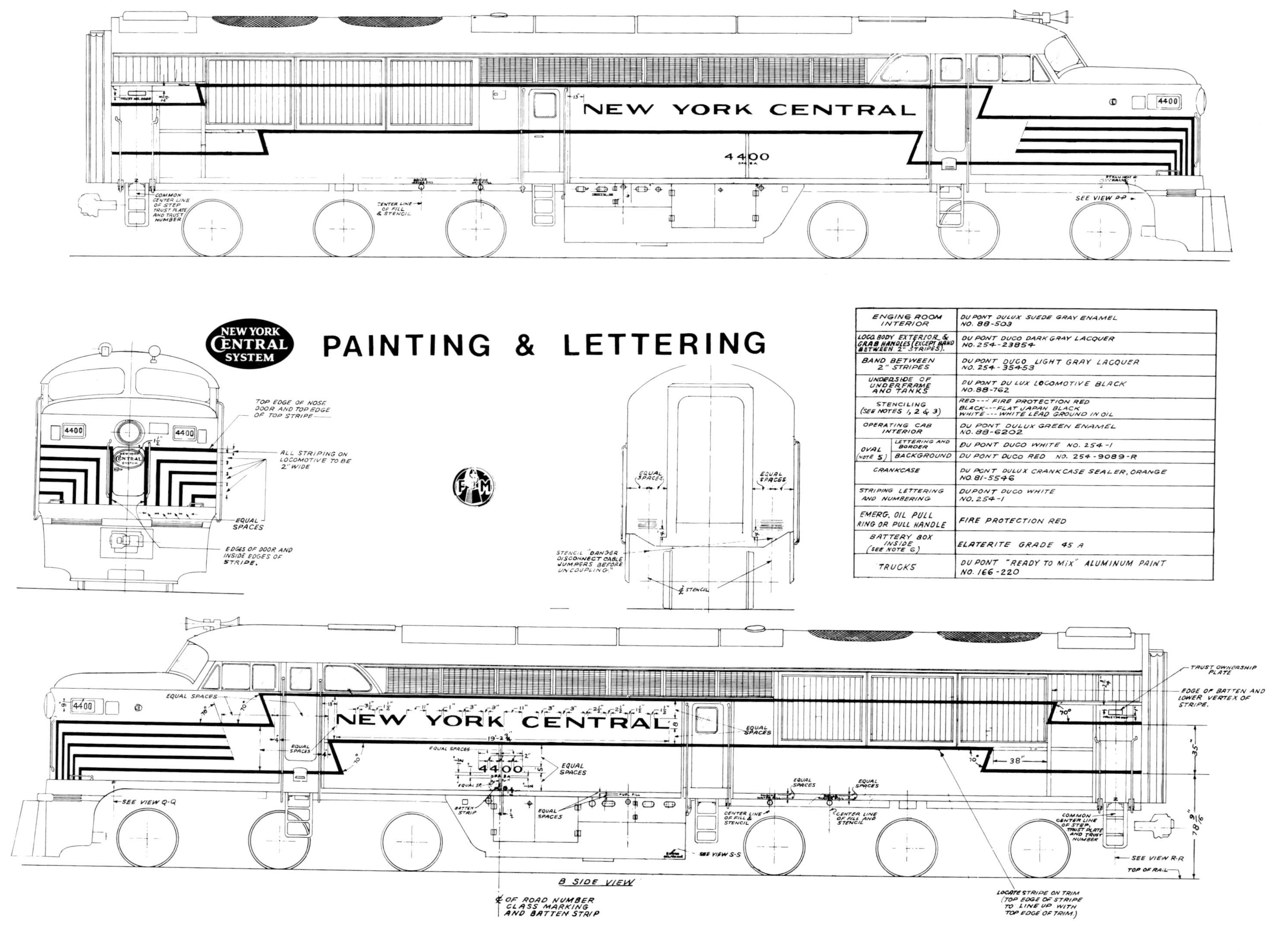

ENGINE ROOM INTERIOR	DU PONT DULUX SUEDE GRAY ENAMEL NO. 88-503
LOCO. BODY EXTERIOR & GRAB HANDLES (EXCEPT BAND BETWEEN 2" STRIPES).	DU PONT DUCO DARK GRAY LACQUER NO. 254-23854
BAND BETWEEN 2" STRIPES	DU PONT DUCO LIGHT GRAY LACQUER NO. 254-35453
UNDERSIDE OF UNDERFRAME AND TANKS	DU PONT DU LUX LOCOMOTIVE BLACK NO. 88-762
STENCILING (SEE NOTES 1, 2 & 3)	RED--- FIRE PROTECTION RED BLACK--- FLAT JAPAN BLACK WHITE--- WHITE LEAD GROUND IN OIL
OPERATING CAB INTERIOR	DU PONT DULUX GREEN ENAMEL NO. 88-6202
OVAL (NOTE 5) LETTERING AND BORDER	DU PONT DUCO WHITE NO. 254-1
OVAL (NOTE 5) BACKGROUND	DU PONT DUCO RED NO. 254-9089-R
CRANKCASE	DU PONT DULUX CRANKCASE SEALER, ORANGE NO. 81-5546
STRIPING LETTERING AND NUMBERING	DUPONT DUCO WHITE NO. 254-1
EMERG. OIL PULL RING OR PULL HANDLE	FIRE PROTECTION RED
BATTERY BOX INSIDE (SEE NOTE 6)	ELATERITE GRADE 45 A
TRUCKS	DU PONT "READY TO MIX" ALUMINUM PAINT NO. 166-220

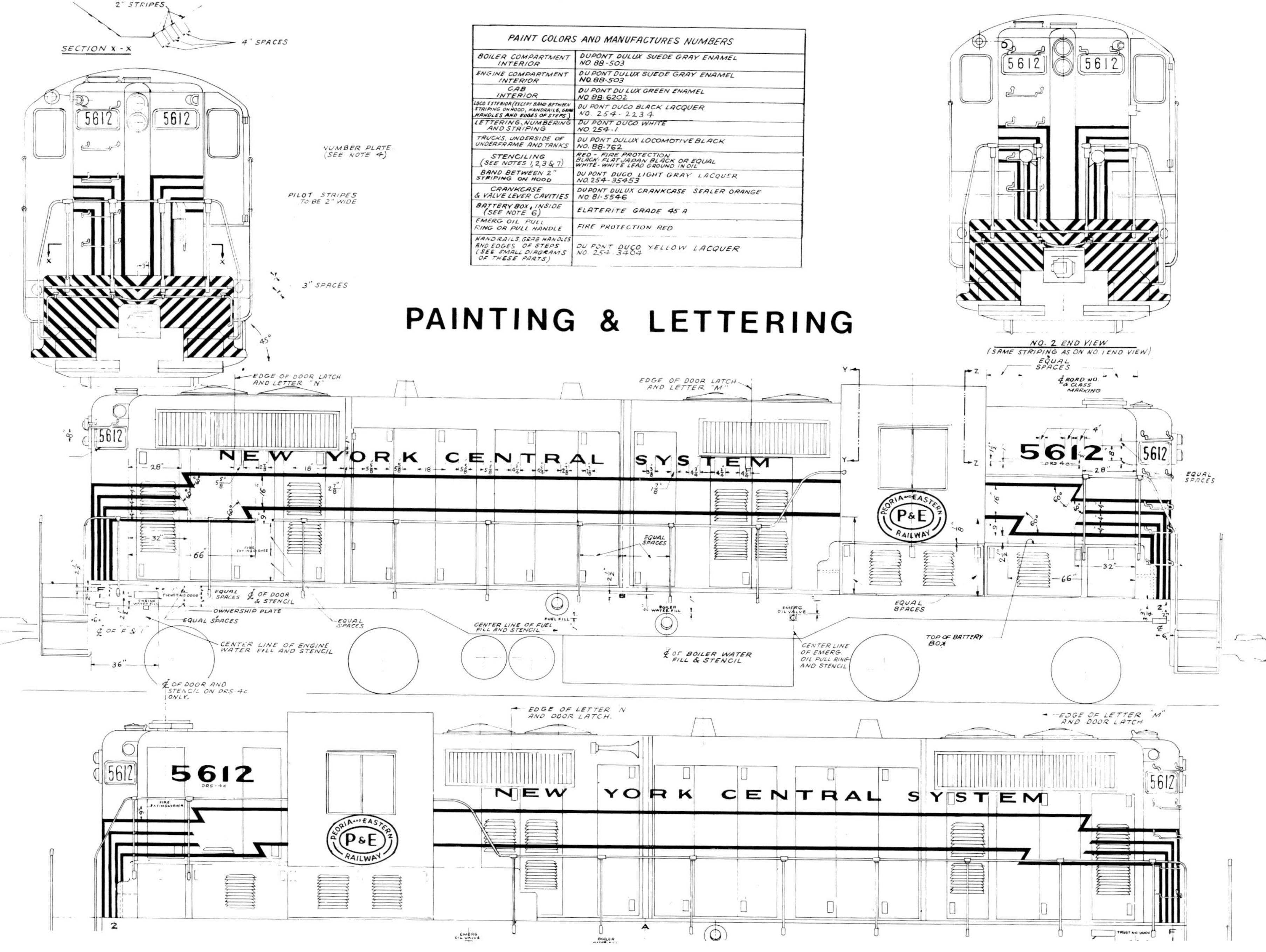

PAINT COLORS AND MANUFACTURES NUMBERS	
BOILER COMPARTMENT INTERIOR	DUPONT DULUX SUEDE GRAY ENAMEL NO. 88-503
ENGINE COMPARTMENT INTERIOR	DU PONT DULUX SUEDE GRAY ENAMEL NO. 88-503
CAB INTERIOR	DU PONT DU LUX GREEN ENAMEL NO 88-6202
LOCO EXTERIOR (EXCEPT BAND BETWEEN STRIPING ON HOOD, HANDRAILS, GRAB HANDLES AND EDGES OF STEPS.)	DU PONT DUCO BLACK LACQUER NO. 254-2234
LETTERING, NUMBERING AND STRIPING	DU PONT DUCO WHITE NO. 254-1
TRUCKS, UNDERSIDE OF UNDERFRAME AND TANKS	DU PONT DULUX LOCOMOTIVE BLACK NO. 88-762
STENCILING (SEE NOTES 1, 2, 3 & 7)	RED - FIRE PROTECTION BLACK - FLAT JAPAN BLACK OR EQUAL WHITE - WHITE LEAD GROUND IN OIL
BAND BETWEEN 2" STRIPING ON HOOD	DU PONT DUCO LIGHT GRAY LACQUER NO. 254-35453
CRANKCASE & VALVE LEVER CAVITIES	DUPONT DULUX CRANKCASE SEALER ORANGE NO. 81-5546
BATTERY BOX, INSIDE (SEE NOTE 6)	ELATERITE GRADE 45 A
EMERG OIL PULL RING OR PULL HANDLE	FIRE PROTECTION RED
HANDRAILS, GRAB HANDLES AND EDGES OF STEPS (SEE SMALL DIAGRAMS OF THESE PARTS)	DU PONT DUCO YELLOW LACQUER NO. 254-3404

PAINTING & LETTERING

NEW YORK CENTRAL SYSTEM

SEE SEPARATE VIEW FOR LETTERING OF CAB CLASS GF-25, GF-28

℄ CAB NUMBERING ℄ OVAL

OVAL X-87067 LINE 2

FIRE EXTINGUISHER

TRUST OR OWNERS No.

℄ EMERG. OIL PULL RING & DECAL

℄ FUEL FILL & DECAL

SEE NOTE 7

"FIRE EXTINGUISHER" DECAL TO BE APPLIED TO HOOD DOORS ADJACENT TO EXTINGUISHERS AS REQUIRED.

"FIRE EXTINGUISHER" DECAL TO BE APPLIED IN THIS LOCATION ON ALCO. & G.E. UNITS ONLY

℄ DOOR & DECAL

℄ ENGINE WATER FILL & DECAL

OVAL X-87067 LINE 1

℄ CAB, NUMBERING ℄ OVAL

LETTERING OF CAB GF-25, GF-28

NOTE No 1
LETTERING AND NUMBERING: USE WHITE ON BLACK OR GREEN BACKGROUND AND BLACK ON WHITE BACKGROUND.
STENCILING AND DECALS: USE WHITE ON BLACK OR GREEN BACKGROUND AND BLACK ON GRAY OR WHITE BACKGROUND EXCEPT WHERE RED IS CALLED FOR.

NOTE No 2
ANY APPARATUS OR CABINET CONTAINING APPARATUS CARRYING MORE THAN 100 VOLTS ARE TO USE METAL WARNING SIGN TO DRG. S-86759.

NOTE No 3
DECAL FOR "EMERG. OIL VALVE" TO BE APPLIED ADJACENT TO EACH LOCATION WHERE PULL CORDS TRIPPING THE EMERGENCY FUEL OIL CUT-OFF VALVE CAN BE OPERATED.

NOTE No 4
"FIRE EXTINGUISHER" AND "EMERG. BRAKE VALVE" TO HAVE DECAL IN RED LETTERS.

NOTE No 5
BEFORE PAINTING INSIDE OF BATTERY BOX, FILL ALL COUNTERBORES IN BUFFERS AND NON-DRAINABLE POCKETS IN FLOOR WITH ACID RESISTING BATTERY BOX COMPOUND, 150°F MELTING POINT, JOHNS-MANVILLE CORP.

NOTE No 6
SEE CURRENT LETTER OF INSTRUCTION FOR LIST OF APPROVED PAINTS.

NOTE No 7
CLASS MARKING TO BE OFF CENTER TO CLEAR LATCHES. CLASS AF-20

NEW YORK CENTRAL SYSTEM

USED ON

LOCO. Nos.	CLASS
2822-2823	GF-28
3000-3049	EF-30
2020-2044	AF-20
2369-2399	EF-25
2188-2197	EF-22
2100-2172	EF-20
2500-2569	GF-25

D	C	B	A	STYLE No	LINE No
59"	42"	40"	4"	1	1
41"	47"	40"	4"	2	2
54"	47"	40"	4"	3	3
45	34	42"	4"	4	4
72	47	37"	6"	5	5

Index By Unit Number

Index By Unit Number

Louis A. Marre Collection

No. 2501 a GE U25B along with two more units was in charge of train SV-9 through Vickers, Ohio in August 1966. Note the two TOFC ahead of the Flexi-vans.